高等职业教育"十三五"规划教材

Qiche Zhuanye Yingyu
汽车专业英语

(第2版)

边浩毅 主 编
黄国潮 冯 谣 副主编

人民交通出版社股份有限公司
China Communications Press Co.,Ltd.

内 容 提 要

本书是高等职业教育"十三五"规划教材之一，内容包括：四冲程发动机基础知识介绍、发动机构造认识、燃油直喷系统、发动机冷却系统和润滑系统认识、发动机点火系统和起动系统认识、底盘构造认识、汽车检测设备认识、KT600 汽车诊断系统、汽车市场调查分析、进出口交易的一般流程、来人来店购车接待、汽车产品配置介绍、汽车保险办理、汽车销售礼仪、汽车产品售后服务、出国手续办理，共 16 个任务。

本书可作为高等职业院校汽车相关专业教材，也可作为汽车销售企业的培训教材。

图书在版编目(CIP)数据

汽车专业英语 / 边浩毅主编. —2 版. —北京：
人民交通出版社股份有限公司，2019.7
ISBN 978-7-114-15391-4

Ⅰ. ①汽⋯ Ⅱ. ①边⋯ Ⅲ. ①汽车工程—英语 Ⅳ.
①U46

中国版本图书馆 CIP 数据核字(2019)第 050858 号

书　　　名：	汽车专业英语(第 2 版)
著 作 者：	边浩毅
责任编辑：	时　旭
责任校对：	刘　芹
责任印制：	张　凯
出版发行：	人民交通出版社股份有限公司
地　　　址：	(100011)北京市朝阳区安定门外外馆斜街 3 号
网　　　址：	http://www.ccpress.com.cn
销售电话：	(010)59757973
总 经 销：	人民交通出版社股份有限公司发行部
经　　　销：	各地新华书店
印　　　刷：	北京市密东印刷有限公司
开　　　本：	787×1092　1/16
印　　　张：	15.5
字　　　数：	360 千
版　　　次：	2009 年 9 月　第 1 版 2019 年 7 月　第 2 版
印　　　次：	2019 年 7 月　第 2 版　第 1 次印刷　总第 5 次印刷
书　　　号：	ISBN 978-7-114-15391-4
定　　　价：	38.00 元

(有印刷、装订质量问题的图书由本公司负责调换)

第2版前言

本教材第1版于2009年1月出版发行,多年来数次印刷,一直深受广大高等职业院校师生的欢迎,在此对长期使用本教材的师生表示感谢。为适应高职汽车类专业课程建设和教学改革的需要,同时不断追赶现代汽车技术和市场的发展步伐,根据人民交通出版社股份有限公司和广大用书院校的要求,编者对此书进行再版修订。此次修订的内容主要包括:

(1)将原"任务三"燃油系统中关于化油器的知识全部删除,更新为缸内燃油直喷系统。

(2)"任务五"中,将点火系统和起动系统相关部件都配上插图,并增加了汽车微机控制点火系统的内容。

(3)将原"任务八"中2ZZ-GE发动机模拟器内容全部删除,替换为目前高职院校汽车专业常用的KT600汽车诊断系统内容。

(4)补充、更新了部分图片,音标、推荐书目部分也做了更新。

(5)降低了部分文章内容的难度,并增加了中文翻译。

本教材由浙江机电职业技术学院边浩毅担任主编,浙江交通职业技术学院黄国潮、冯谣担任副主编。边浩毅负责修订任务二、任务十、任务十一、任务十四、任务十五;黄国潮负责修订任务一、任务三、任务四、任务五、任务八;冯谣负责修订任务六、任务七、任务九、任务十二、任务十三、任务十六。

由于编写时间紧迫,经验不足,水平有限,缺点错误在所难免,恳请广大师生和读者批评指正。

编者
2018年9月

目录

任务一　四冲程发动机基础知识介绍 ……………………………………………………… 1
Task 1　Introduction to the Elementary Knowledge of the Four-stroke Engine ………… 2

任务二　发动机构造认识 …………………………………………………………………… 13
Task 2　Engine Structure Understanding ………………………………………………… 14

任务三　燃油直喷系统 ……………………………………………………………………… 26
Task 3　Gasoline Direct-injection Systems ……………………………………………… 27

任务四　发动机冷却系统和润滑系统认识 ………………………………………………… 36
Task 4　Engine Cooling System and Lubricating System Understanding ……………… 37

任务五　发动机点火系统和起动系统认识 ………………………………………………… 49
Task 5　Engine Ignition System and Starting System Understanding …………………… 50

任务六　底盘构造认识 ……………………………………………………………………… 64
Task 6　Chassis Structure Understanding ………………………………………………… 65

任务七　汽车检测设备认识 ………………………………………………………………… 79
Task 7　Automotive Testing Equipment Understanding ………………………………… 80

任务八　KT600 汽车诊断系统 ……………………………………………………………… 91
Task 8　KT600 Diagnostic Systems for Motor Vehicles ………………………………… 92

任务九　汽车市场调查分析 ………………………………………………………………… 108
Task 9　Research Report on Automobile Market GM Reports Income of ＄2.4 Billion
　　　　and EBIT-adjusted of ＄3.2 Billion ……………………………………………… 109

任务十　进出口交易的一般流程 …………………………………………………………… 122
Task 10　General Procedures of Export and Import Transaction ………………………… 122

任务十一	来人来电购车接待	144
Task 11	Reception for Guest & Telephone Purchasing	144
任务十二	汽车产品配置介绍	161
Task 12	Introduction to Automobile Product	161
任务十三	汽车保险办理	175
Task 13	Handle with Automobile Insurance	176
任务十四	汽车销售礼仪	190
Task 14	The Car Sales Etiquette	191
任务十五	汽车产品售后服务	200
Task 15	Automotive Product After-sales Service	200
任务十六	出国手续办理	213
Task 16	Service of Procedure For Going Abroad	214

部分练习题参考答案 …… 232

任务一
四冲程发动机基础知识介绍

1. 掌握与发动机四冲程的工作过程、发动机分类相关的专业术语、词汇。
2. 能就发动机四个行程的内容进行中英互译。
3. 能对简单的相关内容进行阅读和翻译。
4. 能辨认汽车实物上英语词汇。
5. 正确完成课后练习。

以四冲程发动机为例，介绍发动机四个行程的工作过程、发动机分类等专业术语、词汇。通过完成该任务，能阅读关于发动机工作过程的英文文献，并掌握简单翻译技巧。

本学习任务沿着以下脉络进行学习：

通读全文 → 学习单词和语法 → 完成课后练习 → 分组讨论 → 课后阅读

Task 1　Introduction to the Elementary Knowledge of the Four-stroke Engine

Internal Combustion Engine

The engine is a self-contained power unit which converts the heat energy of fuel into mechanical energy for moving the vehicle(Fig. 1-1).[1] Because fuel is burned within the engine, it is known as an internal combustion engine. In the internal combustion engine, air/fuel mixture is introduced into a closed cylinder where it is compressed and then ignited. The burning of the fuel causes a rapid rise in cylinder pressure which is converted to useful mechanical energy by the piston and crankshaft. The most common engine is the four-stroke piston engine. These four strokes are intake stroke, compression stroke, power stroke and exhaust stroke.

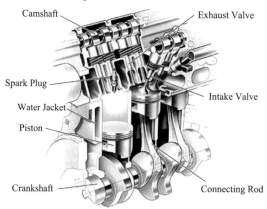

Fig. 1-1　Internal Combustion Engine

Intake Stroke

The intake stroke of a four-stroke engine begins with the piston at top dead center (TDC). The starter causes the crankshaft to rotate in a clockwise direction. The crankshaft, through the connecting rod, forces the piston to move downward. This downward movement of the piston creates a vacuum, a difference in pressure, in the space above the piston. The engine manufacturer times the intake valve action so that it opens automatically at or slightly before the piston starts down. Therefore, a mixture of gasoline and air, pushed by the atmospheric pressure outside the engine, rushes through the intake manifold and into the engine cylinder. At the same time, the exhaust valve remains closed during this downward stroke of the piston. This valve closure prevents the entering air/fuel charge from escaping through the exhaust port. After the piston reaches the bottom of its first stroke, the cylinder is practically full of an air/fuel charge. The drawing of an air/fuel charge into the cylinder in this manner, during the downward movement of the piston, constitutes the intake stroke of the piston(Fig. 1-2).[2]

Compression Stroke

After the piston reaches bottom dead center (BDC), it moves upward again as the starter continues to turn the crankshaft in a clockwise direction. As the piston is beginning to move upward, the intake valve closes, and the exhaust valve remains closed. Since both valves are closed, the piston compresses the air/fuel mixture in the small space between the top of the piston and the cylinder head. As the piston reaches TDC again during its upward travel, the compression stroke of the piston is over. The air/fuel charge is now under compression so that it will produce a great deal of power when the spark plug ignites it (Fig. 1-3).

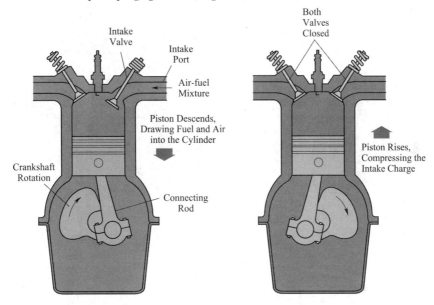

Fig. 1-2　Engine Intake-stroke　　　Fig. 1-3　Engine Compression-stroke

Power Stroke

Just as or slightly before the piston reaches TDC on the compression stroke with the air/fuel mixture fully compressed, a timed electrical spark appears at the spark plug. This spark ignites the compressed air/fuel mixture. The burning mixture begins to expand; the pressure in the combustion chamber above the piston immediately increases. This results in a high pressure applied to the top of the piston. Now, both valves remain closed during the power stroke. This assures that the total force of the expanding gas applies itself to the head of the piston. This tremendous force pushes the piston downward on the power stroke, causing the connecting rod to rotate the crankshaft.[3] In other words, the force resulting from the expansion of the burning air/fuel mixture is turning the crankshaft (Fig. 1-4).

Exhaust Stroke

Near the end of the downward movement of the piston on the power stroke, the camshaft opens the exhaust valve, but the intake valve remains closed. Although much of the gas pressure has expended itself driving the piston downward, some pressure still remains when the exhaust valve opens. This remaining pressurized gas flows comparatively freely from the cylinder through the passage (port) opened by the exhaust valve.[4] Then, as the piston again moves up in the cylinder, it drives any remaining gases out of the cylinder past the open exhaust valve. As the piston travels through the TDC position and starts downward again in the cylinder, a new operating cycle begins. The four strokes are continuously repeated in every cylinder as long as the engine remains running(Fig. 1-5).

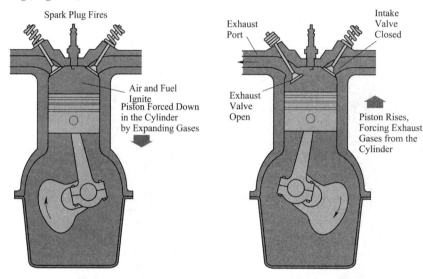

Fig. 1-4   Engine Power-stroke   Fig. 1-5   Engine Exhaust-stroke

Flywheel

The engine cycle has only one power stroke where the piston is actually driving the crankshaft. During the other three strokes, the rotating crankshaft is moving the piston up or down in its cylinder. Thus, during the power stroke, the crankshaft tends to speed up; during the other three strokes, it tends to slow down. To keep the crankshaft turning smoothly between two power strokes, the flywheel is attached to the end of the crankshaft.[5] This wheel resists any effort to change its speed of rotation. When the crankshaft tends to speed up or slow down, flywheel inertia resists it.

Multiple-Cylinder Engines

The single-cylinder engine just described as above provides only one power stroke during every two crankshaft revolutions or delivers power only one-fourth of the time. To provide a more even and continuous flow of power, automobiles have engines with four, six, or eight cylinders.

Engine Classification

For identification purposes, manufacturers classify automobile engines by their cylinder arrangement, valve arrangement, and type of system used to cool the engine.[6]

Engine manufacturers basically use three distinct ways to arrange the cylinders in an engine: in-line, V-shape, or opposed(Fig. 1-6).

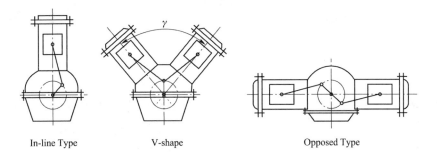

In-line Type   V-shape   Opposed Type

Fig. 1-6 Engine Arrangement

Automobile engines have their valves arranged in one of three ways. In an L-head engine, the valves are in the block, sitting side by side, adjacent to the cylinder. This engine design was at one time very common, but because of its limited compression ratio, the usage now has been confined. The F-type engine has one valve in the cylinder head and one in the engine block. Modern automotive engines utilize the third type of valve arrangement, with both valves in the cylinder head.

Manufacturers also classify engines as being either air-cooled or water-cooled(Fig. 1-7). In these air-cooled engines, the cylinders are cooled by the air flowing around. A liquid-cooled engine uses a liquid coolant as the medium to remove heat from the engine. With this system, the engine has the water jackets in the block and head, which surround the cylinders and combustion chambers and through which coolant circulates freely.[7] This coolant enters the engine from the

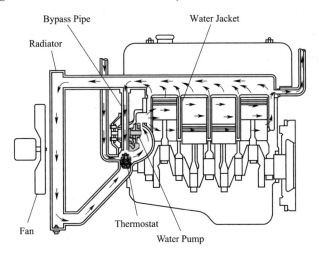

Fig. 1-7 Water-cooled Engine

bottom of the radiator and circulates throughout the engine, where it absorbs heat. Then it exits from the upper water jackets and pours into the upper portion of the radiator. As the coolant passes through the radiator, it picks up the heat contained in the coolant and passes this heat to the air flowing around the radiator passages or tubes. Thus, the coolant leaving the lower tank is cool ready to flow through the engine again.

Word List

1. introduction [ˌɪntrəˈdʌkʃ(ə)n]   *n.* 介绍,传入,初步,导言,绪论,入门
2. unit [ˈjuːnɪt]   *n.* 元件,部件,零件,装置
3. vehicle [ˈviːɪkəl]   *n.* 交通工具,车辆
4. engine [ˈendʒɪn]   *n.* 发动机
5. cylinder [ˈsɪlɪndə]   *n.* 汽缸,圆筒,圆柱体
6. combustion [kəmˈbʌstʃ(ə)n]   *n.* 燃烧
7. burn [bɜːn]   *vi. /vt.* 燃烧
8. convert [kənˈvɜːt]   *vt.* 使转变,转换……
9. piston [ˈpɪst(ə)n]   *n.* 活塞
10. crankshaft [ˈkræŋkʃɑːft]   *n.* 曲轴
11. ignition [ɪgˈnɪʃ(ə)n]   *n.* 点火,点燃
12. intake [ˈɪnteɪk]   *n.* 入口,进口
13. starter [ˈstɑːtə]   *n.* 起动机
14. clockwise [ˈklɒkwaɪz]   *adj.* 顺时针方向的;*adv.* 顺时针方向地
15. movement [ˈmuːvm(ə)nt]   *n.* 运动,动作,运转
16. vacuum [ˈvækjuəm]   *n.* 真空;*adj.* 真空的
17. gasoline [ˈgæsəliːn]   *n.* 汽油
18. manifold [ˈmænɪfəʊld]   *n.* 进、排气歧管
19. stroke [strəʊk]   *n.* 冲程,行程
20. remain [rɪˈmeɪn]   *vi.* 保持,逗留,剩余
21. charge [tʃɑːdʒ]   *n.* 充气,装料
22. draw [ˈdrɔː]   *vt.* 吸引,吸入
23. constitute [ˈkɒnstɪtjuːt]   *vt.* 组成,构成
24. compress [kəmˈpres]   *vt.* 压缩,浓缩
25. travel [ˈtræv(ə)l]   *v.* 旅行,传播,行进
26. power [ˈpaʊə]   *n.* 能量,动力
27. ignite [ɪgˈnaɪt]   *v.* 点火,点燃
28. spark [spɑːk]   *n.* 火花

29. revolution [ˌrevəˈluːʃ(ə)n]   n. 旋转,转数,旋转一周
30. expand [ɪkˈspænd; ek-]   vt. 使膨胀,详述,扩张
31. expend [ɪkˈspend; ek-]   vt. 消耗,花费,支出
32. passage [ˈpæsɪdʒ]   n. 通道,通路
33. port [pɔːt]   n. 通道,港口,端口
34. continuously [kənˈtɪnjuəslɪ]   adv. 不断地,连续地
35. attach [əˈtætʃ]   vt. 安装上,系上,贴上
36. resist [rɪˈzɪst]   vt. 抵抗,反抗,抗,忍得住
37. inertia [ɪˈnɜːʃə]   n. 惯性,惯量
38. even [ˈiːv(ə)n]   adj. 平滑的,偶数的,平均的
39. automobile [ˈɔːtəməbiːl]   n. 汽车
40. arrange [əˈreɪndʒ]   v. 排列,安排
41. flywheel [ˈflaɪwiːl]   n. 飞轮
42. arrangement [əˈreɪn(d)ʒm(ə)nt]   n. 排列,安排
43. adjacent [əˈdʒeɪs(ə)nt]   adj. 邻近的,接近的
44. coolant [ˈkuːl(ə)nt]   n. 冷却液
45. medium [ˈmiːdɪəm]   n. 媒体,媒介,介质
46. radiator [ˈreɪdɪeɪtə]   n. 散热器
47. tank [tæŋk]   n. 水箱
48. camshaft [ˈkæmʃɑːft]   n. 凸轮轴

Proper Names

1. self-contained   自备的
2. internal combustion engine   内燃机
3. heat energy   热能
4. mechanical energy   机械能
5. air/fuel mixture   空气燃油混合物(可燃混合气)
6. intake stroke   进气行程
7. compression stroke   压缩行程
8. power stroke   做功行程
9. exhaust stroke   排气行程
10. top dead center (TDC)   上止点
11. connecting rod   连杆
12. intake valve   进气门
13. atmospheric pressure   大气压力

14. intake manifold 进气歧管
15. exhaust valve 排气门
16. bottom dead center (BDC) 下止点
17. spark plug 火花塞
18. combustion chamber 燃烧室
19. compression ratio 压缩比
20. cylinder head 汽缸盖
21. engine block 汽缸体
22. water jacket 水套

Useful Expressions

1. so that 所以,因此
2. at the same time 同时,但是
3. because of 因为
4. speed up 加速
5. slow down (使)慢下来
6. result in 导致
7. side by side 并排,并肩

Key Vocabulary

1. expand

vt. 使膨胀,详述,扩张,扩大

The business has expanded from having one office to having twelve. 这个公司已从一个分公司发展到拥有12个分公司了。

vi. 张开,发展

expand on 详述

expand to 扩大为

2. arrange

vt. 排列,整理

He arranged the books on the shelf. 他把书架上的书整理了一下。

vt. 安排,准备

We have arranged a party. 我们准备了一个晚会。

vi. 商定

Arranged with her to meet at 8. 和她商定8点钟见面。

arrange for 安排

Notes

1. The engine is a self-contained power unit which converts the heat energy of fuel into mechanical energy for moving the vehicle.

翻译:发动机为自备动力型装置,该装置将燃料的热能转换成机械能,用于推动车辆前进。

语法:which converts…引导定语从句。

2. The drawing of an air/fuel charge into the cylinder in this manner, during the downward movement of the piston, constitutes the intake stroke of the piston.

翻译:在活塞向下运动时,可燃混合气以上述方式被吸入汽缸,该过程就是进气行程。

语法:during the downward movement of the piston 作时间状语从句。

3. This tremendous force pushes the piston downward on the power stroke, causing the connecting rod to rotate the crankshaft.

翻译:在作功行程时,巨大的气体压力推动着活塞向下运动,带动连杆转动曲轴。

语法:causing the connecting rod to rotate the crankshaft 是现在分词作结果状语从句。

4. This remaining pressurized gas flows comparatively freely from the cylinder through the passage (port) opened by the exhaust valve.

翻译:带残余压力的废气从已被排气门开启的排气道中较为顺畅地排出。

5. To keep the crankshaft turning smoothly between two power strokes, the flywheel is attached to the end of the crankshaft.

翻译:为了使曲轴在两个相邻的作功行程间平稳地转动,在曲轴的后端安装了飞轮。

6. For identification purposes, manufacturers classify automobile engines by their cylinder arrangement, valve arrangement, and type of system used to cool the engine.

翻译:发动机制造商将汽车发动机按汽缸排列、气门布置以及冷却系统的类型进行分类。

语法:for identification purposes 作目的状语。

7. With this system, the engine has the water jackets in the block and head, which surround the cylinders and combustion chambers and through which coolant circulates freely.

翻译:在水冷式发动机上,发动机汽缸体和汽缸盖内均有水套,水套包围着汽缸和燃烧室,水套内部有自由循环流动的冷却液。

语法:which 引导的定语从句修饰 the water jackets。

Exercises

1. Choose the best answer from the following choices according to the text.

1) In the internal combustion engine, air/fuel mixture is introduced into a closed _____ where it is compressed and then ignited.

    A. tank   B. spark   C. cylinder   D. flywheel

2) The air/fuel charge is now under _____ so that it will produce a great deal of power when the spark plug ignites it.

    A. compression   B. inflation   C. vacuum   D. ignition

3) Thus, the coolant leaving the lower tank is _____ ready to flow through the engine again.

    A. hot   B. cool   C. cold   D. warm

2. Translate the following into Chinese

1) internal combustion engine   2) vehicle   3) power stroke

4) exhaust valve   5) gasoline   6) liquid-cooled engine

7) flywheel   8) air-cooled engine   9) crankshaft

3. Translate the following into English

1) 四冲程发动机   2) 进气行程   3) 排气行程

4) 燃烧室   5) 汽缸   6) 活塞

7) 可燃混合气   8) 火花塞   9) 连杆

4. Translate the following sentences into Chinese

1) In the internal combustion engine, an air-fuel mixture is introduced into a closed cylinder where it is compressed and then ignited.

2) The intake stroke of a four-stroke engine begins with the piston at top dead center (TDC).

3) After the piston reaches bottom dead center (BDC), it moves upward again as the starter continues to turn the crankshaft in a clockwise direction.

5. Translate the words or phrases in the following figure into Chinese

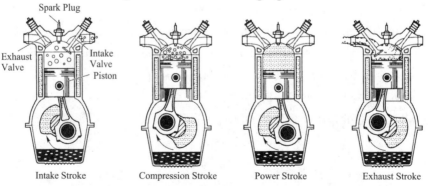

Intake Stroke   Compression Stroke   Power Stroke   Exhaust Stroke

Practical Reading

2ZZ-GE ENGINE

Description

The 2ZZ-GE engine is an in-line, 4-cylinder, 1.8-liter, 16-valve DOHC engine.[1] This engine meets the European STEP Ⅲ regulations.

The VVTL-i system (Variable Valve Timing and Lift-intelligent) system, the DIS (Direct Ignition System), and an Air Injection system have been adopted on this engine in order to improve performance, fuel economy and reduce exhaust emissions.[2]

Layout of Main Engine Components (Fig. 1-8)

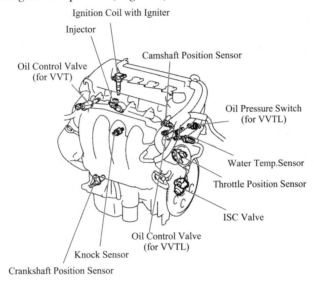

Fig. 1-8 Layout of Main Engine Components

Word List

1. regulation [ˌregjuˈleɪʃ(ə)n]   n. 规则,规章
2. layout [ˈleɪaʊt]   n. 设计,布置,版面安排
3. component [kəmˈpəʊnənt]   n. 元件,组件,部件

Proper Names

engine component   发动机零部件

Notes

1. The 2ZZ—GE engine is an in-line, 4-cylinder, 1.8-liter, 16-valve DOHC engine.

翻译:2ZZ—GE 发动机是一种直列4缸、1.8升排量、16气门、双顶置凸轮轴发动机。

2. The VVTL-i system (Variable Valve Timing and Lift-intelligent) system, the DIS (Direct Ignition System), and an Air Injection system have been adopted on this engine in order to improve performance, fuel economy and reduce exhaust emissions.

翻译:为提高发动机动力性,燃油经济性及降低排放,本发动机采用了VVTL-i(可变气门正时—智能气门升程系统)、DIS(直接点火系统)、空气喷射系统。

学习资料:
相关链接及网址
1. http://65.201.178.38
2. http://www.a-car.com

推荐书目
1. William K. Toboldt, & Larry Johnson. Automotive Encyclopedia. South Holland, Illinois: The Goodheart-willcox Company, Inc. 1983.
2. 马林才.汽车实用英语.[M].2版.北京:人民交通出版社,2014.
3. 王凤丽.汽车专业英语.[M].北京:人民邮电出版社,2015.

任务二 发动机构造认识

1. 掌握关于发动机构造相关的专业术语、单词和词汇。
2. 掌握发动机中零部件的固定表达方法。
3. 能对发动机上各大总成进行中英互译。
4. 能对与发动机构造相关的英语资料进行简单的阅读和翻译。
5. 能辨认汽车实物上英语词汇。

任务描述

以四冲程发动机为例,介绍发动机的构造,如汽缸体、汽缸盖、活塞、连杆、曲轴、配气机构以及飞轮等。通过完成该任务,能阅读关于发动机构造及其零部件的外文文献,并掌握相应内容的翻译技巧。

本学习任务沿着以下脉络进行学习:

通读全文 → 学习单词和语法 → 完成课后练习 → 分组讨论 → 课后阅读

Task 2 Engine Structure Understanding

Engine Block

The engine block forms the main framework, or foundation, of the engine (Fig. 2-1).[1] The block is cast mainly from gray iron or iron alloyed with other metals such as nickel or chromium. However, some blocks have been made from aluminum. In any case, the block itself has many components.

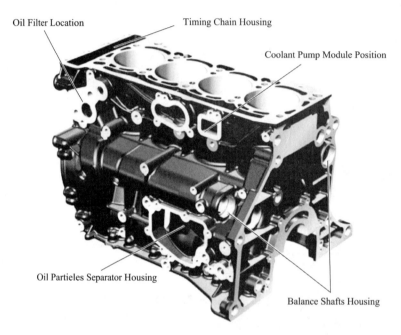

Fig. 2-1 Engine Block

The cylinders are cast into the block. The cylinders are circular, tubelike openings in the block, which act as guides for the pistons as they move up and down. In aluminum blocks, the manufacturer usually installs cast-iron or steel cylinder sleeves (liners). The water jackets are also cast into the block. Finally, the block has cast-in bores for both the camshaft and crankshaft.

Many parts are also attached by fastening devices to the engine block. These items include the water pump, oil pan, the flywheel or clutch housing, the ignition distributor, oil and fuel pump, and the cylinder head.

Cylinder Head

The cylinder head is bolted to the block (Fig. 2-2). The manufacturer casts the cylinder head in one piece from iron, from iron alloyed with other metals, or from aluminum alloy. Aluminum has the advantage of combining lightness with rather high heat conductivity. Depending on the style of engine, the cylinder head serves many functions.

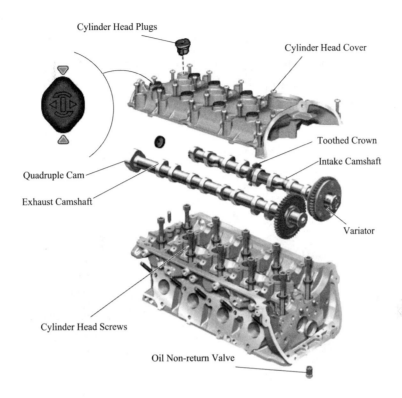

Fig. 2-2 Cylinder Head

Pistons

The engine manufacturer fits a piston into each cylinder of the engine. The piston is a movable part or plug that receives the pressure from the burning air/fuel mixture and converts this pressure into reciprocating (up-and-down) motion (Fig. 2-3). [2] Manufacturers make most engine pistons from aluminum, which is less than half the weight of iron. Iron pistons were common in early automotive engines.

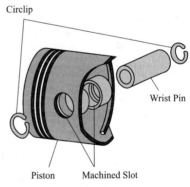

Fig. 2-3 piston

Piston Clearance

Piston clearance is the distance between the outer circumference of the piston and the cylinder wall itself (Fig. 2-4). [3] In operation, oil fills this clearance so that the piston moves on films of lubricating oil. If this clearance is too small, several problems can develop. On the other hand, excessively large clearance can result in piston slap as the piston starts down on the power strokes. The piston itself operates many degrees hotter than the adjacent cylinder wall and therefore expands more. Manufacturers must control this expansion in order to avoid the loss of adequate piston clearance.

Piston Rings

Some operating clearance must exist between the piston and the cylinder wall; however, some form of seal is necessary between the piston and the cylinder wall to prevent blowby. Consequently, piston rings are used to provide the necessary seal to eliminate blowby and to control oil consumption. [4] Automotive pistons have two kinds of rings: compression and oil control. The compression rings primarily seal against the loss of air/fuel mixture as the piston compresses it and also the combustion pressure as the mixture burns. While the function of the oil control ring is to prevent excessive amounts of oil from working up into the combustion chamber (Fig. 2-5).

Fig. 2-4 Piston Clearance   Fig. 2-5 Piston Rings

Connecting Rods

As mentioned earlier, the piston moves up and down in the cylinder, in a reciprocating motion. In order to rotate the drive wheels, a connecting rod and crankshaft must change the reciprocating motion to rotary. The connecting rod itself attaches at one end to the piston and on the other end to the crankpin section of the crankshaft (Fig. 2-6). [5]

Fig. 2-6 Connecting Rods

Crankshaft

The crankshaft is the main rotating member, or shaft, of the engine (Fig. 2-7). Its function, along with the connecting rod, is to change the reciprocating motion of the piston to rotary. In addition, the crankshaft is responsible for driving the camshaft through timing gears, plus operating the accessories via a system of belts and pulleys. Lastly, the crankshaft carries the total torque-turning or twisting effort and delivers it to the flywheel. From the flywheel, the torque then passes either to the friction clutch assembly or to the torque converter.

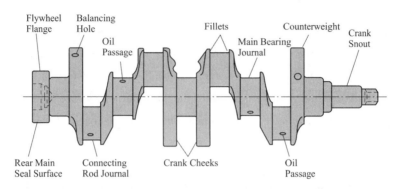

Fig. 2-7　Crankshaft

Designed into the one-piece crankshaft are areas for main bearing journals, crankpins, counterweights, flywheel flange, and driving hub.

Flywheel

The flywheel is a comparatively heavy wheel, bolted to the flange on the rear end of the crankshaft(Fig. 2-8). Its function is to keep the engine running smoothly between power strokes. Its inertia tends to keep the flywheel rotating at a constant speed. The flywheel also has several other functions. For example, the flywheel has gear teeth around its outer circumference. These teeth mesh with teeth located on the starting motor drive pinion in order to crank the engine over. In addition, the rear surface of the flywheel serves as the driving member of the clutch assembly.[6]

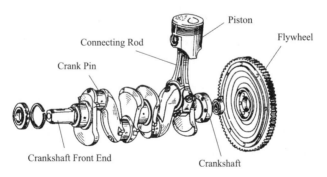

Fig. 2-8　Flywheel

Vibration Damper

Manufacturers usually install a vibration damper and fan pulley assembly onto the drive end of the crankshaft. This damping device controls torsional vibrations.

Valve

Modern engines have cylinder heads that contain valves. These valves open and close ports to allow or stop the flow of gases into or from the combustion chamber. Each cylinder requires at least two: an intake and exhaust.

Camshaft

The camshaft is another rotating shaft within the engine; it serves usually three functions. First, the camshaft has a series of cams that can change rotary motion to straight-line motion which cause the intake and exhaust valves to open. The camshaft will have one cam for each valve, or, in most engines, two cams per cylinder. Second, the camshaft has an eccentric, or special cam, designed to operate the fuel pump. Finally, the camshaft has a gear that drives the oil pump and ignition distributor.

Lifters

A lifter is a cylindrical part within an engine that rests on a cam of the camshaft. As the camshaft rotates, the cam raises the lifter, and the lifter in turn opens a valve. The lifter may be in direct contact with the tip of the valve stem, or it may bear against a push rod that functions along with a rocker-arm assembly to open a valve. [7]

Push Rodsand Rocker Arms

Along with the camshaft, valves, valve seats, and valve springs, some valve trains have several other components-the push rods and rocker arms. The push rod is a metal rod that fits between the lifter and the rocker arm. Its function is to transmit cam lobe lift from the camshaft to the rocker arm assembly. The rocker arm is nothing more than a precision-designed lever. Its function is to convert the upward motion of a push rod into downward motion that compresses the spring and opens the valve.

Valve Timing

Duration is the length of time a valve is open. The measurement of this open period is not in units of time because the actual time a valve remains open varies with engine speed. Therefore, this measurement is in degrees of crankshaft rotation, which does not change with speed. To lengthen the time and to accelerate the air/fuel mixture flow into the cylinders, both the intake and exhaust valves must be open at the same time for a short period. [8] The overlap is provided in order to take advantage of the inertial forces in the escaping exhaust gases. These gases create strong suction as they rush out of the combustion chamber.

Timing Gears

The manufacturer machines a cam lobe into a given shape that produces a given amount of valve-open duration and overlap. Furthermore, meshing the timing gears or installing the chain onto the sprockets at a specific place will time the valves to open and close at the proper moment in the engine's cycle(Fig. 2-9).

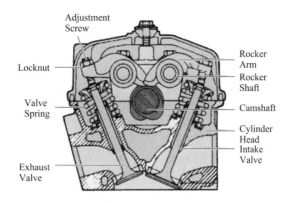

Fig. 2-9　Valve Gear

Word List

1. framework ['freɪmwɜːk]　　　　　　　　n. 构架，框架，结构
2. foundation [faun'deɪʃ(ə)n]　　　　　　n. 基础，根本
3. nickel ['nɪk(ə)l]　　　　　　　　　　　　n. 镍
4. chromium ['krəumɪəm]　　　　　　　　n. 铬
5. aluminum [ə'luːmɪnəm]　　　　　　　　n. 铝
6. cast [kɑːst]　　　　　　　　　　　　　v. 浇铸
7. sleeve [sliːv]　　　　　　　　　　　　n. 套管，轴套，衬套，缸套
8. bore [bɔː]　　　　　　　　　　　　　　n. 内径，枪膛；v. 钻孔
9. serve [sɜːv]　　　　　　　　　　　　　vt. 服务，可做，适于，具有……作用
10. crankcase ['kræŋkkeɪs]　　　　　　　n. 曲轴箱
11. bolt [bəult]　　　　　　　　　　　　　n. 螺钉；v. 用螺栓紧固
12. seal [siːl]　　　　　　　　　　　　　　n. 封铅，封条，密封
13. reciprocating [rɪ'sɪprə,keɪtɪŋ]　　　　adj. 往复的
14. circumference [sə'kʌmf(ə)r(ə)ns]　　n. 圆周，周围
15. slap [slæp]　　　　　　　　　　　　vt. 拍，拍击
16. expansion [ɪk'spænʃ(ə)n; ek-]　　　n. 扩充，膨胀
17. plus [plʌs]　　　　　　　　　　　　　prep. 加上，以及
18. accessory [ək'ses(ə)rɪ]　　　　　　　n. 附件，零件，附加物
19. via ['vaɪə, 'viːə]　　　　　　　　　　prep. 经，通过，经由
20. sprocket ['sprɔkɪt]　　　　　　　　　n. 链轮齿
21. chain [tʃeɪn]　　　　　　　　　　　　n. 链（条）
22. crankpin ['kræŋkpɪn]　　　　　　　　n. 曲柄销，连杆轴颈
23. counterweight ['kauntəweɪt]　　　　　n. 平衡物，平衡重

24. flange [flæn(d)ʒ]   n. 凸缘,边缘,轮缘
25. function [ˈfʌŋ(k)ʃ(ə)n]   n. 功能,作用
26. cam [kæm]   n. 凸轮
27. eccentric [ɪkˈsentrɪk; ek-]   n. 偏心轮
28. gear [gɪə]   n. 齿轮,传动装置
29. lifter [ˈlɪftə]   n. 挺杆
30. component [kəmˈpəunənt]   n. 部分,部件,零件,元件

Proper Names

1. gray iron	灰口铁
2. water pump	水泵
3. oil pan	机油盘
4. heat conductivity	热传导性
5. fastening device	紧固件
6. drive wheel	驱动轮
7. valve timing	气门正时
8. friction clutch assembly	摩擦式离合器
9. torque converter	液力变矩器
10. main bearing journal	主轴承轴颈
11. driving hub	驱动毂
12. fan pulley	风扇皮带轮
13. timing gear	正时齿轮
14. fuel pump	燃油泵
15. piston clearance	活塞间隙
16. piston ring	活塞环
17. compression ring	气环
18. oil control ring	油环
19. vibration damper	扭转减振器
20. torsional vibration	扭转振动
21. oil pump	机油泵
22. ignition distributor	点火分电器
23. valve stem	气门杆
24. push rod	气门推杆
25. valve tip	气门杆顶端
26. valve seat	气门座

27. valve spring　　　　　　　　　　　气门弹簧
28. rocker arm　　　　　　　　　　　气门摇臂
29. cam lobe　　　　　　　　　　　　凸轮凸起部,凸轮工作部分

Useful Expressions

1. responsible for　　　　　　　　　　负责
2. along with　　　　　　　　　　　　连同……一起,随同……一起
3. convert into　　　　　　　　　　　转变,变换
4. in turn　　　　　　　　　　　　　　依次,轮流

Key Vocabulary

1. alloy

n. 合金

vt. 使成合金,减低成色

vt. 使减弱,使减轻

Pleasure alloyed with pain. 欢乐因痛苦削弱了。

2. cast

vt./vi. 投,掷,抛

cast a net 撒网

cast the fishing line into the water 把钓鱼线抛入水中

vt./vi. 舍弃,脱落

Every year the snake casts (off) its skin. 蛇每年都要蜕皮。

n. 演员

He was in the cast of the school play. 他在学校演的剧里扮演角色。

cast away 遭遇海难而流落某地

cast down 使心烦意乱;气馁;沮丧

cast off 解缆放船;解缆

cast on（编织毛衣等）起针;编织成第一行针脚

Notes

1. The engine block forms the main framework, or foundation, of the engine.

翻译:发动机汽缸体构成发动机的主要框架或基础。

2. The piston is a movable part or plug that receives the pressure from the burning air/fuel

mixture and converts this pressure into reciprocating (up-and-down) motion.

翻译:活塞是运动部件,它承受可燃混合气燃烧时产生的压力,并将该力转化成活塞的上下往复式运动。

3. Piston clearance is the distance between the outer circumference of the piston and the cylinder wall itself.

翻译:活塞间隙是指活塞外圆表面到汽缸壁之间的距离。

4. Consequently, piston rings are used to provide the necessary seal to eliminate blowby and to control oil consumption.

翻译:因此,使用活塞环来对活塞和汽缸壁间进行必要的密封,以防止发动机窜气和减小发动机机油消耗。

5. The connecting rod itself attaches at one end to the piston and on the other end to the crankpin section of the crankshaft.

翻译:连杆一头与活塞相连,另一头与曲轴的曲柄销相连。

6. In addition, the rear surface of the flywheel serves as the driving member of the clutch assembly.

翻译:此外,飞轮的后端面还作为离合器总成的驱动件。

7. The lifter may be in direct contact with the tip of the valve stem, or it may bear against a push rod that functions along with a rocker-arm assembly to open a valve.

翻译:气门挺杆或者直接与气门杆顶端接触,或者与推杆相连,推动推杆与摇臂总成一起开启气门。

8. To lengthen the time and to accelerate the air/fuel mixture flow into the cylinders, both the intake and exhaust valves must be open at the same time for a short period.

翻译:为了延长可燃混合气进入汽缸的时间和加速混合气的进入,在同一小段时间内使进、排气门同时开启。

Exercises

1. Choose the best answer from the following choices according to the text.

1) The _____ are circular, tubelike openings in the block, which act as guides for the pistons as they move up and down.

  A. chambers   B. cylinders   C. bores   D. rings

2) Manufacturers make most engine pistons from _____, which is less than half the weight of iron.

  A. iron   B. nickel   C. chromium   D. aluminum

3) _____ describes the escape of unburned and burned gases from the combustion chamber, past the piston, and into the crankcase.

　　　　A. Timing　　　　　　B. Cranking　　　　　C. Blowby　　　　　D. Leaking

4）Flywheel _____ tends to keep it rotating at a constant speed.

　　　　A. inertia　　　　　　B. quality　　　　　　C. movement　　　　D. weight

5）The _____ is a metal rod that fits between the lifter and the rocker arm.

　　　　A. timing gear　　　　B. cam lobe　　　　　C. push rod　　　　　D. rocker arm

2. Translate the following into Chinese

1）gray iron　　　　　　　2）timing gear　　　　　　3）water pump

4）compression ring　　　　5）valve timing　　　　　　6）crankpin

7）counterweight　　　　　8）vibration damper　　　　9）fan pulley

3. Translate the following into English

1）发动机汽缸体　　　　　2）摩擦式离合器　　　　　3）曲轴箱

4）油底壳　　　　　　　　5）活塞间隙　　　　　　　6）活塞环

7）点火分电器　　　　　　8）凸轮工作部分　　　　　9）气门推杆

4. Translate the following sentences into Chinese

1）The cylinders are circular, tubelike openings in the block, which act as guides for the pistons as they move up and down.

2）Many parts are also attached by fastening devices to the engine block.

3）If this clearance is too small, for whatever reason, several problems can develop.

5. Translate the words or phrases in the following figure into Chinese

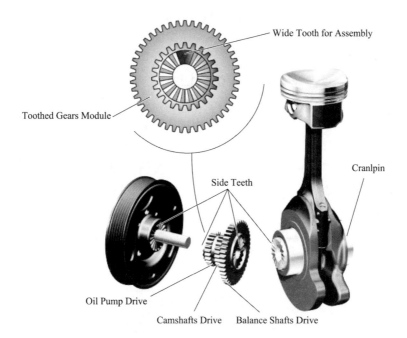

Practical Reading

Engine Gaskets and Engine Radiator

In an automobile, gaskets are thin sheets of flexible materials that are used to separate two metal components.[1] They allow metal parts to be mated together without losing fluids that are transferred between the two. Normally when two pieces of metal are mated, there are minute machining differences in the surfaces that would allow high-pressure fluids or gasses to escape and relieve pressure. In an internal combustion engine, fluid flow between parts is vital for engine operation. Gaskets help the engine transfer these fluids with less loss. Gaskets are commonly made from brass, steel, and rubber compounds. In addition to proving more conducive passages for fluids to flow, they also serve as insulation to isolate some parts from shock or vibrations that could cause leaks, and create tighter fitting parts that are more likely to stay in place.[2]

A radiator is a long copper or aluminum tube that is bent many times to form a rectangular shape. This tube is then surrounded by many small aluminum fins. The aluminum draws heat readily from the warm cooling fluid inside the tube. Once the fins are heated air is directed across them releasing their heat into the air and cooling the engine. A radiator also has a neck that ends in a cap. This cap is called a pressure cap. Once overheats to a certain degree the fluid may expand exerting pressure on the entire system.[3] The cap is manufactured in such a way that if the pressure reaches a predetermined level it will give way releasing the pressure of the system preventing a larger explosion. *CAUTION* never remove a hot radiator cap.[4]

Word List

1. gasket ['gæskɪt]   n. 垫圈,衬垫
2. minute ['mɪnɪt]   adj. 微小的
3. brass [brɑːs]   n. 黄铜,黄铜制品
4. compound ['kɔmpaund]   n. 混合物,化合物
5. cap [kæp]   n. 盖,罩
6. insulation [ɪnsjuˈleɪʃ(ə)n] n. 绝缘
7. copper ['kɔpə]   n. 铜

Proper Names

engine gasket   发动机垫圈

Notes

1. In an automobile, gaskets are thin sheets of flexible materials that are used to separate two metal components.

   翻译:在汽车上,垫圈是既薄又软的材料,用于分隔两个金属部件。

2. In addition to proving more conducive passages for fluids to flow, they also serve as insulation to isolate some parts from shock or vibrations that could cause leaks, and create tighter fitting parts that are more likely to stay in place.

   翻译:除了给液体流动提供更好的通道外,垫圈还可作为缓冲材料,将某些部件从振动和冲击处隔离开,以免产生泄漏,以及使接合件配合更紧密,便于零件更好地安装就位。

3. Once overheats to a certain degree the fluid may expand exerting pressure on the entire system.

   翻译:液体一旦过热到一定程度,它将膨胀,以至于在整个冷却系统里产生压力。

4. *CAUTION* never remove a hot radiator cap.

   翻译:注意,切勿在冷却液沸腾时拆卸散热器盖。

学习资料:

1. 王怡民. 汽车专业英语[M]. 北京:人民交通出版社,2003
2. 马林才. 汽车实用英语(下)[M]. 北京：人民交通出版社,2005
3. William K. Toboldt, & Larry Johnson. Automotive Encyclopedia. South Holland, Illinois：The Goodheart-willcox Company, Inc. 1983.
4. Robert N. Brady. Electric and Electronic Systems for Automobiles and Trucks. Virginia：Reston Publishing Company, Inc. 1983.
5. 陈文华. 汽车发动机构造与维修[M]. 北京:北京航空航天大学出版社,2007

任务三 燃油直喷系统

学习目标

1. 掌握缸内直喷发动机燃油供给系统的组成、作用、优缺点等英语术语、单词和词汇。
2. 掌握关于高压泵、高压传感器的词汇。
3. 能读懂汽车燃油供给系统的资料,并能进行中英互译。
4. 能进行相关内容的简单阅读和翻译。
5. 能对汽车实物上的英语单词和词汇进行辨认。

任务描述

以目前最新的缸内直喷发动机为例,介绍汽油缸内直喷发动机的优缺点,燃油系统的组成、工作原理等。通过完成该任务,能阅读关于发动机燃油供给系统的外文文献,并掌握相应内容的翻译技巧。

学习引导

本学习任务沿着以下脉络进行学习:

Task 3　Gasoline Direct-injection Systems

Direct Fuel Injection

Several vehicle manufacturers such as Audi, Mitsubishi, Mercedes, BMW, Toyota/Lexus, Mazda, Ford, and General Motors are using gasoline direct injection (GDI) systems, which General Motors refers to as a Spark Ignition Direct Injection (SIDI) system.[1] A direct injection system sprays high-pressure fuel, up to 2900 PSI, into the combustion chamber as the piston approaches the top of the compression stroke. With the combination of high-pressure swirl injectors and modified combustion chamber, almost instantaneous vaporization of the fuel occurs. This combined with a higher compression ratio allows a direct-injected engine to operate using a leaner-than-normal air-fuel ratio, which results in improved fuel economy with higher power output and reduced exhaust emissions (Fig. 3-1).

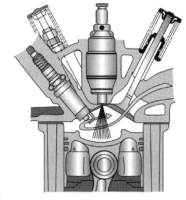

Fig. 3-1　Gasoline Direct-injection System

Advantages of Gasoline Direct Injection

The use of direct injection compared with port fuel-injection has many advantages including:

1. Improved fuel economy due to reduced pumping losses and heat loss. Allows a higher compression ratio for higher engine efficiency[2].

2. Allows the use of lower-octane gasoline.

3. The volumetric efficiency is higher.

4. Less need for extra fuel for acceleration.

5. Improved cold starting and throttle response.

6. Allows the use of a higher percentage of EGR to reduce exhaust emissions.

7. Up to 25% improvement in fuel economy.

8. 12% to 15% reduction in exhaust emissions.

Disadvantages of Gasoline Direct Injection

1. Higher cost due to high-pressure pump and injectors

2. More components compared with port fuel injection

3. Due to the high compression, a NO_x storage catalyst is sometimes required to meet emission standards, especially in Europe (Fig. 3-2).

4. Uses up to six operating modes depending on engine load and speed, which requires more calculations to be performed by the powertrain control module (PCM).

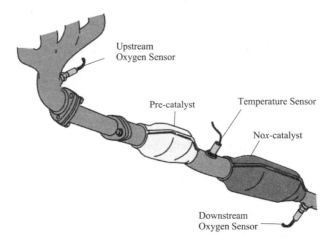

Fig. 3-2　Catalytic Conversion Device

Direct Injection Fuel Delivery System

Low-pressure Fule Pump

The fuel pump in the fuel tank supplies fuel to the high-pressure fuel pump at a pressure of approximately 60 PSI[3]. The fuel filter is located in the fuel tank and is part of the fuel pump assembly. It is not usually serviceable as a separate component. The engine control module (ECM) controls the output of the high-pressure pump, which has a range between 500 PSI (3440 kPa) and 2900 PSI (15200 kPa) during engine operation (Fig. 3-3).

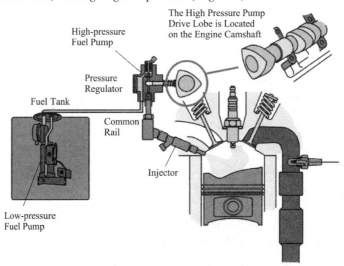

Fig. 3-3　Typical Direct-injection System

High Pressure Fuel Pump

In a General Motors system, the engine control module (ECM) controls the output of the high-pressure pump[4], which has a range between 500 PSI (3440 kPa) and 2900 PSI (15200 kPa) during engine operation. The high-pressure fuel pump connects to the pump in the fuel tank through the low-pressure fuel line. The pump consists of a single-barrel piston pump, which is driven by the engine camshaft. The pump plunger rides on a three-lobed cam on the camshaft. The high-pressure pump is cooled and lubricated by the fuel itself. (Fig. 3-4).

Fuel Rail

The fuel rail stores the fuel from the high-pressure pump and stores high-pressure fuel for use to each injector. All injectors get the same pressure fuel from the fuel rail.

Fuel Pressure Regulator

An electric pressure-control valve is installed between the pump inlet and outlet valves. The fuel rail pressure sensor connects to the PCM with three wires:

1. Five-volt reference
2. Ground
3. Signal

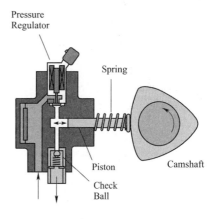

Fig. 3-4　High-pressure Fuel Pressure

The sensor signal provides an analog signal to the PCM that varies in voltage as fuel rail pressure changes. Low pressure results in a low-voltage signal and high-pressure results in a high-voltage signal. The PCM uses internal drivers to control the power feed and ground for the pressure control valve. When both PCM drivers are deactivated, the inlet valve is held open by spring pressure. This causes the high-pressure fuel pump to default to low-pressure mode. The fuel from the high-pressure fuel pump flows through a line to the fuel rail and injectors. The actual operating pressure can vary from as low as 900 PSI (6200 kPa) at idle to over 2000 PSI (13800 kPa) during high speed or heavy load conditions (Fig. 3-5).

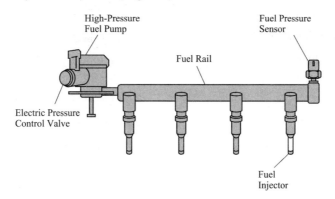

Fig. 3-5　Fuel Pressure Regulator

Word List

1. manufacturer [ˌmænjuˈfæktʃ(ə)rə(r)]　　　　n. 制造商, 厂商

2. sprays [spreɪz]　　　　　　　　　　　v. 喷;扫射
3. economy [ɪ'kɒnəmɪ]　　　　　　　　n. 经济,节约;理财
4. emission [ɪ'mɪʃ(ə)n]　　　　　　　　n.(光、热等的)发射,散发;排放
5. pump [pʌmp]　　　　　　　　　　　n. 泵,抽水机;打气筒
6. injection [ɪn'dʒekʃ(ə)n]　　　　　　n. 注射,喷射
7. acceleration [əkselə'reɪʃ(ə)n]　　　n. 加速,促进
8. percentage [pə'sentɪdʒ]　　　　　　n. 百分比;百分率,百分数
9. sensor ['sensə]　　　　　　　　　　n. 传感器
10. reduction [rɪ'dʌkʃ(ə)n]　　　　　　n. 减少;下降;缩小
11. calculation [kælkju'leɪʃ(ə)n]　　　n. 计算;估计
12. approximately [ə'prɒksɪmətlɪ]　　 adv. 大约,近似地;近于
13. located [ləu'keɪtɪd]　　　　　　　 adj. 处于,位于;坐落的
14. module ['mɔdjuːl]　　　　　　　　n. [计] 模块;组件;模数
15. upstream ['ʌpstriːm]　　　　　　　n. 上游部门;adj. 向上游的,逆流而上的
16. downstream ['daun'striːm]　　　　adj. 下游的;顺流的
17. injector [ɪn'dʒektə]　　　　　　　 n. 注射器;注射者;喷油器
18. range [reɪn(d)ʒ]　　　　　　　　　n. 范围;幅度;排;山脉
19. signal ['sɪgn(ə)l]　　　　　　　　　n. 信号;暗号;导火线
20. assembly [ə'semblɪ]　　　　　　　n. 装配;集会,集合

Proper Names

1. volumetric efficiency　　　　　　　充气效率
2. gasoline direct injection　　　　　　燃油直接喷射
3. high-pressure fuel　　　　　　　　　高压燃油
4. compression ratio　　　　　　　　　压缩比
5. fuel economy　　　　　　　　　　　燃油经济性
6. EGR　　　　　　　　　　　　　　　废气再循环
7. powertrain control module　　　　　动力控制模块
8. pre-catalyst　　　　　　　　　　　　三元催化器
9. oxygen sensor　　　　　　　　　　　氧传感器
10. fuel pump　　　　　　　　　　　　高压泵
11. fuel tank　　　　　　　　　　　　　燃油箱
12. fuel rail　　　　　　　　　　　　　燃油轨
13. pressure regulator　　　　　　　　　压力调节器
14. fuel pump　　　　　　　　　　　　高压泵

Useful Expressions

1. such as　　　　　　　　　　　例如，诸如，比如，像
2. the top of　　　　　　　　　　在……的顶部；在……的巅峰
3. due to　　　　　　　　　　　由于；应归于

Key Vocabulary

1. pump

n. 泵，抽水机，打气筒

Here is an old-fashioned pump for drawing water from a well. 这里有一个旧式水泵可从井里抽水。

　　pump abuses upon sb. 破口大骂

　　pump away at 努力干

　　pump out 抽空

2. injection

n. 注射，注射剂，注射液，引入

It's time for another injection. 又该打针了。

The doctor prescribed three injections. 医生开了三支注射液的处方。

Many scholars were annoyed by his injection of politics into academic discussions. 他把政治引进学术讨论中，使很多学者感到恼火。

Did you get your anticholerainjection?　你打过抗霍乱疫苗了吗？

Will the injection hurt, doctor?　医生，打针会痛吗？

An injection is better than the pill.　注射比服用药片见效快。

An intravenousinjection of a narcotic.　静脉注射麻醉剂

3. actual

adj. 真实的，实际的；现行的，目前的

In the absence of actual data, no reliance can be placed on such figures.

在缺乏实际资料的情况下，这样的数据不可靠。

I can not give the actual figures.

我不能举出实际数字。

If I now scroll down to the actual implementation, now does this work or not work?

如果现在我向下滚动到实际的执行中，这个是可用的还是不可用的呢？

How do we go from theory to actual action steps?

我们应该如何把理论转化为实际行动呢？

Notes

1. Several vehicle manufacturers such as Audi, Mitsubishi, Mercedes, BMW, Toyota/Lexus, Mazda, Ford, and General Motors are using gasoline direct injection (GDI) systems.

翻译:奥迪、三菱、奔驰、宝马、丰田、雷克萨斯、马自达、福特和通用汽车等几家汽车制造商都在使用汽油直接喷射(GDI)系统。

2. Improved fuel economy due to reduced pumping losses and heat loss. Allows a higher compression ratio for higher engine efficiency.

翻译:由于减少了泵的损失和热损失,提高了燃油经济性,从而提高了更高的压缩比,提高了发动机的效率。

3. The fuel pump in the fuel tank supplies fuel to the high-pressure fuel pump at a pressure of approximately 60 PSI.

翻译:燃料箱中的燃油泵向高压燃料泵提供燃料,压力约为60 PSI。

4. In a General Motors system, the engine control module (ECM) controls the output of the high-pressure pump.

翻译:在通用汽车系统中,发动机控制模块(ECM)控制高压泵的输出。

Exercises

1. Choose the best answer from the following choices according to the text.

1) The _____ has the job of supplying a combustible mixture of air and fuel to the engine.

   A. starting system   B. cooling system

   C. lubricating system   D. fuel system

2) Electronic Fuel injection system can be divided into _____ basic sub-systems.

   A. two   B. three   C. four   D. five

3) To maintain precise fuel metering, the fuel _____ regulator maintains a constant fuel.

   A. pressure   B. flow   C. velocity   D. quality

4) The _____ monitors variables such as coolant temperature, engine speed, throttle angle, and exhaust oxygen content.

   A. sensor   B. ECU

   C. terminal   D. motor

2. Translate the following into Chinese.

1) electronic fuel injection   2) high-pressure   3) air flow meter

4) ECU   5) tank   6) fuel economy

7) pressure regulator

3. Translate the following into English.

1）燃油供给系统　　　　2）燃油滤清器　　　　3）高压泵

4）燃油压力传感器　　　5）燃油压力调节阀　　6）喷油器

7）压缩比

4. Translate the following sentences into Chinese.

1）The fuel filter is located in the fuel tank and is part of the fuel pump assembly.

2）The fuel rail stores the fuel from the high-pressure pump and stores high-pressure fuel for use to each injector.

3）The sensor signal provides an analog signal to the PCM that varies in voltage as fuel rail pressure changes.

Practical Reading

Engine Measurement and Performance Characteristics

The former chapter presented the scientific principles upon which the automobile engine operates. It is time to expand on the topic of engine operation by exploring the many factors that influence engine performance. These factors include a bore, stroke, displacement, compression ratio, compression pressure, volumetric efficiency, thermo efficiency, and mechanical efficiency. There are a few negative factors that adversely affect the normal combustion process and can cause power loss and serious engine damage. [1] These factors are, of course, detonation and surface ignition.

Bore

The bore of an engine is a measurement taken inside the cylinder. Actually, the bore is the diameter of the cylinder itself. The larger the cylinder bore, of course, the more powerful will be the power stroke because a bigger piston has more area on which the high-pressure combustion gases can push down.

Stroke

Stroke is also a basic cylinder measurement. However, in this case, the measurement is that of the actual piston travel within the cylinder as it moves from TDC to BDC or back again. A square engine is one that has a bore and stroke of the same dimension; whereas, an oversquare engine has a bore greater than its stroke. [2]

Displacement

Manufacturers commonly use displacement to indicate engine size; this specification is really a measurement of cylinder volume. In other words, when the piston moves up from BDC to TDC, it displaces or pushes away a given volume of gases. Of course, the number of cylinders that an engine has, will determine total engine displacement. Therefore, engine displacement is always equal to the piston displacement of one cylinder multiplied by the number of cylinders in the engine.[3]

Compression Ratio

Another design feature of an engine that determines the total power output of an engine is the compression ratio. Compression ratio is a measure of the cylinder volume in cubic inches above the piston when it is at TDC (its clearance volume) compared to the cylinder volume above the piston when it is at BDC. When considering this statement, total cylinder volume appears to be the same thing as piston displacement, but it is not. Total cylinder volume is equal to piston displacement plus combustion chamber volume. The combustion chamber volume, with the piston at top dead center (TDC) is commonly known as clearance volume. Compression ratio is nothing more than the total volume of a cylinder divided by the clearance volume. The formula for finding compression ratio is then (total volume)/(clearance volume).

Word List

1. explore [ɪkˈsplɔː; ek-]   v. 探测,探究
2. displacement [dɪsˈpleɪsm(ə)nt]   n. 工作容积,排量
3. detonation [detəˈneɪʃ(ə)n]   n. 爆燃,爆震

Proper Names

1. volumetric efficiency   容积效率
2. thermo efficiency   热效率
3. mechanical efficiency   机械效率
4. surface ignition   表面点火
5. square engine   等径发动机,方型发动机
6. oversquare engine   短行程发动机

Notes

1. There are a few negative factors that adversely affect the normal combustion process and can cause power loss and serious engine damage.

翻译:一些负面因素会影响发动机的正常燃烧过程,并且导致功率损失和严重的发动机损坏。

2. A square engine is one that has a bore and stroke of the same dimension; whereas, an oversquare engine has a bore greater than its stroke.

翻译:等径发动机是指发动机的缸径等于活塞行程,然而,短行程发动机的缸径要比它的行程大。

3. Therefore, engine displacement is always equal to the piston displacement of one cylinder multiplied by the number of cylinders in the engine.

翻译:因此,发动机排量总是等于单个发动机的排量乘以发动机的汽缸数。

学习资料:
相关链接及网址
1. http://65.201.178.38
2. http://www.a-car.com
推荐书目
1. William K. Toboldt, & Larry Johnson. Automotive Encyclopedia. South Holland, Illinois: The Goodheart-willcox Company, Inc. 1983.
2. 马林才.汽车实用英语[M].2版.北京:人民交通出版社,2014.
3. 王凤丽.汽车专业英语[M].北京.人民邮电出版社,2015.

任务四

发动机冷却系统和润滑系统认识

1. 掌握与发动机冷却系统和润滑系统组成相关的专业术语、词汇。
2. 掌握发动机冷却系统和润滑系统的专有词汇。
3. 能对关于发动机冷却系统和润滑系统的资料进行中英互译。
4. 能对相关内容的英文资料进行简单阅读和翻译。
5. 能对汽车实物上的英语单词或词汇进行辨认。

任务描述

以四冲程发动机为例,介绍发动机冷却系统的水套、节温器、水泵、散热器、散热器盖和风扇等,以及润滑系统中主要零部件等相关专业术语、词汇。通过完成该任务,能阅读关于发动机冷却系统和润滑系统的外文文献,并掌握简单翻译技巧。

本学习任务沿着以下脉络进行学习:

通读全文 → 学习单词和语法 → 完成课后练习 → 分组讨论 → 课后阅读

Task 4 Engine Cooling System and Lubricating System Understanding

Engine Cooling System

A cooling system of some kind is necessary in the internal combustion engine (Fig. 4-1). The cooling system of a water-cooled engine consists of the engine water jacket, thermostat, water pump, radiator, radiator cap, fan, fan drive belt and necessary hoses.

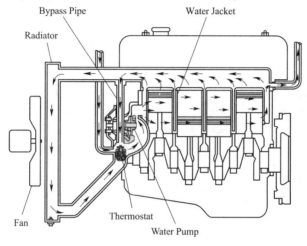

Fig. 4-1 Engine Cooling System

Heat transfer

In an automobile engine, heat flows or transfers from the iron or aluminum cylinder to the cooling water, and from the coolant to the copper or aluminum radiator (Fig. 4-2).[1]

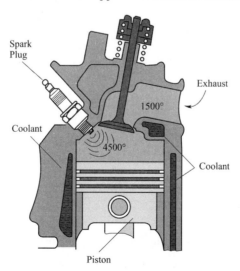

Fig. 4-2 Engine Heat Transfer

Cooling System Pump

Automobile engine water pumps are of many designs, but most are the centrifugal type. Sometimes the fan is installed on the water pump shaft (Fig. 4-3).

Radiator

The radiator is a device designed to dissipate the heat that the coolant has absorbed from the engine (Fig. 4-4). It is constructed to hold a large amount of water in tubes or other passages which provide a large area in contact with the atmosphere.[2]

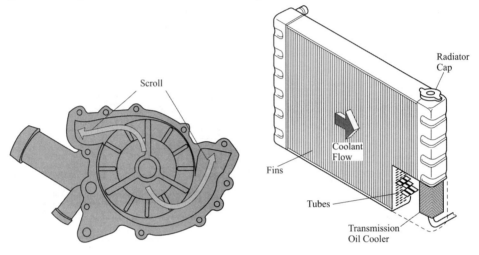

Fig. 4-3 Cooling System Pump   Fig. 4-4 Radiator

Radiator Cap

The radiator cap is designed to seal the cooling system so that it operates under some pressure (Fig. 4-5). This improves cooling efficiency and prevents evaporation of the coolant.

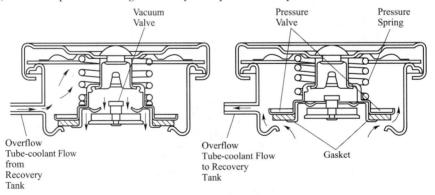

Fig. 4-5 Radiator Cap

Cooling Fan

The fan is designed to draw cooling air through the radiator core (Fig. 4-6). This is necessary at low speeds or when the engine is idling since there is not enough air motion under those conditions to provide adequate cooling.

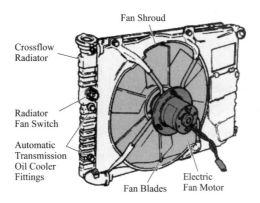

Fig. 4-6 Fan

Thermostat

Automotive internal combustion engines operate more efficiently when a high temperature is maintained within narrow limits. To attain this objective, a thermostat is inserted in the cooling system(Fig. 4-7). In operation, the thermostat is designed to close off the flow of water from the engine to the radiator until the engine has reached the desired operating temperature.[3]

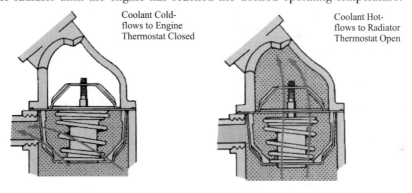

Fig. 4-7 Thermostat

Antifreeze Solution

When water freezes, it expands approximately nine percent in volume. Because of this great rate expansion, it will break or seriously distort the shape of the vessel in which it is contained. Because of this characteristic, it is necessary to use a nonfreezing solution in the cooling system of water-cooled engines operated in climates where the temperature is below the freezing point of water(Fig. 4-8).[4]

Engine Lubricating System

Excessive friction in the engine, however, would mean rapid destruction(Fig. 4-9). We cannot eliminate internal friction, but we can reduce it to a controllable degree through the use of friction reducing lubri-

Fig. 4-8 Refrigerant

cants.[5] the lubricating oil in an automobile engine has several tasks to perform:

1. By lubrication, reduce friction between moving parts of an/the engine.
2. By acting as a seal to prevent leakage between parts such as pistons, rings, and cylinders.
3. By flowing between friction-generating parts to carry away heat.
4. By washing away abrasive metal worn from friction surfaces.

Engine oil is available in different viscosities. Viscosity is considered to be the internal friction of a fluid. An oil of low viscosity will flow more easily than an oil of high viscosity. Oil is supplied to moving parts of the engine by pump pressure or splashing, or by a combination of both.

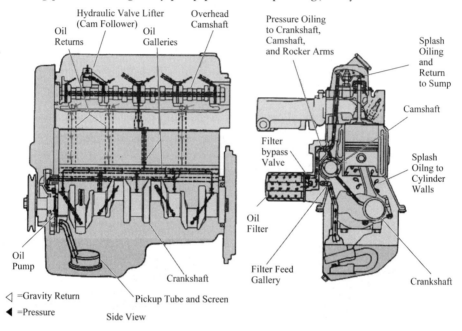

Fig. 4-9 Engine Lubricating System

Oil Pump

The pumps used to circulate the oil are of the positive displacement type in several designs (Fig. 4-10). Since these pumps handle oil, they are well lubricated at all times and do not suffer from excessive wear. Most cases of lost oil pressure are due to excessive clearance in the bearings of the engine rather than worn oil pumps.[6] Another reason for a lack of oil pressure is a stoppage in the oil pump supply line or screen. A typical cause is the accumulation of sludge in a screen.

Oil Sludge

Sludge is a mixture of water, oil, dirt and other products of combustion. (Fig. 4-11) It is most likely to form in an engine that seldom reaches a satisfactory operating temperature. Slow speed, stop-and-go operation means that the engine seldom gets hot enough to drive the water and vapor out of the crankcase.[7] Sludge formation can be held to a minimum by using the correct cooling system thermostat to maintain a high engine operating temperature. Using engines oils of high detergency and making frequent changes of oil and filter are necessary. Adequate crankcase ventilation is also important.

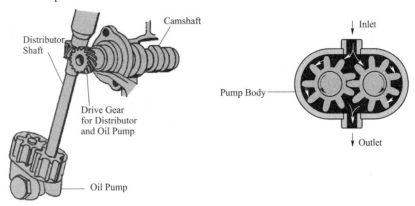

Fig. 4-10 Oil Pump

Oil Filter

The Oil filter is placed in the engine oil system to remove dirt and abrasives from the oil (Fig. 4-12). Diluents, such as gasoline and acids, are not removed. However, by removing the solid materials, the possibility of acids forming is reduced, and the rate of wear of engine parts is greatly reduced. Oil filters installed on modern passenger car engines are full-flow type; all oil passes through the filter before it reaches the bearings. However, in the event the filter becomes clogged or obstructed, a bypass valve is provided so that oil will continue to reach the bearings.

Fig. 4-11 Oil Sludge

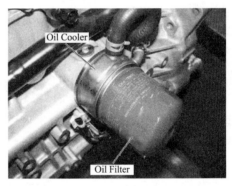

Fig. 4-12 Oil Filter

Word List

1. thermostat [ˈθəːməstæt]   n. 节温器,温度自动调节器
2. fan [fæn]   n. 风扇
3. transfer [trænsˈfəː; trɑːns-; -nz-]   vt. 转移,传递
4. copper [ˈkɔpə]   n. 铜,铜制品

5. rust [rʌst] n. 铁锈
6. centrifugal ['sentrɪ'fjuːg(ə)l] adj. 离心的,离心力的
7. dissipate ['dɪsɪpeɪt] v. 驱散,消散
8. idle [aɪd(ə)l] adj. 空闲的,懒惰的,怠速的
9. objective [əb'dʒektɪv] n. 目标,目的
10. antifreeze ['æntɪfriːz] n. 防冻剂
11. vessel [ves(ə)l] n. 容器,器皿
12. climate ['klaɪmɪt] n. 气候,风土
13. inhibitor [ɪn'hɪbɪtə] n. 抑制剂
14. corrosion [kə'rəʊʒ(ə)n] n. 腐蚀
15. generous ['dʒen(ə)rəs] adj. 慷慨的,大方的,大量的
16. destruction [dɪ'strʌkʃ(ə)n] n. 破坏,毁灭
17. friction ['frɪkʃ(ə)n] n. 摩擦,摩擦力
18. lubricant ['luːbrɪk(ə)nt] n. 滑润剂
19. task [tɑːsk] n. 任务,作业
20. abrasive [ə'breɪsɪv] adj. 研磨的; n. 研磨剂
21. viscosity [vɪ'skɒsɪtɪ] n. 黏度
22. accumulation [əkjuːmju'leɪʃ(ə)n] n. 积聚,堆积物
23. detergency [dɪ'təːdʒənsɪ] adj. 清净性
24. varnish ['vɑːnɪʃ] n. 漆膜,清漆
25. lacquer ['lækə] n. 漆膜,涂膜
26. substance ['sʌbst(ə)ns] n. 物质,实质
27. regularly ['regjuləlɪ] adv. 有规律地,有规则地
28. screen [skriːn] n. 筛子
29. diluent ['dɪljuənt] n. 稀释液,冲淡剂
30. acid [æsɪd] n. 酸

Proper Names

1. cooling system 冷却系统
2. lubricating system 润滑系统
3. radiator cap 散热器盖
4. radiator core 散热器芯
5. fan blade 风扇叶片
6. positive displacement type 容积式
7. oil sludge 油泥

8. crankcase ventilation　　　　　　　曲轴箱通风
9. break down　　　　　　　　　　　　分解
10. pour point depressant　　　　　　降凝剂
11. detergent-dispersant　　　　　　　清净分散剂
12. foam inhibitor　　　　　　　　　　抗泡剂
13. oxidation inhibitor　　　　　　　　抗氧剂
14. viscosity index improver　　　　　黏度指数改进剂
15. antiwear additive　　　　　　　　　抗磨添加剂

Useful Expressions

1. in contact with　　　　　　　　　　与……在接触中，接触
2. because of　　　　　　　　　　　　因为，由于
3. coat with　　　　　　　　　　　　　给某物涂、盖、包上

Key Vocabulary

1. transfer

vt. 搬，转换，调动，使换车，使转校，改变，转变，转让，让渡

She has been transferred to another department. 她已被调往另一部门。

At the port, the goods were transferred onto a ship. 货物在港口被转移到一艘船上。

Her father transferred her to a better school. 她父亲把她转到了一所更好的学校。

Within a few years, they had transferred barren wastes into fertile fields. 几年之内他们就把荒地变成了良田。

To preserve the farm intact, he transferred it to one heir. 为了保持这个农场的完整，他将它移交给一个继承人。

vi. 搬迁，转移，调任，转校，转学科

The company has transferred to the west coast. 公司已迁往西海岸。

June transferred to an American college in 1990. 琼在1990年转学到一所美国的大学。

n. 迁移，移交，转让，转账

The transfer of money by bank check is very common today. 用银行支票汇钱现在很普遍。

2. provide

vt. 供给，提供，装备，准备，规定

Sheep provide us with wool. 羊供给我们羊毛。

They are ill provided with food. 他们的食品不足。

The agreement provides that three months notice shall be given on either side. 协议规定任何

一方应在3个月前发出通知。

vi. 抚养,赡养,规定

He tried to earn more money to provide for a large family. 他设法多挣钱以供养一个子女众多的家。

He has a large family to provide for. 他有一大家子人要养活。

The constitution provides for citizens' rights and obligations. 宪法规定了公民的权利与义务。

provide against 为…作好准备,预防(灾荒,困难)

provide for 提供生活费;养活;为…作准备;防备;规定

provide with 给…提供;以…装备

3. prevent

vt. 防止,预防,阻止,制止,妨碍

Vitamin C is supposed to prevent colds. 维生素C被认为能预防感冒。

Who prevents their plans from being carried out? 谁阻止他们的计划不让实施?

Of course, I can't prevent your going. 当然,我不能阻止你去。

vi. 妨碍,阻止

We must take steps to prevent such crimes. 我们必须采取步骤去防止这样的罪行。

prevent…from 使……不做某事,阻止……做某事

4. additive

adj. 附加的,加法的

additive information 补充报告

additive samples 附加样本

completely additive 完全添加

n. 添加剂,添加物

An additive that improves the flow of plastics during fabrication. 助熔剂是在制塑过程中提高塑料流动性的添加剂

Notes

1. In an automobile engine, heat flows or transfers from the iron or aluminum cylinder to the cooling water, and from the coolant to the copper or aluminum radiator.

翻译:在汽车发动机里面,铁或铝制的汽缸将热量传导到冷却液,再由冷却液将热量传递到铜或铝制的散热器中。

2. It is constructed to hold a large amount of water in tubes or other passages which provide a large area in contact with the atmosphere.

翻译:结构上,散热器要有能容纳大量水的管道,这些管道能提供很大的散热面积,便于与空气接触。

语法：which 引导定语从句，修饰 tubes or passages。

3. In operation, the thermostat is designed to close off the flow of water from the engine to the radiator until the engine has reached the desired operating temperature.

翻译：工作时，在发动机还未达到合适的工作温度前，节温器切断从发动机水套流向散热器的水路。

语法：until the engine has reached the desired operating temperature 引导时间状语从句。

在用法上：A till (until) B 。A 所表示的动作或状态一直持续下去，到 till (until) B 出现时即停止并向相反方向转化。

4. Because of this characteristic, it is necessary to use a nonfreezing solution in the cooling system of water-cooled engines operated in climates where the temperature is below the freezing point of water.

翻译：由于冷却液会在低温下冻结，所以，水冷式发动机在水的凝固点以下的气候条件下运行时，需要向冷却系统中加入防冻液。

语法：Because of 后接短语表原因。

it is necessary to use 是 it 作形式主语，为了避免全句的头重脚轻。真正主语是 to 不定式，本句亦是 To use…is necessary。

5. We cannot eliminate internal friction, but we can reduce it to a controllable degree by the use of friction reducing lubricants.

翻译：虽然不能消除发动机内的摩擦，但可以通过使用减摩润滑剂，将摩擦减小到一定的程度。

6. Most cases of lost oil pressure are due to excessive clearance in the bearings of the engine rather than worn oil pumps.

翻译：多数情况下，机油压力不足是由于发动机内轴承间隙过大造成的，而不仅仅是由于机油泵磨损造成的。

7. Slow speed, stop-and-go operation means that the engine seldom gets hot enough to drive the water and vapor out of the crankcase.

翻译：低速、停停开开等工况意味着发动机温度不高，不能将曲轴箱内的水和水蒸气排出。

语法：that 引导的从句作谓语 mean 的宾语。

Exercises

1. Choose the best answer from the following choices according to the text.

1) In an automobile engine, heat flows or transfers from the iron or aluminum cylinder to the cooling water, and from the coolant to the copper or aluminum _____ .

  A. pump   B. radiator   C. piston   D. fan

2) When water freezes, it expands approximately _____ percent in volume.

  A. seven   B. eight   C. nine   D. ten

3) Oils used in automobiles need some _____ to improve their characteristics.

    A. additives   B. antifreeze   C. lubricant   D. coolant

2. Translate the following into Chinese.

1) cooling system   2) thermostat   3) radiator cap

4) radiator core   5) lubricating system   6) crankcase ventilation

7) viscosity index improver   8) varnish   9) oil sludge

3. Translate the following into English.

1) 水泵   2) 防冻液   3) 水冷式发动机

4) 润滑系统   5) 滑润剂   6) 抗氧剂

7) 发动机沉积物   8) 机油滤清器   9) 金属与金属接触

4. Translate the following sentences into Chinese.

1) Excessive friction in the engine, however, would mean rapid destruction.

2) In order to reduce the formation of rust, commercial antifreeze contains an inhibitor designed to prevent corrosion.

5. Translate the words or phrases in the following figure into Chinese

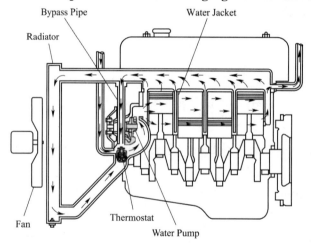

Practical Reading

Air Conditioning System

Not only do we depend on our cars to get us where we want to go, but also we depend on them to get us there without discomfort.[1] We expect the heater to keep us warm when it's cold outside, and the air conditioning system to keep us cool when it's hot.

Despite its relatively small size, the cooling system has to deal with an enormous amount of heat to protect the engine from friction and the heat of combustion. The cooling system has to remove a lot of heat per minute. This is more than we need to heat a large home in cold weather. It's good to know that some of this heat can be put to the useful purpose of keeping us warm.

Air conditioning makes driving much more comfortable in hot weather. Your car's air conditioner cleans and dehumidifies, the outside air entering your car. It also has the task of keeping the air at the temperature you select. The job of the air conditioning system is really to "remove" the heat that makes us uncomfortable, and return the air to the car's interior in a "un-heated" condition. [2] Air conditioning, or cooling, is really a process of removing heat from an object.

A compressor circulates a liquid refrigerant called Refrigerant-12. The compressor moves the Refrigerant-12 from an evaporator, through a condenser and expansion valve, right back to the evaporator. [3] The evaporator is right in front of a fan that pulls the hot, humid air out of the car's interior. The refrigerant makes the hot air's moisture condense into drops of water, removing the heat from the air. Once the water is removed, the "cool" air is sent back into the car's interior.

Word List

1. discomfort [dɪsˈkʌmfət]　　　　　　　　n. 不便之处，不适，不舒服
2. enormous [ɪˈnɔːməs]　　　　　　　　　adj. 巨大的，庞大的
3. dehumidify [diːhjuːˈmɪdɪfaɪ]　　　　　　vt. 除湿，使干燥
4. compressor [kəmˈpresə]　　　　　　　n. 压缩机
5. refrigerant [rɪˈfrɪdʒ(ə)r(ə)nt]　　　　　adj. 制冷的；n. 制冷剂
6. evaporator [ɪˈvæpəreɪtə]　　　　　　　n. 蒸发器
7. condenser [kənˈdensə]　　　　　　　　n. 冷凝器
8. humid [ˈhjuːmɪd]　　　　　　　　　　　adj. 充满潮湿的，湿润的
9. moisture [ˈmɔɪstʃə]　　　　　　　　　　n. 潮湿，湿气

Proper Names

1. air conditioning system　　　　　　　　空调系统
2. expansion valve　　　　　　　　　　　膨胀阀

Notes

1. Not only do we depend on our cars to get us where we want to go, we also depend on them to get us there without discomfort.

翻译：我们不仅要用汽车把我们送到目的地，同时还需旅途舒适。

2. The job of the air conditioning system is really to "remove" the heat that makes us uncomfortable, and return the air to the car's interior in a "un-heated" condition.

翻译:空调系统的作用实际上是将令人不适的热量带走,同时在寒冷的天气下将热量送回到汽车内部。

3. The compressor moves the Refrigerant-12 from an evaporator, through a condenser and expansion valve, right back to the evaporator.

翻译:压缩机将R12从蒸发器中压入冷凝器,经过膨胀阀,然后直接回到蒸发器中。

学习资料:
相关链接及网址
1. http://65.201.178.38
2. http://www.a-car.com

推荐书目
1. William K. Toboldt, & Larry Johnson. Automotive Encyclopedia. South Holland, Illinois: The Goodheart-willcox Company, Inc. 1983.
2. 马林才.汽车实用英语[M].2版.北京:人民交通出版社,2014.
3. 王凤丽.汽车专业英语[M].北京.人民邮电出版社,2015.

任务五 发动机点火系统和起动系统认识

1. 掌握与发动机点火系统和起动系统组成相关的专业术语、词汇。
2. 掌握发动机点火系统和起动系统特殊的英语表达方法。
3. 能对关于发动机点火系统和起动系统的资料进行中英互译。
4. 能进行相关简单内容的英文资料进行阅读和翻译。
5. 能对汽车实物上已标识出的英语单词或词汇进行辨认。

任务描述

介绍发动机点火系统的蓄电池、点火线圈、分电器、电容器、点火开关、火花塞、电阻和必要的高/低压线圈以及起动系统的电磁开关和起动机等相关专业术语、词汇。通过完成该任务，能阅读关于发动机点火系统和起动系统的外文文献，并掌握简单翻译技巧。

本学习任务沿着以下脉络进行学习：

通读全文 → 学习单词和语法 → 完成课后练习 → 分组讨论 → 课后阅读

Task 5 Engine Ignition System and Starting System Understanding

Engine Ignition System

The ignition system on an internal combustion engine provides the spark that ignites the combustible air/fuel mixture in the combustion chamber (Fig. 5-1). [1] Most ignition systems operate from a battery. Conventional systems consist of the battery, ignition coil, distributor, condenser, ignition switch, spark plugs, resistor and the necessary low and high tension wiring.

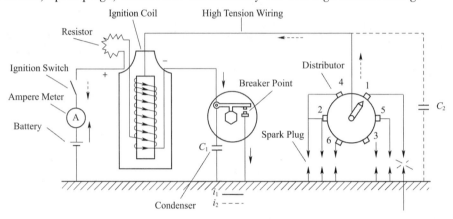

Fig. 5-1 Conventional Ignition System

Ignition Coil

The ignition coil is a transformer designed to set up the primary voltage of 12V to approximately 20000V required to jump the spark plug gap in the combustion chamber. It is composed of a primary winding, secondary winding, and core of soft iron.

Ignition Condenser

The purpose of the ignition condenser is to reduce arcing at the breaker points and prolong their life.

Ignition Distributor

The ignition distributor opens and closes the primary ignition circuit. It also distributes high tension current to the proper spark plug at the correct time. The distributor is usually driven by the camshaft and rotates at one half-crankshaft speed on four-cycle engines.

Distributor Cap

The distributor cap should be carefully checked to see that sparks have not been arcing from point to point within the cap. Both the interior and exterior must be clean. The firing points should not be eroded and the interior of the towers must be clean and free from corrosion.

Distributor Rotor

A distributor rotor is a conductor designed to rotate and distribute the high tension current to the towers of the distributor cap (Fig. 5-2). The distributor rotor is provided with some sort of spring connection to the center tower or terminal of the distributor cap.[2] This spring must have ample tension to provide good electrical contact.

Ignition Switch

The purpose of the ignition switch is to connect and disconnect the ignition system from the battery, so the engine can be started and stopped as desired.

Spark Plug

The spark plug in a spark ignition engine provides the gap across which the high tension voltage jumps, to create the spark ignites the compressed air/fuel mixture (Fig. 5-3).[3] The spark plug contains a center electrode, which is connected to the ignition coil secondary through the distributor. The side electrode protrudes from the bottom edge of the spark plug shell. There is a gap between the side electrode and the center electrode.

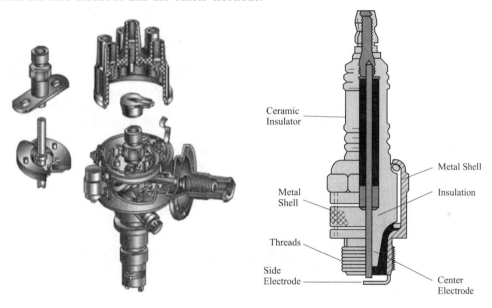

Fig. 5-2 Distributor   Fig. 5-3 Spark Plug

Ignition Resistor

In most 12V systems, a resistor is connected in series with the primary circuit of the ignition coil during normal operation. However, during the starting period, the resistor is cut out of the circuit so that full voltage is applied to the coil. This insures a strong spark during the starting period, and in that way quicker starting is provided.

Ignition Timing

The ignition system must be timed accurately so that the spark occurs in the combustion chamber at the correct instant. Incorrect timing results in loss of efficiency and power.

Spark Advance

A mechanism is provided to automatically advance and retard the spark as conditions require.

On automotive engines, two methods usually are employed to actuate that mechanism, centrifugal force, and engine vacuum.[4] The corresponding devices are a centrifugal advance component and vacuum advance unit.

Coil-On-Plug ignition

Coil-on-plug (COP) ignition uses one ignition coil for each spark plug(Fig. 5-4). This system is also called coil-by-plug, coil-near-plug, or coil-over-plug ignition, The coil-on-plug system eliminates the spark plug wires that are often the source of electromagnetic interference (EMI) that can cause problems to some computer signals. The vehicle computer controls the timing of the spark. Ignition timing also can be changed (retarded or advanced) on a cylinder-by-cylinder basis for maximum performance and to respond to knock sensor signals.

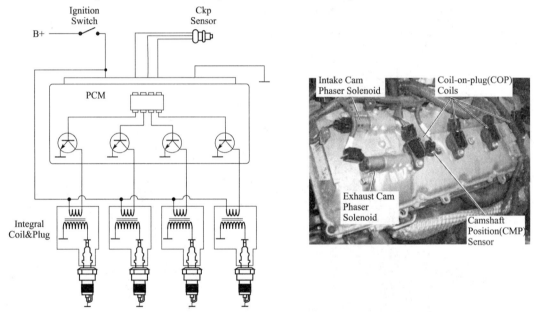

Fig. 5-4 Coil-on-plug (COP) Ignition

Engine Starting System

The starting system provides the power to turn the internal combustion engine over until it can operate under its own power(Fig. 5-5).[5] To perform this task, the starting motor receives electrical power from the battery, and it converts this energy into mechanical energy, which transmits through the drive mechanism to the engine's flywheel. The typical starting system has five components: battery, starting switch, battery cables, starter solenoid or switch, and starting a motor.

Battery

The battery supplies electrical energy in the form of current flow for the starting circuit (Fig. 5-6). The starting motor can draw a large amount of current from the battery in order to turn the engine over.

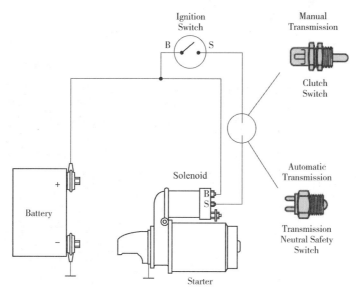

Fig. 5-5　Engine Starting System

Starting Switch

The starting switch activates the system (Fig. 5-7). In the modern automobiles, this switch is part of the keyed ignition. The ignition switch usually has four positions: accessories, off, on (run), and start. All the ignition switch positions except start have detents. That is, the switch remains in those positions until moved by the operator.

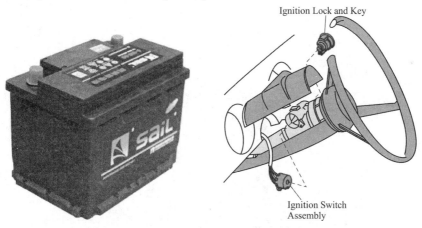

Fig. 5-6　Battery　　　　Fig. 5-7　Starting Switch

Cables

The starting circuit requires two or more cables (Fig. 5-8). Two of these cables attach directly to the battery. One cable connects between the battery negative terminal and a good ground. If this cable does not directly attach to the engine, the vehicle usually has additional cables running from the engine to the vehicle frame or body.

Starter Solenoid

The starter solenoid is an electromagnetically operated heavy-duty switch that can have two distinct functions (Fig. 5-9). [6] First and most important of all, the solenoid switch opens and closes the circuit between the battery and cranking motor. The battery must supply a great deal of current flow to the starter before it can crank the engine. Second, many solenoids also shift the cranking pinion into mesh with the flywheel ring gear.

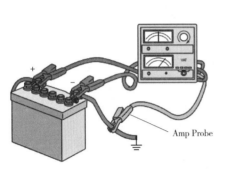

Fig. 5-8 Cables

Fig. 5-9 Solenoid

Starting Motor

The starting or cranking motor itself is nothing but a device that converts electrical energy to mechanical energy in order to turn the engine over for starting (Fig. 5-10). [7] The starter is a special type of electric motor designed to operate under great overloads and to produce high horsepower. All starting motors are much the same in general design and operation, differing mainly in the type of drive mechanism used. Basically, starter motor consists of a housing, fields, armature and brushes, end frames, and drive mechanism.

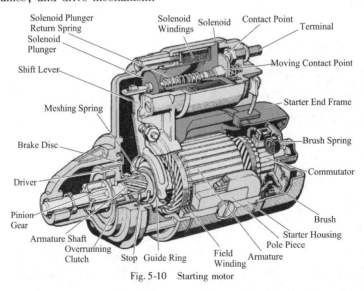

Fig. 5-10 Starting motor

Armature

The armature is the only rotating component within the starter. When the starter is in operation, the current flowing through the armature produces a magnetic field in each of its conductors; the reaction between the armature's magnetic field and that produced by the field coils causes the armature to rotate.

Brushes

The starting motor has two to six brushes. These devices ride on the commutator segments; they carry the heavy current flow from the stationary field coils to the rotating armature windings via the commutator segments.

Commutator End Frame

The commutator end frame is a metal plate that bolts to the commutator end of the starter housing. Depending on the starter design, this component has several functions.

Driving Housing

The driving housing, sometimes known as the drive end frame, has several functions. First of all, this housing supports the driving end of the armature shaft by means of a bushing. Second, this heavy iron component contains the mounting flange by which the starter motor attaches to the engine.

Starter Drive

Cranking motors can use three types of drives. The most common type of drive moved in and out of mesh by the shift lever is the overrunning clutch. The shift lever activates the drive pinion, and the pinion along with the overrunning clutch mechanism moves endwise along a splined armature shaft, moving the gear into or out of mesh with the flywheel teeth (Fig. 5-11).

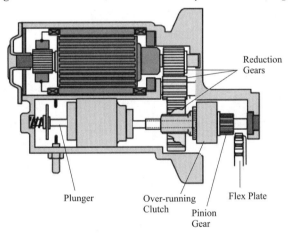

Fig. 5-11 Starter Drive

Word List

1. battery [ˈbætrɪ]   n. 蓄电池
2. distributor [dɪˈstrɪbjutə]   n. 分电器
3. condenser [kənˈdensə]   n. 电容器
4. resistor [rɪˈzɪstə]   n. 电阻器

5. transformer [trænsˈfɔːmə; trɑːns-; -nz-]   n. 变压器
6. insulation [ˌɪnsjuˈleɪʃ(ə)n]   n. 绝缘;隔离,孤立
7. thread [θred]   n. 线;螺纹;思路;衣服
8. ample [ˈæmp(ə)l]   adj. 充足的,丰富的
9. protrude [prəˈtruːd]   v. 突出
10. detent [dɪˈtent]   n. 棘爪,制动器
11. ground [graund]   vt. 接地,搭铁,路面
12. electromagnetic [ɪˌlektrə(u)mægˈnetɪk]   adj. 电磁的
13. horsepower [ˈhɔːspauə]   n. 马力
14. field [fiːld]   n. 磁场
15. armature [ˈɑːmətʃə; -tj(u)ə]   n. 电枢
16. brush [brʌʃ]   n. 电刷
17. reaction [rɪˈækʃ(ə)n]   n. 相互作用力
18. commutator [ˈkɔmjuˌteɪtə]   n. 换向器
19. stationary [ˈsteɪʃ(ə)n(ə)rɪ]   n. 定子
20. bushing [buʃɪŋ]   n. 轴承

Proper Names

1. ignition coil   点火线圈
2. ignition switch   点火开关
3. primary voltage   初级电压
4. primary winding   初级线圈
5. secondary winding   次级线圈
6. breaker point   断电器触点
7. distributor cap   分电器盖
8. distributor rotor   分火头
9. center electrode   中心电极
10. side electrode   侧电极
11. ignition timing   点火正时
12. spark advance   点火提前
13. coil-on-plug   独立点火线圈
14. starting switch   起动开关
15. starter solenoid   起动机电磁开关
16. starting motor   起动机
17. negative terminal   负极

18. ring gear　　　　　　　　　　　　　齿圈
19. end frame　　　　　　　　　　　　　端盖
20. field coil　　　　　　　　　　　　　励磁线圈
21. commutator segment　　　　　　　　 换向器片
22. shift lever　　　　　　　　　　　　 传动杠杆
23. magnetic field　　　　　　　　　　　磁场
24. overrunning clutch　　　　　　　　　单向离合器
25. mesh with　　　　　　　　　　　　　与……相啮合

Useful Expressions

1. compose of　　　　　　　　　　　　　由……组成
2. in series with　　　　　　　　　　　 与……串联,与……相连
3. first of all　　　　　　　　　　　　 首先

Key Vocabulary

1. transformer

n. 促使变化的(或人物),改革者,变压器,变形金刚

Do you enjoy the transformer? 你喜欢变形金刚?

the voltage regulating devices of the transformer 变压器调压装置

Open tender for purchasing power transformer. 公开招标购买电力运输设备。

Burn out a fuse, motor, transformer. 烧坏熔断丝、发动机、变压器。

to subject to the action of a transformer 变压使……经过变压器的转换

We can quite easily understand what a transformer is. 我们能够很容易地懂得变压器是什么。

The transformer is more expensive than the toy train. 变形金刚比玩具火车贵得多。

to couple(electric circuits) by means of a transformer 通过变压器连接电路

2. arc

n. 弧(线,形,度,拱),电弧,弧光(灯),拱(洞),扇形物,弧形板,电弧振荡器

trench arc and back-arc-basin system 沟弧盆系

It is an arc. 这是一段弧。

to form an arc 形成拱状物

the vivid arc of a rainbow 彩虹清晰的拱

This is one section of an arc. 这是一段弧。

arc profile gear for watch and clock 钟表齿形

Do electric-arc furnace need water too? 电弧炉也需要水吗?

An arc is a part of the circumference of a circle or other curved lines. 弧是圆周或曲线的一部分。

3. drive

n. 驾车旅行,车程,车道,汽车路,运动,(人的)本能需要,欲望,魄力,干劲

We went for a drive in the afternoon. 我们下午开车出去兜风。

We saw a red car parked on his drive. 我们看到一辆红色轿车停在他的私人车道上。

The manager decided to launch a sales drive. 经理决定开展一次推销活动。

He was dominated by an insatiable drive for fame. 他被一种难以满足的成名欲支配着。

He is a man of great drive. 他是一个劲头十足的人。

vt. 驾驶(汽车等),用车送(人),驱赶,赶走,挖掘(隧道),迫使

I don't know how to drive a carriage. 我不会驾马车。

He'll drive us to the airport. 他会开车送我们去机场。

He drove the sheep up the hill. 他把羊群往山上赶。

The machine is driven by electricity. 这机器用电力驱动。

The farmers drove wells to water the crops. 农民打井灌溉庄稼。

He drove her to admit it. 他逼迫她承认。

vi. 开车,疾驰

It is dangerous to drive after drinking. 酒后开车危险。

The rain was driving in our faces. 大雨猛打着我们的脸。

drive against 敲打,进攻

drive at 暗示,意指

drive away 驱车离开

Notes

1. The ignition system on an internal combustion engine provides the spark that ignites the combustible air/fuel mixture in the combustion chamber.

翻译:内燃机的点火系统产生电火花,点燃燃烧室内的可燃混合气。

2. The distributor rotor is provided with some sort of spring connection to the center tower or terminal of the distributor cap.

翻译:分火头借助弹簧作用力连接到分电器盖的中心触头上。

3. The spark plug in a spark ignition engine provides the gap across which the high tension voltage jumps, to create the spark ignites the compressed air/fuel mixture.

翻译:在点燃式发动机中,火花塞提供了给高压电跳火的间隙,跳火产生电火花,点燃压缩后的可燃混合气。

4. On automotive engines, two methods usually are employed to actuate that mechanism, centrifugal force, and engine vacuum.

翻译:在汽车发动机点火系统中,通常有两种方法可用来驱动点火提前装置:即离心力和发动机的真空度。

5. The starting system provides the power to turn the internal combustion engine over until it can operate under its own power.

翻译:起动系统提供动力来转动内燃机,直到发动机可以依靠自身的动力运行。

6. The starter solenoid is an electromagnetically operated heavy-duty switch that can have two distinct functions.

翻译:起动机电磁开关是一个靠电磁感应力运行的大功率开关,它有两个突出的作用。

7. The starting or cranking motor itself is nothing but a device that converts electrical energy to mechanical energy in order to turn the engine over for starting.

翻译:起动机只是一个将电能转化成机械能的装置,用手起动发动机。

Exercises

1. Choose the best answer from the following choices according to the text.

1) The _____ on an internal combustion engine provides the spark that ignites the combustible air/fuel mixture in the combustion chamber.

  A. starting system   B. cooling system

  C. ignition system   D. fuel system

2) The purpose of the ignition switch is to connect and disconnect the ignition system from the _____, so the engine can be started and stopped as desire.

  A. battery   B. starter

  C. radiator   D. distributor

3) The _____ provides the power to turn the internal combustion engine over until it can operate under its own power.

  A. fuel system   B. cooling system

  C. ignition system   D. starting system.

4) The battery supplies _____ in the form of current flow for the starting circuit.

  A. electrical energy   B. mechanical energy

  C. chemical energy   D. heat energy

2. Translate the following into Chinese.

1) spark plug   2) battery   3) distributor

4) armature   5) commutator   6) ignition system

7) starting system   8) brush   9) field coil

3. Translate the following into English.

1) 点火线圈 2) 初级线圈 3) 分电器盖

4) 起动机电磁开关 5) 点火提前 6) 点火正时

7) 点火分电器 8) 起动机 9) 点火开关

4. Translate the following sentences into Chinese.

1) The purpose of the ignition condenser is to reduce arcing at the breaker points, and prolong their life.

2) A distributor rotor is a conductor designed to rotate and distribute the high tension current to the towers of the distributor cap.

3) The armature is the only rotating component within the starter.

Practical Reading

Light, Wires and Seat Adjuster

The various components in the electric system also include wiring circuits, lighting systems, power seat and window adjuster, horns, and other electrical accessories. [1]

Wiring Circuits

With the increasing number of electrically operated devices in the modern automobile, the wiring circuits have become rather complex. The wires between components are bound together into a harness. Each wire is marked by means of special colors in the insulation; for example, light green, dark green, blue, red, black with a white tracer, and so on. [2] These markings permit identification of the various wires in the harness.

The circuits between the engine-compartment components and the instrument panel are completed through connector plugs and receptacles. As many as a dozen separate wires are gathered together and connected to a receptacle. It becomes a simple matter, then, to push the plug into the receptacle to complete many connections at one time. Matching tangs and holes complete the connections between the wires. The plugs and receptacles have locking devices that prevent their coming loose in operation.

Light

The lighting system in a typical automobile includes the headlights, parking lights, direction-signal lights, side marker lighter, stoplights, backup lights, tail lights, and the interior lights. [3] The interior lights include instrument-panel lights, various warning, indicator, and courtesy lights which turn on when a car door is opened.

When the light switch is pulled out, the circuit from the battery to the headlights is completed. This circuit is through the foot selector switch. The switch has two positions, low beam and driving beam. These are also called passing beam and high beam. The backup lights come on when the driver shifts into reverse. This closes a switch linked to the selector lever which connects the backup lights to the battery. Blinker lights are installed on many cars to provide a means of signaling when a car is stalled on the highway or has pulled off to the side. The blinking is much more noticeable than a steady light and provides a warning to approaching cars.

Seat Adjuster

Electric seat adjusters are used on front seats to adjust the seat height, and position, and tilt (on some models). The adjuster that moves the seat up and down and from front to rear is called a four-way adjuster.[4] The adjuster includes a drive motor, a transmission, drive cables, jack screws, slides, tracks, and supports. When the up-down switch is pushed up to raise the seat, the motor starts to turn and, at the same time, the up-down solenoid is actuated to throw the up-down gears into the mesh. The up-down gear turns in the proper direction to raise the seat.

Word List

1. horn [hɔːn] 　　　　　　　　　　 n. 喇叭
2. bind [baɪnd] 　　　　　　　　　　 v. 绑,捆
3. harness [ˈhɑːnɪs] 　　　　　　　　 n. 电线束
4. insulation [ɪnsjuˈleɪʃ(ə)n] 　　　　 n. 绝缘,隔离
5. tracer [ˈtreɪsə] 　　　　　　　　　 n. 描线
6. receptacle [rɪˈseptək(ə)l] 　　　　 n. 插座
7. tang [tæŋ] 　　　　　　　　　　　 n. 凸口,(定位用的)突起部
8. headlight [ˈhedlaɪt] 　　　　　　　 n. (汽车的)前照灯
9. stoplight [ˈstɒplaɪt] 　　　　　　　 n. 制动灯
10. selector [sɪˈlektə] 　　　　　　　 n. 选择器
11. blinker [ˈblɪŋkə] 　　　　　　　　 n. 闪光信号灯
12. tilt [tɪlt] 　　　　　　　　　　　　 v. (使)倾斜
13. slide [slaɪd] 　　　　　　　　　　 n. 滑道
14. track [træk] 　　　　　　　　　　 n. 导轨

Proper Names

1. lighting system 　　　　　　　　　照明系统
2. window adjuster 　　　　　　　　　车窗调节器
3. parking light 　　　　　　　　　　　驻车灯

4. direction-signal light	转向信号灯
5. side marker lighter	示廓灯
6. backup light	倒车灯
7. tail light	尾灯
8. interior light	车内灯
9. courtesy light	门控灯
10. low beam	近光
11. driving beam	远光
12. passing beam	通过光
13. high beam	强光
14. four-way adjuster	四维调节器
15. jack screw	千斤顶螺丝钉

Notes

1. The various components in the electric system also include wiring circuits, lighting systems, power seat and window adjuster, horns, and other electrical accessories.

翻译：电气系统中的各种元件还包括电线、照明系统、座位和车窗调节器、喇叭以及其他电器附件。

2. Each wire is marked by means of special colors in the insulation; for example, light green, dark green, blue, red, black with a white tracer, and so on.

翻译：每根线都标以特殊颜色以便于区分。例如，浅绿色、深绿色、蓝色、红色、带有白线的黑色等。

3. The lighting system in a typical automobile includes the headlights, parking lights, direction-signal lights, side marker lighter, stoplights, backup lights, tail lights, and the interior lights.

翻译：普通车的照明系统包括前照灯、驻车灯、转向信号灯、示廓灯、制动灯、倒车灯、尾灯以及车内灯。

4. The adjuster that moves the seat up and down and from front to rear is called a four-way adjuster.

翻译：能够把座位升高、降低和向前后倾斜的调节器称为"四维调节器"。

学习资料：
相关链接及网址
1. http://65.201.178.38
2. http://www.a-car.com

推荐书目

1. Robert N. Brady. Electric and Electronic Systems for Automobiles and Trucks. Virginia：Reston Publishing Company，Inc. 1983.
2. 陈文华.汽车发动机构造与维修[M].北京:北京航空航天大学出版社,2007.
3. 马林才.汽车实用英语[M].2版.北京：人民交通出版社,2014.
4. 王凤丽.汽车专业英语[M].北京.人民邮电出版社,2015.

任务六

底盘构造认识

1.掌握汽车底盘中关于传动系统、行驶系统、转向系统和制动系统等专业术语、单词和词汇。

2.掌握各个系统中具体结构的英语表达方法。

3.能对关于汽车底盘的资料进行中英互译。

4.能对简单相关内容的英语资料进行阅读和翻译。

5.能对汽车实物上已经标识出的英语单词或词汇进行辨认。

任务描述

介绍关于变速器、离合器、差速器、传动轴、制动器、轮胎和悬架等汽车底盘的总成以及零部件等的相关专业术语、词汇。通过完成该任务,能阅读关于底盘构造的外文文献,并掌握简单翻译技巧。

本学习任务沿着以下脉络进行学习:

通读全文 → 学习单词和语法 → 完成课后练习 → 分组讨论 → 课后阅读

Task 6 Chassis Structure Understanding

The power train carries power from the engine crankshaft to the car wheels so the wheels rotate and car moves(Fig. 6-1).[1] For many years, on most cars, the engine has been mounted in the front and the rear wheels were driven. The power train includes transmission, clutch, differential and drive shaft.

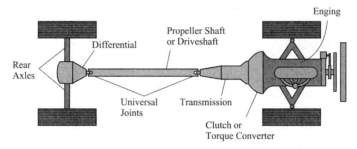

Fig. 6-1 Power Train

Manual Transmission

The manual transmission provides a means of varying the relationship between the speed of the engine and the speed of the wheels(Fig. 6-2). Varying these gear ratios allows the right amount of engine power at many different speeds. Manual transmission requires the use of a clutch to apply and remove the engine torque to the transmission input shaft.

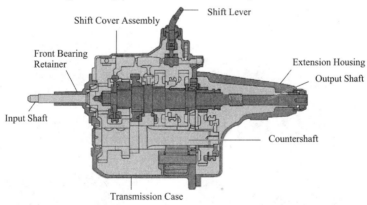

Fig. 6-2 Manual Transmission

Clutch

The clutch allows you to connect and disconnect the engine and the transmission, both starting up and during shifts(Fig. 6-3).

Automatic Transmission

In an automatic transmission, gear ratios are changed automatically(Fig. 6-4). This eliminates the need for the driver to operate the clutch and manually "shift gears". The typical automatic transmission combines a fluid torque converter, a planetary gear system, and a hydraulic control system in a single unit.

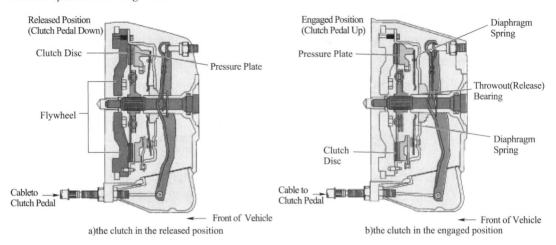

a) the clutch in the released position   b) the clutch in the engaged position

Fig. 6-3   Clutch

Differential

Differentials are used at the rear of vehicles with rear-wheel drive and used at the front in the transaxles of vehicles with front-wheel drive(Fig. 6-5). When the car is on the straight road, the ring gear, differential case, differential pinion gears, and two differential side gears all turn as a unit without any relative motion.[2] However, when the car begins to round a curve, the differential pinion gears rotate on the pinion shaft. This permits the outer wheel to turn faster than the inner wheel.

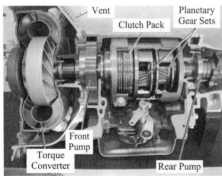

Fig. 6-4   Automatic Transmission

Fig. 6-5   Differential

Drive Shaft

A drive shaft also called a propeller shaft, is used to connect and transmit engine torque from the transmission to the rear differential(Fig. 6-6). Universal joints (U-joints) are used to allow the rear differential to move up and down on the rear suspension and still be able to transmit engine torque

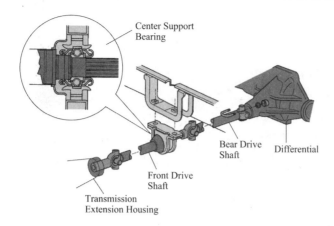

Fig. 6-6　Drive Shaft

Steering System

The steering system must deliver precise directional control (Fig. 6-7). And it must do so requiring little driver effort at the steering wheel. The key components that make up the steering system are the steering wheel, steering column, steering shaft, steering gear, pitman arm, drag link, steering arm, ball joints, and tie-rod assembly.

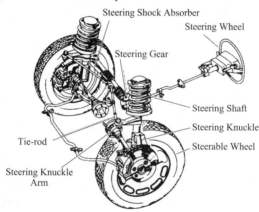

Fig. 6-7　Steering System

Steering wheel

The steering wheel, which consists of a rigid rim and a number of spokes connecting the rim to a center hub, attaches to the top of the steering shaft at its center. Most steering wheel hubs have internal splines that fit over external splines on the steering shaft. A bolt or nut at the center of the hub secures the wheel to the shaft. The steering wheel may also contain controls for the cruise control and audio controls, as well as the driver's airbag.

Steering Column

The steering shaft is at the center of the steering column (Fig. 6-8) The top end of the steering shaft splines to the center of the steering wheel, and a large nut fastens the steering wheel to the shaft. The lock housing, which contains the ignition lock cylinder, encases the top part of the steering shaft. The steering column jacket covers the shaft under the ignition lock housing, and the gear selector lever housing fits over a portion of the column jacket.

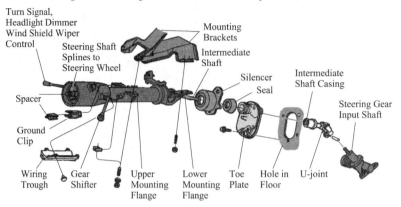

Fig. 6-8　Steering Column

A U-joint connects the lower end of the steering shaft to a small intermediate shaft, often called a stub shaft. Because this steering column includes a gear selector lever, the lower end of the column also incorporates an attachment point that connects the shift tube to the gear shift rod. The intermediate shaft extends through a hole in the floor where it is coupled to the steering gear input shaft by a U-joint.

Steering Shaft

The steering shaft is basically a rod, usually jointed, that runs from the top of the steering column to the steering gear. U-joints in the shaft accommodate any angular variations between the steering shaft and the steering gear input shaft.

Steering Gear

This gearbox multiplies steering torque and changes its direction as received through the steering shaft from the steering wheel. There are two widely used types of gears: worm and roller, and recirculating ball.

Pitman Arm

The pitman arm is a steel arm clamped to the output shaft of the steering gear (Fig. 6-9). The outer end of the pitman arm moves through an arc in order to change the rotary motion of the steering gear output shaft into linear motion. [5] The length of the pitman arm affects steering quickness. A longer pitman arm will generate more steering motion at the front wheels for a given amount of steering wheel movement.

Drag Link

This forged rod connects the pitman arm to the steering arm. The drag link is connected at each end by ball joints.

Steering Arm

Sometimes called a steering lever, this forged steel component connects the drag link to the top portion of the driver's side steering knuckle and spindle.[6] As the steering arm moves, it changes the angle of the steering knuckle.

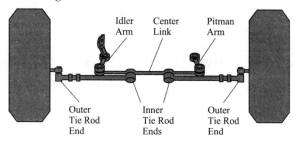

Fig. 6-9　Pitman Arm

Ball Joints

This ball-and-socket assembly consists of a forged steel ball with a threaded stud attached to it. A socket shell grips the ball. The ball stud moves around to provide the freedom of movement needed for various steering links to accommodate relative motion between the axle and the frame rail when the front axle springs flex.

Tie Rod Assembly

The steering arm or lever controls the movement of the driver's side steering knuckle. There must be some method of transferring this steering motion to the opposite, passenger side steering knuckle. This is done through the use of a tie-rod assembly that links the two steering knuckles together and forces them to act in unison(Fig. 6-10).

Fig. 6-10　Tie Rod Assembly

Brake System

Each vehicle must have two independent brake systems for safety. The main brake system is hydraulically operated and is called the service brake system. The secondary or parking brake system is mechanically operated. The automobile brake systems are divided into three types of service brake combinations: drum brakes, disc brakes, and disc-drum combinations.

Drum Brake

Drum brakes use an internal expanding brake shoe with the lining attached, working within the confines of a rotating brake surface called a brake drum(Fig. 6-11).[7] The brake shoe diameter is expanded to contact the brake surface by a hydraulic cylinder that is referred to as a wheel cylinder. Fluid pressure from the master cylinder supplies fluid to the wheel cylinders causing them to expand. The expansion of the wheel cylinder through mechanical linkage forces the brake linings into contact with the rotating brake drum to provide braking action.

Disc Brake

Disc brakes employ a brake disc that rotates with the wheel (Fig. 6-12). The brake disc is usually referred to as a brake rotor. A hydraulically operated caliper is used to force the lining friction material against the braking surface of the rotor for stopping wheel rotation.[8] Disc brake shoes move perpendicular to the face of the brake rotor to provide a clamping action on the rotor to slow the vehicle motion.

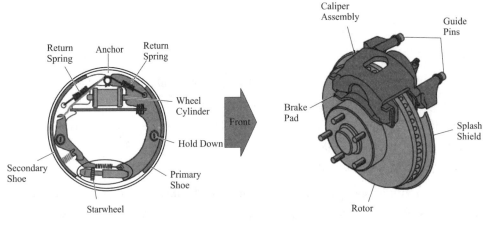

Fig. 6-11　Drum Brake　　　　Fig. 6-12　Disc Brake

Hydraulic Brake system

Hydraulic brake systems utilize liquid to transfer force from the driver's foot to the brake shoes. Depressing the brake pedal creates a mechanical force that is transmitted through a pushrod to a piston in the master cylinder. The piston, in turn, pushes the brake fluid through the brake lines to pistons in a caliper or a cylinder on each wheel. The pressure acting on these pistons pushes brake shoes against a rotating disc or drum. This friction generated by the contacting brake shoes and rotating disc/drum slows and eventually stops the wheels. Releasing the brake pedal causes this action to reverse-with brake fluid returning to the master cylinder.

Air Brake System

The second type of system-the air brake system-utilizes compressed air as a source of force to stop the truck. A complete air brake system, includes foundation brakes, air system, and optional brake equipment.

Parking Brakes

The parking brake system is used to hold one or more of the vehicle brakes in an applied position for an extended period of time. This brake system must be capable of holding the vehicle on a grade and bringing the vehicle to a stop if the service brakes fail.[9]

Tires and Wheels

Tires and wheels are important to vehicle ride, handling, and fuel economy. The tires and wheels must first support the vehicle weight. The tires are also required to change the vehicle direction while the vehicle is in motion. In addition, the tires and wheels have to transfer the engine and braking torque to the road surface for driving and braking the vehicle.

Suspension System

The suspension system has two basic functions, to keep car's wheels in firm contact with the road and to provide a comfortable ride for the passengers. A lot of the system's work is done by the springs. The springs used on today's cars and trucks include leaf springs, coil springs, air springs, and torsion bars.

Word List

1. chassis ['ʃæsɪ]   n. 底盘
2. transmission [trænz'mɪʃ(ə)n]   n. 变速器
3. clutch [klʌtʃ]   n. 离合器
4. differential [ˌdɪfə'renʃ(ə)l]   n. 差速齿轮,差速器
5. torque [tɔː(r)k]   n. 转矩
6. disconnect [ˌdɪskə'nekt]   v. 断开,分离,拆开
7. shift [ʃɪft]   vt. 换挡,替换,改变,变速
8. transaxle [træns'æksl]   n. 变速驱动桥
9. round [raund]   vt. 绕行,拐弯
10. suspension [sə'spenʃ(ə)n]   n. 悬架,悬挂装置
11. axle ['æks(ə)l]   n. 轮轴,车轴,车桥
12. spoke [spəuk]   n. 轮辐
13. diameter [daɪ'æmɪtə(r)]   n. 直径
14. cab [kæb]   n. 司机室,驾驶室
15. angular ['æŋgjulə(r)]   adj. 有角的
16. accommodate [ə'kɔmədeɪt]   vt. 使适应,容纳
17. gearbox ['gɪə(r)bɔks]   n. 齿轮箱,变速器
18. multiply ['mʌltɪplaɪ]   v. 乘,增加
19. worm [wɔː(r)m]   n. 蜗杆
20. roller ['rəulə(r)]   n. 蜗轮,滚筒
21. socket ['sɔkɪt]   n. 窝,孔,插座
22. thread [θred]   n. 螺纹
23. stud [stʌd]   n. 柱头螺栓,螺柱
24. frame [freɪm]   n. 车架
25. unison ['juːnɪs(ə)n]   n. 和谐,一致

26. grade [greɪd] n. 斜坡
27. caliper [ˈkælɪpə] n. 卡钳
28. perpendicular [ˌpəː(r)pənˈdɪkjulə(r)] adj. 垂直的，正交的
29. optional [ˈɒpʃ(ə)nəl] adj. 可选择的，随意的
30. tire [taɪə] n. 轮胎
31. handle [ˈhænd(ə)l] vi. 搬运，易于操纵
32. passenger [ˈpæsɪndʒə(r)] n. 乘客，旅客

Proper Names

1. power train 动力传动系统
2. drive shaft 传动轴
3. manual transmission 手动变速器
4. automatic transmission 自动变速器
5. planetary gear system 行星齿轮系统
6. ring gear 冠状齿轮
7. differential case 差速器壳
8. differential pinion gears 差速器行星小齿轮
9. differential side gears 差速器半轴齿轮
10. propeller shaft 汽车传动轴
11. universal joint 万向节
12. steering system 转向系统
13. brake system 制动系统
14. steering wheel 转向盘
15. steering column 转向管柱
16. steering shaft 转向轴
17. steering gear 转向齿轮，转向器
18. pitman arm 转向摇臂
19. drag link 转向直拉杆
20. steering arm 转向节臂
21. ball joint 球形接头
22. tie-rod 转向横拉杆
23. steering knuckle 转向节
24. service brake system 行车制动系统
25. parking brake system 停车制动系统
26. drum brake 鼓式制动器

27.	disc brake	盘式制动器
28.	brake shoe	制动蹄
29.	wheel cylinder	轮缸,分泵
30.	master cylinder	主缸,总泵
31.	hydraulic brake system	液压制动系统
32.	brake pedal	制动踏板
33.	suspension system	悬架系统
34.	leaf spring	钢板弹簧
35.	coil spring	螺旋弹簧
36.	air spring	减振气囊
37.	torsion bar	扭杆弹簧

Useful Expressions

make up　　　　　　　　　　　弥补,整理,和解,化妆,补足,拼凑

Key Vocabulary

1. accommodate

vt. 能容纳,能提供⋯膳宿,(飞机等)可搭载,给⋯方便,向⋯提供,调和

The hotel can accommodate 500 tourists. 这家旅馆可住500名观光客。

You will have to accommodate yourself to the changed situation. 你必须适应变化了的形势。

The policeman accommodated us when we asked for help. 我们请求警察帮忙,他爽快地答应了。

The bank will accommodate him with a loan. 银行将向他提供一笔贷款。

accommodate oneself to 使自己适应于

accommodate(sb.)with 向(某人)供应(提供)

2. handle

n. 柄,把手,柄状物,可乘之机

I turned the handle and opened the door. 我转了转拉手,把门打开。

Don't let your conduct give any handle for gossip. 别让你的行为成为人家说三道四的话柄。

vt. 触,弄,搬动,操作,指挥,处理,对待

Do not handle the exhibits. 请勿触摸展品。

He knows how to handle the machine. 他会操作这台机器。

I didn't know how to handle these people. 我不知道如何对付这些人。

Handle children kindly, if you want them to trust you. 假如你要孩子们信任你,就要对他们和气些。

Notes

1. The power train carries power from the engine crankshaft to the car wheels so the wheels rotate and car moves.

翻译:从发动机曲轴输出的动力经传动系统传递给车轮,使车轮转动,驱动汽车前进。

2. When the car is on the straight road, the ring gear, differential case, differential pinion gears, and two differential side gears all turn as a unit without any relative motion.

翻译:当汽车行驶在直线道路上时,环形齿轮、差速器壳、差速器行星小齿轮以及差速器半轴齿轮等作为无相对运动的整体而转动。

语法:when 引导时间状语从句。as a unit 表示运动的方式。

3. Since all roads are not perfectly smooth, and the transmission is fixed, the drive shaft has to be flexible to absorb the shocks of bumps in the road.

翻译:因为不是所有的路面都是平整的,而变速器又是固定的,这样,传动轴不得不具有柔性以吸收来自路面的颠簸振动。

语法:since…引导原因状语从句。

4. Spokes extend from the wheel to the wheel hub, which is fastened securely at the top of the steering column.

翻译:转向盘辐条从转向盘轮缘延伸到转向盘的轮毂,而轮毂则被紧紧地安装在转向管柱的顶端。

语法:which is fastened securely at the top of the steering column 是非限定性定语从句,修饰先行词 the wheel hub。

5. The outer end of the pitman's arm moves through an arc in order to change the rotary motion of the steering gear output shaft into linear motion.

翻译:转向摇臂的外端沿着弧向运动,以便将转向器输出轴的旋转运动变成直线运动。

6. Sometimes called a steering lever, this forged steel component connects the drag link to the top portion of the driver's side steering knuckle and spindle.

翻译:由钢铁铸造的转向节臂有时又称为转向杆,它将转向直拉杆与驾驶员侧的转向节和转向轮轴的上端部分连接在一起。

7. Drum brakes use an internal expanding brake shoe with the lining attached, working within the confines of a rotating brake surface called a brake drum.

翻译:鼓式制动器使用一个内张型的带摩擦片的制动蹄,以制动鼓内圆柱面为工作表面,摩擦片在工作表面的限定区域内接触。

语法:working…是现在分词短语,作用相当于状语从句。

8. A hydraulically operated caliper is used to force the lining friction material against the braking surface of the rotor for stopping wheel rotation.

翻译:液压式制动钳是用来迫使摩擦片上的摩擦材料紧靠在制动盘的端面上,以使汽车车轮停止旋转。

9. This brake system must be capable of holding the vehicle on a grade and bringing the vehicle to a stop if the service brakes fail.

翻译:驻车制动系统必须能保证汽车在斜坡上原地停驻,并在行车制动系统失效时仍能实现汽车停车。

语法:be capable of doing 中的 doing 即为句中的 holding 和 bringing,它们是并列关系。

Exercises

1. Choose the best answer from the following choices according to the text.

1) For many years, on most cars the engine has been mounted in the _____ and the rear wheels were driven.

  A. front   B. rear   C. left   D. right

2) Manual transmission requires use of a _____ to apply and remove the engine torque to the transmission input shaft.

  A. chassis   B. differential   C. clutch   D. axle

3) The steering gear multiplies steering _____ and changes its direction as received through the steering shaft from the steering wheel.

  A. power   B. torque   C. friction   D. wheel

4) Hydraulic brake systems utilize _____ to transfer force from the driver's foot to the brake shoes.

  A. air   B. liquid   C. solid   D. linkage

5) _____ system has two basic functions, to keep car's wheels in firm contact with the road and to provide a comfortable ride for the passengers.

  A. Steering   B. Brake   C. Ignition   D. Suspension

2. Translate the following into Chinese.

1) pitman arm   2) automatic transmission   3) planetary gear system

4) chassis   5) universal joint   6) steering system

7) brake system   8) service brake system   9) parking brake system

3. Translate the following into English.

1) 传动系统   2) 手动变速器   3) 差速器

4) 后轮驱动   5) 转向盘   6) 钢板弹簧

7) 制动蹄   8) 悬架系统   9) 制动踏板

4. Translate the following sentences into Chinese.

1) The universal joint or U-joint is used to connect the drive shaft to the transmission output

shaft.

2) Truck steering systems are either manual or power assisted, with power assist units using either hydraulic or air assist setups to make steering effort easier.

3) The larger the steering wheel diameter, the more torque is generated from the same amount of drive effort.

5. Translate the words or phrases in the following figure into Chinese.

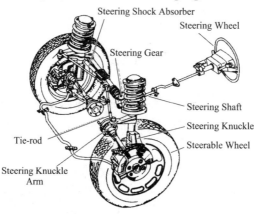

Practical Reading

Body Construction

An automobile body is generally divided into four sections-the fronts the upper or top, rear and the underbody. These sections are further divided into small units, called assemblies, which in turn are divided into even smaller units, called parts.

The front section is composed of a number of assemblies, such as the grille, the hood, the right, and left fender, and the cowl assembly. [1] The cowl assembly, one of the largest of all assemblies, is composed of the shroud upper panel, shroud vent panel, a windshield glass support, instrument panel, front body hinge pillar to rocker panel, and the dash panel. The roof panel is usually the largest of all body panels and is supported by the upper inner windshield frame, the front body hinge pillars, the longitudinal roof bows on its sides, and the inner back window panel at the rear. The center of the roof panel is reinforced by the roof bow. The quarter-panel assemblies are located in the rear section of the automobile and are composed of the lower inner rear quarter panel, wheelhouse panel, and outer rear quarter side panel. The automobile body is divided into three distinctly separate compartments and these are serviced by the following assemblies. [2] Doors provide easy access to the body compartment, hoods to the engine compartment, and the deck lids to the luggage compartment. They are all similar in design and construction in that each is made with an outer panel hood flanged edges are not only folded over but are also spot-welded to a box-type frame or inner construction, thus giving them a great deal of strength. [3] All are mounted on hinges and equipped with locks for easy opening and closing. Rocker panels are rust-proofed assemblies of box-type construction and are composed of the outer door-opening rocker panel, the rear outer rocker panel reinforcement, and the front outer-rocker panel reinforcement. They are located directly below the doors and are not only spot-welded to the sides of the floor pans, thereby greatly reinforcing the underbody section, but also to the cowl assembly in front and the rear quarter-panel assembly at the rear.

The front and rear bumpers not only provide a certain amount of protection to the automobile but also enhance its appearance. [4] The bumpers are held in position by means of brackets, shock absorbers or insulators that are bolted to each end of the frame side rails, commonly called frame horns.

Word List

1. grille [grɪl] n. 格子,铁格子
2. hood [hud] n. (汽车的)篷盖
3. fender ['fendə(r)] n. 挡泥板
4. cowl [kaul] n. 壳,套,罩,盖
5. shroud [ʃraud] n. 遮蔽物,侧板,罩
6. windshield ['wɪn(d)ʃɪːld] n. 风窗玻璃
7. hinge [hɪndʒ] n. 铰链,折页
8. pillar ['pɪlə(r)] n. 柱子,柱状物,支柱
9. bumper ['bʌmpə(r)] n. 保险杠

Proper Names

1. dash panel 仪表盘安装面板
2. roof panel (车身)顶板
3. wheelhouse panel 车轮拱罩
4. outer rear quarter side panel 后侧外围板
5. inner rear quarter panel 后侧内围板
6. spot-welded 点焊

Notes

1. The front section is composed of a number of assemblies, such as the grille, the hood, the right, and left fender, and the cowl assembly.

翻译:车前部由许多组件组成,如格栅、车盖、左右护板和外壳总成。

2. The automobile body is divided into three distinctly separate compartments and these are serviced by the following assemblies.

翻译:车身可分为三个明显的独立部分,而各部分又用于以下装置。

3. They are all similar in design and construction in that each is made with an outer panel hood flanged edges are not only folded over but are also spot-welded to a box-type frame or inner construction, thus giving them a great deal of strength.

翻译:它们在设计和结构上相似,每个都制造成外部板板合边,不仅折合而且点焊成箱形框架或箱形内部结构,这样就提供了足够的强度。

4. The front and rear bumpers not only provide a certain amount of protection to the automobile but also enhance its appearance.

翻译:前后保险杠不仅对汽车提供了一定的保护,而且也改善了汽车的外观。

学习资料:

相关链接及网址

1. http://65.201.178.38

2. http://www.a-car.com

推荐书目

1. 王怡民.汽车专业英语[M].北京:人民交通出版社,2003.

2. 马林才.汽车实用英语(下)[M].北京：人民交通出版社,2005.

3. 金加龙.汽车底盘构造与维修[M].4 版.北京:电子工业出版社,2016.

4. 刘汉涛.陪你充电每一天:图解汽车维修英语[M].北京:电子工业出版社,2016.

5. 朱派龙.图解汽车专业英语[M].北京:化学工业出版社,2018.

任务七
汽车检测设备认识

1. 掌握汽车检测设备名称、检测内容等专业术语、单词和词汇。
2. 掌握汽车检测设备组成部分的英语表达。
3. 能对关于汽车检测设备的资料进行中英互译。
4. 能对相关内容的英语资料进行阅读和翻译。
5. 能对汽车检测设备实物标识出相应英语单词或词汇。

任务描述

介绍关于泄漏检查器、柴油机烟度计、汽车排气分析仪、底盘测功机、汽车前轮定位仪、汽车侧滑仪和汽车车速表测试仪等相关的专业术语、词汇。通过完成该任务,能阅读关于汽车检测设备结构的外文文献,并掌握简单翻译技巧。

本学习任务沿着以下脉络进行学习:

通读全文 → 学习单词和语法 → 完成课后练习 → 分组讨论 → 课后阅读

Task 7 Automotive Testing Equipment Understanding

The tune-up technician must be very familiar with and competent in the use of various forms of test equipment. With the aid of this equipment, the technician can perform two very important tasks. For instance, the test instruments when properly used quickly pinpoint malfunctions within the engine and the ignition, fuel, electrical, and emission control systems. In addition, this same equipment is an excellent quality control tool.

Leak Detector

This instrument is used for locating leaks in any pressure and vacuum system and is also used to examine the discharge troubles in electric apparatus. [1] The instrument consists of a main body, ultrasonic probe, ultrasonic microphone, and ultrasonic transmitter etc.

Diesel Smoke Meter

This instrument is used for the measurement of smoke emitted from the vehicle with the diesel engine (Fig. 7-1). [2] The instrument is thus suitable for investigating both steady-state and transient conditions but suffers from a lack of sensitivity. The opacimeter is essentially an instrument for use on engine test bed or chassis dynamometer and an exhaust extraction system is needed; this should not cause distortion of the plume. [3] If used in the open air it is clear that the plume must be shielded from the wind.

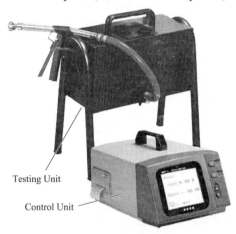

Fig. 7-1 Diesel Smoke Meter

Automotive Emission Analyzer

This is a type of non-dispersive infrared absorption analyzer (Fig. 7-2). The infrared analyzer is a device that measures the number of hydrocarbons (HC) and carbon monoxide (CO) in a vehicle's exhaust. Both of these compounds are harmful to air pollutants. Hydrocarbons in a vehicle's exhaust represent unburned gasoline. If the engine does not burn up all the fuel during the combustion process, raw gasoline goes out the tailpipe and registers as HC on the meter. The meter on the analyzer measures HC emissions in parts per million (ppm). On the analyzer's CO meter, the richness or leanness of a mixture is shown by the position of the needle. The richer the mixture, for example, the higher the needle deflects, indicating a greater percentage of CO in the exhaust sample. [4] The analyzer measures the amount of CO in the exhaust, using a percentage figure.

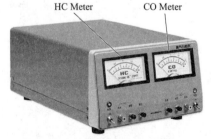

Fig. 7-2 Automotive Emission Analyzer

Microcomputerised Engine Analyzer

It consists of the main part, sensors, and indicator. The main part is a measuring and data-handling system with a microcomputer. There are seven sensors-ignition, power supply, voltage, oil pressure, cylinder pressure, vibration, and fuel injection sensors.

Chassis Dynamometer

The chassis dynamometer is another very important diagnostic tool, found in many tune-up specialty shops(Fig. 7-3). The chassis dynamometer measures the mechanical power of the vehicle at the drive-wheels and provides the operator with a readout in units of road speed and power. [5] In addition, the chassis dynamometer along with an engine analyzer permits the operator to examine engine systems in detail with the vehicle operating under a loaded condition. The typical chassis dynamometer consists of two rollers, a remote control pendant, and readout instruments. The two rollers cradle the vehicle's drive wheels. One of the rollers couples directly to a power absorption unit. The power absorption unit applies a varying load on this roller upon command from the operator. The power absorption unit then acts as a very effective brake, which applies, through the roller, resistance to drive-wheel rotation. The greater the load applied by the absorption unit to the roller, the more horsepower is necessary to turn it at any given speed. Thus, at constant drive-wheel speed, the horsepower output can be made to vary by changing the load, applied by the absorption unit. Also, the operator can vary the horsepower output with a constant load applied to the drive-wheels by changing the engine speed. The remote pendant is a hand-held control used to activate the power absorption unit. The control itself has two buttons: on and off. When the technician pushes the on the button in, the power absorption unit begins to load the roller. The off button, on the other hand, de-energizes the power absorption unit, thus releasing the load from the roller. The speed and power instrument panel contains two large, illuminated meters: speed and power.

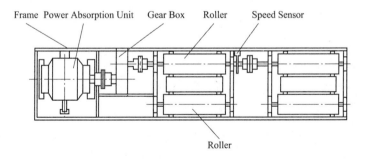

Fig. 7-3 Chassis Dynamometer

Automobile Front Wheel Aligner

This is a special device for measuring the wheel camber, the kingpin caster and the kingpin inclination of the automobile. [6]

Automobile Side-slip Tester

This instrument is used for testing the dynamic location of the front wheels of the automobile (Fig. 7-4). It consists of the testing device, the quantitative indicating device, and the qualitative displaying device of the sideslip.

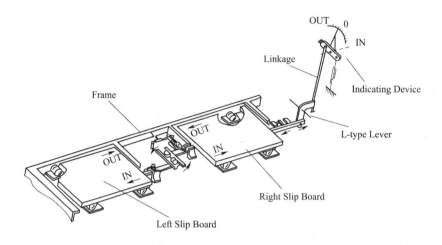

Fig. 7-4　Automobile Side-slip Tester

Automobile Speedometer Tester

This equipment is used for checking the precision and the performance of automobile speedometer. It consists of the speed-test device, speed-display device and speed-alarm device.

Torquemeter

This is a torquemeter with microcomputer; it's used for measuring torque, speed and power of engine, motor, and gearbox, etc.

Reaction Type Automobile Brake Tester

This is an instrument for checking the braking performance of automobile. It consists of the actuating device, braking force supporting device, braking force detecting device and braking force indicating device.

Automobile Comprehensive tester

This instrument is used for the determination of dynamic and economic property in automobile test. It consists of the main part and sensors. The main part consists of a single board computer and an interface circuit plate. Sensors include the fifth wheel sensor, fuel consumption sensor, pulling force sensor, revolution sensor, and brake pedal sensor.

Performance Tester of Internal-Combustion-Engine

This is a tester for measuring the power, fuel consumption and rotational speed of an engine. It consists of a microcomputer and a printing system. It is used in an engine test run in combination with various dynamometers.

Wheel Dynamic Balancer

This is a special equipment for conducting balancing (Fig. 7-5). The electrical logging system analyses and handles signals with a single board computer. Dynamic imbalance, unlike static imbalance, can only be detected when the wheel is rotating. Dynamic balancers of the first type require the tire to be in static balance before any dynamic balancing is attempted. Dynamic imbalance can then be checked as the wheel is spun. The weights of the size indicated are placed on the wheel rim in the proper position (180° from each other on opposite wheel rims). The wheel is respun to make sure that the imbalance has been corrected. Balancers of the second type, those that combine static and dynamic balance functions, use a sensing mechanism that is sensitive to the entire weight characteristic of the tire and wheel assembly. This allows imbalance to be corrected with one weight on each side of the wheel.

Fig. 7-5　Wheel Dynamic Balancer

Word List

1. technician [tek'nɪʃ(ə)n]　　　　　　　　n. 技术员,技师
2. pinpoint ['pɪnpɔɪnt]　　　　　　　　　vt. 指出(原因),指示正确位置
3. instrument ['ɪnstrumənt]　　　　　　　n. 工具,器械
4. apparatus [ˌæpə'reɪtəs]　　　　　　　n. 器械,设备,仪器
5. transient ['trænzɪənt]　　　　　　　　adj. 短暂的,瞬时的
6. sensitivity [ˌsensə'tɪvətɪ]　　　　　　n. 灵敏(度),灵敏性
7. opacimeter [əupə'sɪmɪtə]　　　　　　n. 光密度计,透明度测试仪
8. shield [ʃiːld]　　　　　　　　　　　　vt. (from)保护,防护
9. pollutant [pə'luːt(ə)nt]　　　　　　　n. 污染物质
10. hydrocarbon [ˌhaɪdrəu'kɑː(r)bən]　　n. 烃,碳氢化合物
11. raw [rɔː]　　　　　　　　　　　　　adj. 未加工的,处于自然状态的
12. tailpipe ['teɪlˌpaɪp]　　　　　　　　　n. 排气尾管
13. needle ['niːdl]　　　　　　　　　　　n. 指针
14. deflect [dɪ'flekt]　　　　　　　　　　v. (使)偏转
15. microcomputer ['maɪkrəukəmpjuːtə(r)]　n. 微型计算机
16. pendant ['pendənt]　　　　　　　　　n. 垂饰,下垂物
17. cradle ['kreɪd(ə)l]　　　　　　　　　vt. 将…放在摇篮内,支持,支撑
18. readout ['riːdaut]　　　　　　　　　　n. 读出器,读出

19. dynamic [daɪˈnæmɪk]   *adj.* 动力的,动力学的,动态的
20. quantitative [ˈkwɔntɪtətɪv]   *adj.* 数量的,定量的
21. speedometer [spɪˈdɔmɪtə(r)]   *n.* 速度表
22. torquemeter [ˈtɔːkmiːtə]   *n.* 转矩计,转矩测量仪

Proper Names

1. tune-up   发动机的调整
2. leak detector   泄漏检查器
3. ultrasonic probe   超声波探测器
4. ultrasonic microphone   超声波扩音器
5. ultrasonic transmitter   超声波信号发送器
6. diesel smoke meter   柴油机烟度计
7. chassis dynamometer   底盘测功机
8. infrared absorption analyzer   吸收式红外分析仪
9. engine test bed   发动机试验台
10. engine analyzer   发动机分析仪
11. drive-wheel   驱动轮
12. power absorption unit   动力吸收单元
13. front wheel aligner   前轮定位仪
14. wheel camber   车轮外倾角
15. kingpin caster   主销后倾角
16. kingpin inclination   主销内倾角
17. side-slip tester   侧滑测试仪
18. speedometer tester   车速表测试仪
19. braking performance   制动性能
20. automobile brake tester   汽车制动性能测试仪
21. fifth wheel sensor   五轮传感器
22. fuel consumption sensor   燃油消耗传感器
23. single board computer   单片机
24. performance tester   性能测试仪
25. wheel dynamic balancer   车轮动态平衡机

Useful Expressions

be familiar with   熟悉…的,通晓…的

Key Vocabulary

1. activate

vt. 使…活动,对…起作用,开[起]动,触发,创设,成立(机构等),使之活泼,使激活

His lofty spirit has greatly attracted and activated others. 他的崇高精神大大地吸引并且激励了别人。

A button that you press to activate the reset mechanism. 按下去重新起动机器的按钮。

A similar device used to release or activate a mechanism. 类似扳机的装置用来使机械装置运作。

2. shield

n. 盾,罩,屏,防御(物),保护(物),保护(者)

the lower part of a shield 盾牌的底部

the upper section of a shield 纹章上段盾牌的上面部分

Turn on the wind shield wiper. 开刮水器。

A shield or shield-shaped emblem bearing a coat of arms. 盾状徽章表层带有武器的盾或盾状徽章。

the rocket's ablated head shield 火箭顶部的融化防护罩

Shield of David 大卫王的盾牌(犹太教的六芒星形标志)

vt. 保护,遮蔽,屏蔽,庇护,挡开,避开

vi. 起保护作用

His mother shields him from punishment. 他母亲保护了他,使他免受惩罚。

Lead aprons shield people from radiation. 铅做的工作裙可使人免受辐射。

shield from light; as in photography 避免光线,比如在摄影过程中

be the shield and buckler 做靠山,做后盾,做可靠的保护者

both sides of the shield 盾的正反两面,事物的表里

the other side of the shield 盾的反面,问题的另一面

Notes

1. This instrument is used for locating leaks in any pressure and vacuum system and is also used to examine the discharge troubles in electric apparatus.

翻译:泄露检查器用于查找所有压力和真空系统中的泄露点,也用于查找电气设备中的漏电故障。

2. This instrument is used for the measurement of smoke emitted from the vehicle with the diesel engine.

翻译:该仪器是于柴油机排放炭烟的测定。

3. The opacimeter is essentially an instrument for use on engine test bed or chassis dynamometer and an exhaust extraction system is needed; this should not cause distortion of the plume.

翻译:吸光系数烟度计实际上是用于发动机试验台或底盘测功机上的仪器,它要与废气采集系统同时使用,这种烟度计测量烟度时不会出错。

4. The richer the mixture, for example, the higher the needle deflects, indicating a greater percentage of CO in the exhaust sample.

翻译:混合物的浓度越高,指针偏转得越大,表明所排出样气中 CO 的百分比含量越大。

语法:the richer…the higher 是 the more…the more 的变体形式。在英语中,常用这种类似的方法来表达"越…越…"。

5. The chassis dynamometer measures the mechanical power of the vehicle at the drive-wheels and provides the operator with a readout in units of road speed and power.

翻译:底盘测功机能测量车辆驱动轮上的机械功率,并能给操作员显示车辆的道路行车速度和功率具体读数。

6. This is a special device for measuring the wheel camber, the kingpin caster and the kingpin inclination of an automobile.

翻译:这个是专门用于测量汽车车轮外倾角、主销后倾角和主销内倾角的装置。

Exercises

1. Choose the best answer from the following choice according to the text.

1) Diesel Smoke Meter is used for the measurement of smoke emitted from vehicle with _____ engine.

  A. gasoline   B. diesel   C. Liquefied Petroleum Gas   D. natural gas

2) If the engine does not burn up all the fuel during the combustion process, raw gasoline goes out the tailpipe and registers as _____ on the meter.

  A. CO   B. CO_2 C. NO_x D. HC

3) The typical chassis dynamometer consists of _____ rollers, a remote control pendant, and readout instruments.

  A. two   B. three   C. four   D. five

4) The weights of the size indicated are placed on the wheel rim in the proper position (_____ from each other on opposite wheel rims).

  A. 90°   B. 120°   C. 180°   D. 270°

2. Translate the following into Chinese.

1) microcomputer   2) technician   3) speedometer

4) kingpin inclination   5) wheel camber   6) opacimeter

7) fuel consumption   8) leak detector   9) power absorption unit

3. Translate the following into English.

1) 柴油机烟度计   2) 底盘测功机   3) 发动机试验台

4) 前轮定位仪   5) 发动机分析仪   6) 侧滑测试仪

7) 五轮传感器   8) 单片机   9) 车轮动平衡仪

4. Translate the following sentences into Chinese.

1) The infrared analyzer is a device that measures the amount of hydrocarbons (HC) and carbon monoxide (CO) in a vehicle's exhaust.

2) This instrument is used for testing the dynamic location of the front wheels of automobile.

5. Translate words in the following figure into Chinese.

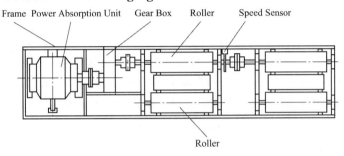

Practical Reading

Engine Noise Diagnosis

The ability to diagnose engine noises with a fair degree of accuracy may be a vital part of the tune-up specialist's job. For instance, it may be necessary for a technician to recognize and locate the cause of noises that may develop due to normal engine wear and tear over long periods of use or may appear because of failure of one or more engine parts. The parts that produce some characteristic noises are loose pistons, excessively worn rings or ring lands, loose piston pins, worn connecting-rod bearings, worn main bearings, loose vibration damper or flywheel, or worn or loose valve-train components.[1] When properly interpreted, these noises are a definite aid in any diagnosis of engine mechanical difficulties. But there are many sources and varieties of engine noises; careful interpretation of these sounds is necessary for several reasons. First, a careful diagnosis of an engine noise can often prevent the expense of tearing down an engine. In this regard, a technician should always make a noise analysis before engine repair begins so that only the needed and correct operations are made with no extra work or charges to the customer. Second, a careful interpretation of abnormal engine sounds can prevent the engine from requiring extensive and costly repair work after continued usage has ruined it. [2]

Stethoscope

All moving mechanical engine parts create some form of sound waves of various pitches, frequencies, qualities, and intensities. Most people can hear many of these sound waves without the assistance of a listening device. On the other hand, some sounds are impossible to hear unless magnifies; even if some sounds are audible, they are frequently difficult to localize and locate. Consequently, most technicians utilize some form of sounding rod or stethoscope when diagnosing engine sounds. A stethoscope, or sound scope, aids in locating the source of engine knocks and noises by magnifying their sound waves. This instrument makes use of a metal prod, about 8 inches long and 1/8 inch in diameter, that passes through a rubber bushing and terminates against a metal diaphragm held in a plastic housing. Furthermore, two ear tubes carry the sound from this diaphragm chamber to the listener's ears. The value of the sound-detecting and amplifying stethoscope is, of course, to help the technician distinguish the difference between normal and abnormal sounds and to find the location and cause of the latter. [3] Even an engine in good operating condition will make noises that the mechanic will be able to hear with a stethoscope. Being familiar with these sounds will be very helpful when the mechanic attempts to pinpoint the location and cause of any abnormal noise due to excessive wear, damage, or maladjustment of engine parts.

Sound tracing with the stethoscope

The best way to trace any type of noise is to follow a systematic procedure. First, for example, always use a stethoscope or other sounding device to amplify the sound. Second, with the listening device, attempt to localize and identify the noise. You can trace both unfamiliar and familiar sounds to the portion of the engine where they originate by following the sound with the prod of the stethoscope until the noise reaches its maximum intensity. [4] After you locate this spot, a knowledge of engine construction and operation will be your best guide as to the most likely cause of the sound.

Word List

1. diagnose ['daɪəgnəʊz]   v. 诊断
2. vital ['vaɪt(ə)l]   adj. 重大的，至关重要的
3. definite ['def(ə)nət]   adj. 明确的，一定的
4. customer ['kʌstəmə(r)]   n. 消费者
5. localize ['ləʊkəlaɪz]   vt. 使局限于某一地方
6. stethoscope ['steθəskəʊp]   n. 听诊器
7. distinguish [dɪ'stɪŋgwɪʃ]   v. 区别，辨别
8. maladjustment [ˌmælə'dʒʌstmənt] n. 失调，不适应

9. intensity [ɪnˈtensɪti]		n. 强度
10. expense [ɪkˈspens]		n. 费用,代价
11. ruin [ˈruːɪn]		v. (使)毁灭
12. pitch [pɪtʃ]		n. 程度
13. audible [ˈɔːdəb(ə)l]		adj. 听得见的
14. originate [əˈrɪdʒəneɪt]		vt. 引起,发生

Proper Names

1. makes use of	使用,利用
2. rubber bushing	橡胶套管
3. engine knock	发动机爆震
4. metal diaphragm	金属膜片

Notes

1. The parts that produce some characteristic noises are loose pistons, excessively worn rings or ring lands, loose piston pins, worn connecting-rod bearings, worn main bearings, loose vibration damper or flywheel, or worn or loose valve-train components.

翻译:产生带某种特征噪声的部件有松动的活塞、过度磨损的活塞环或环岸、松动的活塞销、磨损的连杆轴承、磨损的主轴承、松动的减振器或飞轮以及磨损或松动的配气机构的元件。

2. Second, a careful interpretation of abnormal engine sounds can prevent the engine from requiring extensive and costly repair work after continued usage has ruined it.

翻译:再则,对发动机异常噪声的正确解读能避免发动机在已经损坏的情况下继续使用,否则会导致后续的大量维修工作和昂贵的维修费用。

3. The value of the sound-detecting and amplifying stethoscope is, of course, to help the technician distinguish the difference between normal and abnormal sounds and to find the location and cause of the latter.

翻译:起探测声音和放大声音作用的听诊器,其声音强度有助于技师辨别发动机内的正常声音和异常声音,并发现发出异常声音的部位和原因。

4. You can trace both unfamiliar and familiar sounds to the portion of the engine where they originate by following the sound with the prod of the stethoscope until the noise reaches its maximum intensity.

翻译:用听诊器探针探测噪声,直到所探测到的噪声强度最大,从而发现噪声部位,通过这种方法,你就可以跟踪那些熟悉或不熟悉的噪声从而找到发动机上噪声源。

学习资料：

相关链接及网址

1. http://65.201.178.38

2. http://www.a-car.com

推荐书目

1. Robert N. Brady. Electric and Electronic Systems for Automobiles and Trucks[M]. Virginia：Reston Publishing Company, Inc. 1983.

2. A Tranter. Automobile Electrical Manual[M]. London：Haynes Publishing Group. 1983.

3. William L. Husselbee. Automotive Tune-up Procedures[M]. Virginia：Reston Publishing Company, Inc. 1983.

任务八
KT600 汽车诊断系统

1. 掌握关于 KT600 诊断仪设备结构、使用等方面相关的专业术语、词汇。
2. 掌握 KT600 基本功能。
3. 熟悉 KT600 的基本功能和操作。
4. 能阅读简单的关于故障诊断的英语资料。

任务描述

以某款发动机为例,介绍 KT600 汽车诊断系统中示波器对温度传感器进行测试及波形分析等的相关专业术语、词汇。通过完成该任务,能阅读关于相关发动机诊断的外文文献,对于引进和使用国外教学设备具有一定的辅助作用。本任务完成后,要求学生掌握一定程度的翻译技巧。

本学习任务沿着以下脉络进行学习:

通读全文 → 学习单词和语法 → 完成课后练习 → 分组讨论 → 课后阅读

Task 8　KT600 Diagnostic Systems for Motor Vehicles

Equipment Introductions

Kingtec KT600 oscillograph, special for automobile, is solely developed by Bosch Automotive Diagnostic Equipment (Shenzhen) CO,. LTD. It can collect in real-time the waveform of sensors of ignition, fuel injection, and an electric control system, and can precisely diagnose sensor failures through analysis of waveform of sensors. [1] It can diagnose, through the analysis of ignition waveform, not only the failure of elements of ignition system such as spark plug, high voltage line, and ignition coil but the possible failure of the air intake system and fuel system, providing scientific basis for operating conditions of failure diagnosis of an automobile.

1. Basic Functions

(1) The development of Kingtec KT600 oscillograph function realizes a real-time display of secondary ignition waveform for the first time in China. Equipped with leading 32-bit CPU for main control + high speed digital processing chip, KT600 can process the signal in real time under high sampling frequency of up to 20MHZ.

(2) High-Speed five-channel automobile special oscillograph, with storage function for reference waveform. [2]

(3) Analysis of primary and secondary ignition waveform for automobile; with multiple waveform display modes such as longitudinal, three-dimensional, array and single cylinder modes, with ignition breakdown voltage, dwell angle and combustion time, etc. displayed. Precise ignition synchronization, automatic testing of ignition signal pole; no matter distributor ignition, independent ignition and double end ignition, they can all be tested reliably, equivalent to a hand engine analyzer. [3]

(4) Universal oscillograph functions.

(5) Recorder function.

(6) Engine analyzer function (optional).

2. Technical Features

Adoption of four-layer circuit board technology of International Industrial Standard allows powerful stability and anti-interference ability of product. [4] The first domestic special oscillograph for automobile that displays real waveform in real time. Design of no need to insert card allows easier operation. Unique self-diagnosis function for hardware of equipment. Quick software upgrade through Internet. Special online data stream waveform display and back play makes it possible to capture precisely tiny change of data stream. Equipped with leading 32-bit CPU for main control-high speed digital processing chip to provide fast processing speed. Adoption of programmable VLSI (very large scale integrated circuit) design make hardware design more stable and reliable, and make possible online hardware upgrade.

3. Equipment Configuration and Parameters

1) Main Unit (Tab. 8-1)

Main Unit Tab. 8-1

Item	Index	Item	Index
Voltage of power	12V DC	Serial port	Standard RS232 (ps/2 port)
Operating temperature	-30℃ ~ +50℃	CF card port	CF card for plug and play
Relative humidity	Less than 90%		

2) Performance Parameter of Oscillograph (Tab. 8-2)

Performance Parameter of Oscillograph Tab. 8-2

Item	Index	Item	Index
Number of channel	5 channels	Voltage range	20mV ~ 20v/div
Sampling frequency	20MHz	Scanning time	2.50uS ~ 2S/div
Sampling precision	Double 8 bits		

3) Hardware Configuration (Tab. 8-3)

Hardware Configuration Tab. 8-3

System hardware	Index
CPU	32-bit embedded chip
Main frequency	80MHz
Flash memory	Very large capacity FLASH, rewritable
External memory	CF card, expandable discretionally
Display	6.4 inch LCD touch true color screen
Printer	Thermal sensitive microprinter

4. Equipment Structure

1) KT600 Main Unit

(1) Front view (Fig. 8-1).

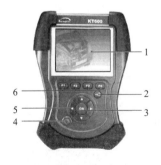

#	Item	Description
1	Touch screen	TFT640×480 6.4-inch touch true color screen
2	ESC	Return to previous menu, exit
3	OK	Enter menu, confirm the selected item
4	⏻	Power switch
5	[▲][▼][▶][◀]	TFT640×480 6.4 inch touch true color screen
6	F4 F1 F2 F3	Return to previous menu, exit

Fig. 8-1 Front View

(2) Back view (Fig. 8-2).

ITEM		INSTRUCTION
1	Print	Thermal printer and 1800mAh lithium battery inside
2	Printer	Press printer clasp, Open printer box plate, Enter papers.
3	Hold	Sunken design looks more humanity, hand hold is available
4	Card	Ensure the connection of diagnoses box and instrument
5	Glue	Protect instruments from abrasion
6	Bracer	Avoid instruments falling down when hold it.
7	Touch	Operate touchscreen

Fig. 8-2 Back View

(3) View of upper interface (Fig. 8-3).

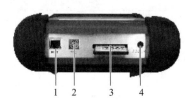

Item		Description
1	Network	Insertion of network cable directly for online upgrade
2	PS/2	For external connection with keyboard and mouse, or used as serial port and USB port through switcher
3	CF card	CF card socket
4	Power	Connection to this port to provide power supply for main

Fig. 8-3 View of Upper Interface

(4) View of lower port (taking oscillographic box as example, Fig. 8-4)。

Item	Description	Item	Description
CH1	Oscillographic channel 1	CH4	Oscillographic channel 4
CH2	Oscillographic channel 2	CH5	Trigger channel
CH3	Oscillographic channel 3		

Fig. 8-4 View of Lower Port

2) Accessories

Accessories of special KT600 oscillograph for an automobile include connecting cable for oscillograph test, power cable, self-diagnostic connector, etc (Tab. 8-4).[5]

Accessories Tab. 8-4

Picture	Name	Function
	Extension lead for power supply	Provide power supply for the main unit, can connect to auto cigar igniter or auto alligator clip.
	Connector for auto cigar igniter	Used to connect extension line for power supply and auto cigar igniter to provide the power supply for the main unit.
	Auto alligator clip	Used to connect extension line for power supply and auto battery to provide the power supply for the main unit.
	Test probe	Used to connect Channel 1, 2, 4 and 5 for input, with the ground line, X1 or X10 attenuation

Continue

Picture	Name	Function
	Extension lead for oscillograph	Can connect Channel CH1, CH2, CH4 and CH5, its main function is to extend input signal line.
	Inductive pickup	Connect Channel CH5, can test engine speed, and consider that the high voltage line clipped is the high voltage line of the first cylinder.
	Secondary pickup	Can connect Channel CH1 and CH2 to induce secondary ignition signal.
	Connecting line for oscillograph	Can extend grounding line or signal line for convenient connection.

Basic Function and Operation

1. Overview of Main Menu

As shown in Fig. 8-5, press [ENTER] button to enter the next menu until you select tested item when you select the item to be tested in KT600 menu using UP or DOWN directional button. Press [EXIT] button to return to the previous menu.

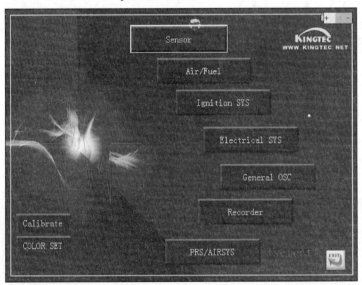

Fig. 8-5　Main Menu

2. Adjusting Method for Universal Oscillograph

Generally, the waveform display of special oscillograph for automobile does not need adjustment. When conducting tests other than the standard menus displayed in special oscillograph for automobile, you can select universal oscillograph function and you need to master specific adjustment method. The adjustment method is the same if there is a similar menu during the test process of special oscillograph for the automobile.

Select universal oscillograph and press [ENTER] to confirm, as shown in Fig. 8-6.

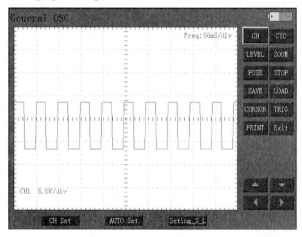

Fig. 8-6 Universal Oscillograph Interface

There are 10 options on the screen: CH, CYC, LEVEL, ZOOM, POSE, STOP, SAVE, LOAD, CURSOR, TRIG, PRINT, EXIT and three function options: CH SET、AUTO SET、Seting_S_L. Press LEFT and RIGHT directional button to adjust the selected item.

1) Channel Adjustment

Pressing function button can select any combination of Channel 1 (CH1), Channel 2 (CH2), Channel 3 (CH3) and Channel 4 (CH4), as shown in Fig. 8-7.

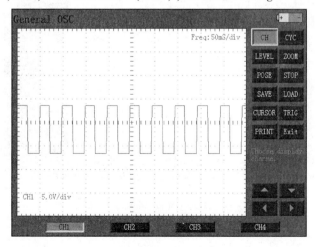

Fig. 8-7 Channel Adjustment Interface

2) Period Adjustment

When the period adjustment is selected, pressing UP and DOWN button can change the time of each single grid. If 10ms/grid is set when the machine is started, it changes to 5ms/grid when the DOWN button is pressed down, and waveform gets sparse; it changes to 20ms/grid when the UP button is pressed down and waveform gets dense.

3) Level Adjustment

When trigger level of the longitudinal axis is adjusted, waveform's position in screen will change when different trigger level is selected for the same the waveform. If the value of trigger level exceeds the limit value of waveform, the waveform will move about and not be steady in the screen.

4) Amplitude Adjustment

Pressing UP and DOWN button can adjust amplitude value of longitudinal waveform, 1:500, 1:200, 1:100, 1:200, 1:0.5, 1:1.0, 1:2.5, 1:5, 1:10 and 1:20 can be selected for KT600.

5) Position Adjustment

Selection of position adjustment can adjust display position of waveform upward or downward. Press UP button to move waveform upward and DOWN button to move downward.

6) Trigger Mode Adjustment

Selection of trigger mode can adjust the starting trigger point of waveform at high frequency (<50ms/grid), and use of function button can select trigger mode: rising edge trigger, falling edge trigger, level trigger, as shown in Fig. 8-8.

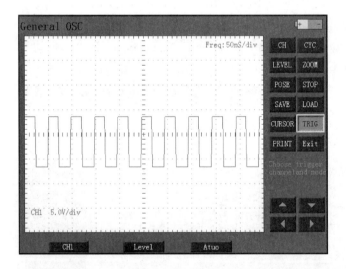

Fig. 8-8 Trigger Mode Adjustment Interface

7) Storage and Loading of Waveform

When selecting a general-purpose oscilloscope, select SAVE to save the current waveform, (if the refresh frequency > =50Hz/grid, the system will freeze the waveform automatically after the current waveform is collected). On the pop-up Save File HMI, the user can name the saved waveform and then save the waveform data (up to 64 files). The system will exit automatically from the Save page after the data is saved.

Select **LOAD**, to load the saved waveform. If there is any waveform file existing, the system will automatically view the saved files. The user can call the waveform as required. Click **Exit/ESC**, to exit from the loading page, as shown in Fig. 8-9.

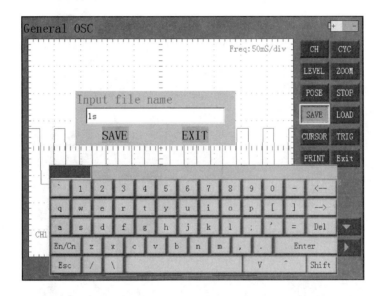

Fig. 8-9 Save the Waveform

8) Save Set

With this function, the user can adjust the waveform parameter easily, for example the user has tested the waveforms of 4 sensorsand used 4 channels: ch1- 200mv/div; ch2 -1v/div; ch3-0.5v/div; ch4-5v/div, simultaneously at 20ms/grid. Relocate each channel to make the waveform be shown clearly. Select Configuration Access, to save the current configuration to the file "4-channel sensor testing", which eliminates the adjustment of fussy data and enables the user to test the waveform of a 4-channel sensor by clicking "**Save Set**" ---〉"**Load Set**". In this way, the waveform will be shown clearly and quickly. As such, any pages with "Configuration Access" can realize this function. Each page can save up to 64 configuration files like this (Fig. 8-10).

Select **Save Set**, to save the current configuration parameters with the file named by letters, figures and Chinese characters, as shown in Fig. 8-11.

Select **Load Set**, to load the configuration parameters to the current page, as shown in Fig. 8-12.

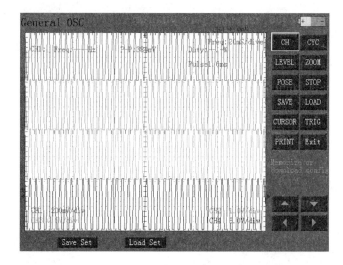

Fig. 8-10 Save Set

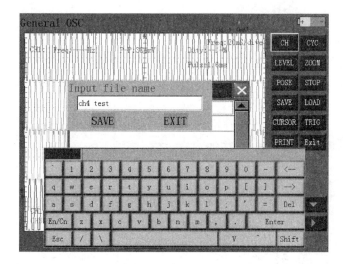

Fig. 8-11 Name the File

3. Selection and Adjustment of Signal Source Parameters of Sensor

In the sensor menu, you can select and adjust the parameters of the channel to be observed by selecting "SIGNAL SOURCE PARAMETER", as shown in Fig. 8-13.

Temperature Sensor Test and Application

They are mainly water temperature sensor and air intake temperature sensor, and most temperature sensors adopt negative temperature coefficient (NTC) thermistor made of semiconducting materials. When temperature changes, its resistance is expected to experience a large change. When the temperature rises, resistance decreases; when temperature decreases, resistance increases.

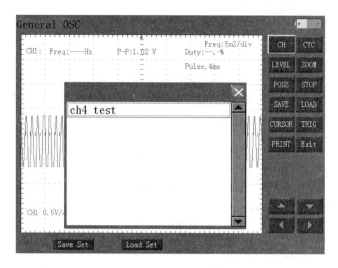

Fig. 8-12 Load the Configuration Parameters

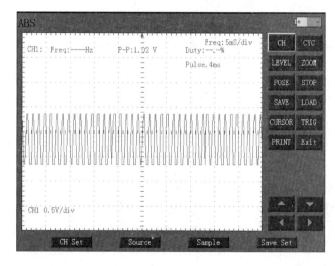

Fig. 8-13 Select "SIGNAL SOURCE PARAMETER"

1. Connecting Equipment

When connecting KT600 to extension line for powersupply, choose battery or cigar igniter as power supply according to the battery position of vehicle mode tested. All connecting diagrams in this users manual take power supply by battery as an example. If choosing cigar igniter connector, confirm that cigar igniter has 12V battery voltage first. Connect test probe to Channel 1 (CH1 port), and then connect the small alligator clip on test probe to the negative of battery or grounding, pierce test probe into the trigger signal line of the temperature sensor. Connecting diagram is shown as Fig. 8-14.

2. Test conditions

(1) Switch on the ignition switch, do not start the engine. Securely connect the temperature

sensor, and measure the output voltage of temperature sensor with the engine in the non-running state.

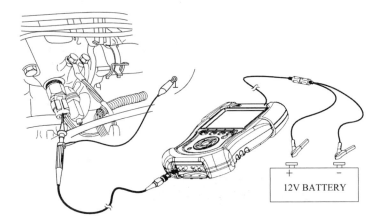

Fig. 8-14 Connecting Equipment

(2) Start engine, observe voltage falling of temperature sensor when the engine gets heated.

(3) You may also disconnect the sensor and use the multimeter to measure resistance value.

3. Test step

(1) Connect equipment according to Fig. 8-14, switch on power supply switch.

(2) In Kingtec instrument menu, press UP and DOWN button to select 2. OSCILLOGRAPH, and press [ENTER] button to confirm.

(3) In the menu of special oscillograph for automobile, select SENSOR and press [ENTER] button to enter selection menu for automobile sensor.

(4) Select TEMPERATURE SENSOR, press [ENTER] button to confirm, and the waveform will be displayed on the screen depending on test conditions.

(5) If necessary, you can select parameters such as period, amplitude value and level, and then press the directional button to change waveform. You may also select STOP button and press it to freeze waveform, select STORE to store the waveform for reference when repair is needed.

4. Waveform Analysis

You can get a precise voltage range of sensor response by referring to standard manual from the manufacturer. Generally, the voltage of the sensor should be 3 ~ 5V (fully cold state) when the engine is not started, and it should have correspondingly variable output voltage signal under different temperature conditions. When temperature sensor circuit is open, voltage increases till it reaches the peak (5V) of reference the voltage; when the temperature sensor is short to ground, voltage decreases till it reaches the peak of grounding voltage. Refer to Fig. 8-15 for temperature characteristics of common thermistor type coolant and air intake temperature sensor, subject to manufacturer's manual.

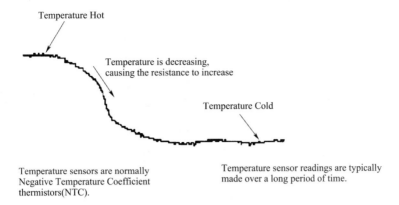

Fig. 8-15 Waveform Analysis

Word List

1. diagnostic [daɪəgˈnɔstɪk]　　　　　　　adj. 诊断的；特征的
2. equipment [ɪˈkwɪpm(ə)nt]　　　　　　n. 设备，装备；器材
3. oscillograph [əˈsɪləgrɑːf]　　　　　　n. [电子] 示波器；记录仪；波形图
4. sensor [ˈsensə]　　　　　　　　　　　n. 传感器
5. ignition [ɪgˈnɪʃ(ə)n]　　　　　　　　　n. 点火，点燃；着火，燃烧
6. scientific [saɪənˈtɪfɪk]　　　　　　　　adj. 科学的，系统的
7. longitudinal [ˌlɔn(d)ʒɪˈtjuːdɪn(ə)l]　　adj. 长度的，纵向的；经线的
8. three-dimensional [ˈθriːdɪˈmenʃənəl]　adj. 三维的；立体的；真实的
9. breakdown [ˈbreɪkdaun]　　　　　　　n. 故障；崩溃；分解；分类；衰弱
10. voltage [ˈvɔltɪdʒ]　　　　　　　　　　n. [电] 电压
11. combustion [kəmˈbʌstʃ(ə)n]　　　　　n. 燃烧，氧化；骚动
12. synchronization [ˌsɪŋkrənaɪˈzeɪʃən]　n. 同步；同时性
13. equivalent [ɪˈkwɪv(ə)l(ə)nt]　　　　adj. 等价的，相等的；n. 等价物，相等物
14. domestic [dəˈmestɪk]　　　　　　　　adj. 国内的；家庭的
15. digital [ˈdɪdʒɪt(ə)l]　　　　　　　　adj. 数字的；手指的
16. programmable [ˌprəuˈgræməbl]　　　adj. 可编程的；可设计的
17. parameter [pəˈræmɪtə]　　　　　　　n. 参数；系数；参量
18. sunken [ˈsʌŋk(ə)n]　　　　　　　　adj. 沉没的；凹陷的；比周围低的

Proper Names

1. electric control system　　　　　　　电气控制系统
2. spark plug　　　　　　　　　　　　火花塞

3. high voltage line 高压线路
4. ignition coil 点火线圈
5. air intake system 进气系统
6. fuel system 燃油系统
7. dwell angle 闭合角,接点闭角;凸轮等半径角
8. distributor ignition 分电器点火
9. Universal oscillograph 通用示波器
10. flash memory 闪速存储器

Useful Expressions

1. not only, but also 不仅,而且
2. such as 比如;诸如
3. no matter 无论;不管
4. used to 惯于;过去经常

Key Vocabulary

1. realize

vt. 实现;认识到;了解;将某物卖得,把(证券等)变成现钱;变卖

All his worst fears were realized.

他最担心的事情都变成了现实。

People don't realize how serious this recession has actually been.

人们没有意识到这次经济衰退有多么严重。

2. return

vt. 返回;报答

Kenny explained the reason for his sudden return to Dallas.

肯尼解释了他突然返回达拉斯的理由。

I enjoyed the book and said so when I returned it.

我很喜欢这本书,归还它的时候就这么说了。

Notes

1. It can collect in real-time the waveform of sensors of ignition, fuel injection, and electric control system, and can precisely diagnose sensor failures through analysis of waveform of sensors.

翻译:它可以实时采集点火系统,燃油喷射系统和电控系统的传感器的波形,通过对传

感器波形的分析,可以精确地诊断传感器的故障。

2. High-Speed five-channel automobile special oscillograph, with storage function for reference waveform.

翻译:高速五通道汽车专用示波器,具有存储参考波形功能。

3. No matter distributor ignition, independent ignition and double end ignition, they can all be tested reliably, equivalent to a hand engine analyzer.

翻译:无论是分配器点火、独立点火和双端点火,都可以可靠地进行测试,相当于一台手摇发动机分析仪。

4. Adoption of four-layer circuit board technology of International Industrial Standard allows powerful stability and anti-interference ability of product.

翻译:采用国际工业标准的四层电路板技术,使产品具有强大的稳定性和抗干扰能力。

5. Accessories of special KT600 oscillograph for the automobile include connecting cable for oscillograph test, power cable, self-diagnostic connector, etc.

翻译:汽车专用KT600示波器配件,包括示波器测试电缆、电力电缆、自诊断连接器等。

Exercises

1. Translate the following into Chinese.

1) diagnostic 2) breakdown 3) sensor
4) domestic 5) voltage 6) ignition
7) parameter 8) oscillograph

2. Translate the following into English.

1) 电气控制系统 2) 进气系统 3) 燃油系统
4) 分电器点火 5) 闪速存储器 6) 火花塞

3. Translate the following sentences into Chinese.

1) the waveform of sensors of ignition, fuel injection, and electric control system, and can precisely diagnose sensor failures through analysis of waveform of sensors.

2) High-Speed five-channel automobile special oscillograph, with storage function for reference waveform.

4. Translate the following sentences into English.

1) 国内第一款实时显示真实波形的汽车专用示波器。

2) 金德KT600的示波器功能的研发在国内首次真正地实现了次级点火波形的实时显示。

Practical Reading

How to use the TCCS Training Board

Setting Engine RPM and Vehicle Speed

(1) The engine speed can be adjusted up to a maximum of 3000 rpm by operating the throttle valve.

(2) The vehicle speed can be adjusted up to the maximum of 80 km/h by operating the throttle valve while the shift lever is in the D, 2, or L position[1].

Setting Water Temperature

The water temperature can be adjusted as described below.

(1) Turn ON the switch.

(2) Turn the water temperature adjustment knob clockwise to increase the water temperature and counterclockwise to decrease the water temperature[2] (Fig. 8-16).

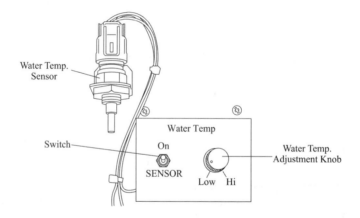

Fig. 8-16 Water Temperature Adjustment

Checking Ignition Timing

Just as on the actual vehicle, the ignition timing can be checked by connecting the pickup clip on the electrical wiring of the ignition coil.

Checking Operation of Injectors

On this training board, the injection conditions of the injectors can be monitored directly.

Word List

counterclockwise [ˌkauntəˈklɔkwaɪz]　　　　　　adv. 反时针方向

Proper Names

1. Toyota Computer-controlled System　　　丰田计算机控制系统
2. engine speed　　　发动机转速

Notes

1. The vehicle speed can be adjusted up to the maximum of 80 km/h by operating the throttle valve while the shift lever is in the D, 2, or L position.

翻译:当变速杆在D、2或L位置时,通过调节节气门,可以调节车速最高至80km/h。

2. Turn the water temperature adjustment knob clockwise to increase the water temperature and counterclockwise to decrease the water temperature.

翻译:转动水温调节旋钮,顺时针转动水温升高,逆时针转动水温降低。

相关链接:
花冠维修手册(Pub. No. RM925E)
参考资料:
1. 马林才.汽车实用英语[M].2版.北京:人民交通出版社,2014.
2. 王凤丽.汽车专业英语[M].北京:人民邮电出版社,2015.

任务九
汽车市场调查分析

1. 掌握汽车市场调查分析等方面相关的专业术语、词汇。
2. 掌握市场调查分析报告的基本构成及表达方法。
3. 能分析国外同类汽车产品市场销售现状及其成因。
4. 能阅读简单的关于汽车市场调查分析的英语资料。

任务描述

以通用 GM 汽车公司为例,通过完成该任务,能阅读国外汽车公司的市场调查分析报告,了解国外汽车市场状况。熟悉该任务是如何进行的,学会分析国外汽车市场状况。

本学习任务沿着以下脉络进行学习:

通读全文 → 学习单词和语法 → 用英语叙述课文 → 完成课后练习 → 分组讨论 → 课后阅读练习

Task 9 Research Report on Automobile Market
GM Reports Income of $2.4 Billion and EBIT-adjusted of $3.2 Billion

DETROIT— General Motors Co. (NYSE: GM) today announced second-quarter 2018 results reflecting profitability in all core operating segments and the second consecutive quarter of records for China and GM Financial. Results included the unfavorable impact of rising commodity costs and foreign currency devaluations in South America.

Second-quarter 2018 Results:

(1) EPS-diluted of $1.66 and EPS diluted-adjusted of $1.81.

(2) Revenue of $36.8 billion.

(3) GM North America EBIT-adjusted of $2.7 billion and margin of 9.4 percent.

(4) GM International EBIT-adjusted of $0.1 billion, includes record equity income in China of $0.6 billion, partially offset by unfavorable foreign exchange impact in South America.

(5) GM Cruise EBIT-adjusted of $(0.2) billion, on plan and reflecting continued spending on autonomous as the company moves to commercialization.

(6) GM Financial EBT-adjusted of $0.5 billion, another record, as earning assets grew 12 percent to $90.4 billion, supporting expected long-term earnings growth.

Recent and significant increases in commodity costs and unfavorable foreign exchange impact of the Argentine peso and Brazilian real have negatively affected business expectations.[1] The company expects these headwinds to continue through 2018 and has revised its full-year outlook to the following:

(1) EPS diluted of approximately $5.14.

(2) EPS diluted-adjusted of approximately $6.

(3) Auto Operating Cash Flow to approximately $11.5 billion.

(4) Adjusted Auto Free Cash Flow to approximately $4 billion.

For complete details and to see reconciliations of non-GAAP measures to their most directly comparable GAAP measures, visit the GM Investor Relations website.

Investor Analyst Conference Call

GM Chairman and CEO Mary Barra and Executive Vice President and CFO Chuck Stevens will host a conference call for investor analysts at 10 a.m. EDT today to discuss second-quarter business results. The call will include introductory remarks followed by a question and answer session for analysts.

Journalists who wish to listen to the call may dial in using the following numbers:

United States:　　　　　　　1-888-808-8618

International: +1-949-484-0645
Name of Call: GM Earnings Call

General Motors (NYSE: GM) is committed to delivering safer, better and more sustainable ways for people to get around. General Motors, its subsidiaries and its joint venture entities sell vehicles under the Cadillac, Chevrolet, Baojun, Buick, GMC, Holden, Jiefang and Wuling brands. More information on the company and its subsidiaries, including OnStar, a global leader in vehicle safety and security services, Maven, its personal mobility brand, and Cruise, its autonomous vehicle ride-sharing company, can be found at https://www.gm.com.

Forward-Looking Statements

This presentation and related comments by management may include forward-looking statements. These statements are based on current expectations about possible future events and thus are inherently uncertain. Our actual results may differ materially from forward-looking statements due to a variety of factors, including:

(1) Our ability to deliver new products, services and experiences that attract new, and are desired by existing, customers and to effectively compete in autonomous, ride-sharing and transportation as a service. [2]

(2) Sales of crossovers, SUVs and full-size pickup trucks.

(3) Our ability to reduce the costs associated with the manufacture and sale of electric vehicles.

(4) The volatility of global sales and operations.

(5) Our significant business in China which subjects us to unique operational, competitive and regulatory risks.

(6) Our joint ventures, which we cannot operate solely for our benefit and over which we may have limited control.

(7) Changes in government leadership and laws (including tax laws and regulations), economic tensions between governments and changes in international trade policies, new barriers to entry and changes to or withdrawals from free trade agreements, changes in foreign exchange rates, economic downturns in foreign countries, differing local product preferences and product requirements, compliance with U.S. and foreign countries' export controls and economic sanctions, differing labor laws and regulations and difficulties in obtaining financing in foreign countries.

(8) Our dependence on our manufacturing facilities.

(9) The ability of suppliers to deliver parts, systems and components without disruption and on schedule.

(10) Prices of raw materials.

(11) Our highly competitive industry.

(12) The possibility that competitors may independently develop products and services similar

to ours despite our intellectual property rights.

(13) Security breaches and other disruptions to our vehicles, information technology networks and systems.

(14) Compliance with laws and regulations applicable to our industry, including those regarding fuel economy and emissions.

(15) Costs and risks associated with litigation and government investigations.

(16) Compliance with the terms of the Deferred Prosecution Agreement.

(17) The cost and effect on our reputation of product safety recalls and alleged defects in products and services.

(18) Our ability to successfully and cost-efficiently restructure operations in various countries, including Korea, with minimal disruption to our supply chain and operations, globally.

(19) Our ability to realize production efficiencies and to achieve reductions in costs.

(20) Our ability to develop captive financing capability through GM Financial.

(21) Significant increases in pension expense or projected pension contributions. A further list and description of these risks, uncertainties and other factors can be found in our Annual Report on Form 10-K for the fiscal year ended December 31, 2017, and our subsequent filings with the U.S. Securities and Exchange Commission. GM cautions readers not to place undue reliance on forward-looking statements. GM undertakes no obligation to update publicly or otherwise revise any forward-looking statements.

Word List

1. profitability [ˈprɒfɪtəˈbɪlətɪ]   n. 盈利能力;盈利性;收益率;利益性
2. segment [ˈsegmənt]   n. 段,部分,片,弓形;v. 分割,划分
3. consecutive [kənˈsekjutɪv]   adj. 连续不断的
4. financial [faɪˈnænʃ(ə)l]   adj. 财政的;财务的;金融的;有钱的
5. unfavorable [ˌʌnˈfeɪvərəbl]   adj. 令人不快的;逆的;不适宜的;不顺利的
6. commodity [kəˈmɒdətɪ]   n. 商品;产品;货物;商品经济
7. revenue [ˈrevənjuː]   n. 收益;营业额;税务署
8. equity [ˈekwətɪ]   n. 公平;公正;资产净值;(公司的)股本
9. partially [ˈpɑː(r)ʃəli]   adv. 部分地;不公平地;偏袒地
10. offset [ɒfˈset]   n.【印】胶印,背面蹭脏,【机】偏置(管),迂回管;v. 抵消,弥补,补偿;adj. 胶印的
11. cruise [kruːz]   n. 航行,乘船游览;v. 乘船游览,以平稳的速度行驶,巡行,轻而易举赢得(或获得)
12. autonomous [ɔːˈtɒnəməs]   adj. 自治的;有自治权的;自主的;有自主权的

13. commercialization ［kəˌməːʃəlaɪˈzeɪʃ(ə)n］ n. 商业化
14. asset ［ˈæset］ n. 资产;财产;有价值的人(或事物);有用的人(或事物)
15. commodity ［kəˈmɔdətɪ］ n. 商品;产品;货物;商品经济
16. headwind ［ˈhedwɪnd］ n. 逆风;顶风
17. approximately ［əˈprɔksɪmətlɪ］ adv. 大约;大概;约莫
18. reconciliation ［ˌrekənsɪlɪˈeɪʃ(ə)n］ n. 和解;协调;调解;和谐一致
19. comparable ［ˈkɔmp(ə)rəb(ə)l］ adj. 类似的;可比较的
20. session ［ˈseʃ(ə)n］ n. 阶段;环节;(正式)会议;(法院)开庭
21. sustainable ［səˈsteɪnəb(ə)l］ adj. (对自然资源和能源的利用)不破坏生态平衡的;可持续的
22. subsidiarity ［səbsɪdɪˈærətɪ］ n. 辅从原则(中央权力机关应只控制地方上无法操控的事务)
23. security ［sɪˈkjuərətɪ］ n. 安全;证券;担保;保证
24. mobility ［məʊˈbɪlətɪ］ n. (住处、社会阶层、职业方面的)流动能力;移动的能力
25. presentation ［ˌprez(ə)nˈteɪʃ(ə)n］ n. 演出;发布会;提交;颁发
26. expectation ［ˌekspekˈteɪʃ(ə)n］ n. 期望;预期;期待;希望
27. inherently ［ɪnˈherəntlɪ］ adv. 内在;固有;本来;从根本上说
28. materially ［məˈtɪərɪəlɪ］ adv. 物质上;【逻,哲】实质上;显著地;相当地
29. effectively ［ɪˈfektɪv(ə)lɪ］ adv. 实际上;有效地;事实上
30. volatility ［ˌvɔləˈtɪlətɪ］ n. 挥发性;挥发度;反复无常;轻浮
31. withdrawal ［wɪðˈdrɔːəl］ n. 撤回;取款;收回;撤走
32. downturn ［ˈdaʊntəː(r)n］ n. (商业经济的)衰退
33. disruption ［dɪsˈrʌpʃ(ə)n］ n. 中断;破裂
34. emission ［ɪˈmɪʃ(ə)n］ n. 排放;辐射;排放物;(书刊)发行
35. litigation ［ˌlɪtɪˈgeɪʃ(ə)n］ n. 诉讼;打官司
36. alleged ［əˈledʒd］ adj. 声称的;有嫌疑的;作为理由[辩解等]的
37. pension ［ˈpenʃ(ə)n］ n. 养老金,退休金,抚恤金;adj. 有关退休金的;v. 给…养老金(恤金,津贴等)
38. description ［dɪˈskrɪpʃ(ə)n］ n. 说明;形容;描写(文字);类型
39. fiscal ［ˈfɪsk(ə)l］ n. 财政年度;财政部长;(苏格兰等的)检察官 adj. 财政的;国库的;国家岁入的
40. publicly ［ˈpʌblɪklɪ］ adv. 公开;由公众;由政府(出资,持有等)

Proper Names

1. foreign currency devaluation   外币贬值
2. EPS（Earnings Per Share）   每股收益
3. EBIT（earnings before interest and tax） 息税前利润
4. long-term earning   长期收入
5. full-year outlook   全年展望
6. Auto Operating Cash Flow   自动操作现金流
7. Auto-Free Cash Flow   自动自由现金流
8. Executive Vice President   执行副总裁
9. introductory remark   介绍性评论
10. dial in   拨入
11. joint venture entity   合资企业实体
12. forward-looking statement   前瞻性声明
13. regulatory risk   监管风险
14. joint venture   合资
15. economic tension   经济紧张
16. local product preference   本地产品优先
17. compliance with   遵守
18. ride-sharing   共享汽车
19. economic sanction   经济制裁
20. obtaining financing   融资
21. manufacturing facilities   生产设施
22. on schedule   按时；按时间表；按照预定计划
23. raw material   原料
24. intellectual property right   知识财产权
25. compliance with   符合；遵守；顺从
26. economic sanction   经济制裁
27. security breaches   安全漏洞
28. government investigation   政府调查
29. the terms of   条款
30. cost-efficiently restructure operation   经济高效的重组操作
31. supply chain   供应链
32. captive financing capability   固定融资能力
33. projected pension contribution   预计养恤金缴款

34. subsequent filing　　　　　　　后续归档
35. Exchange Commission　　　　　外汇委员会
36. undue reliance　　　　　　　　过分依赖

Notes on the Text

1. Recent and significant increases in commodity costs and unfavorable foreign exchange impact of the Argentine peso and Brazilian real have negatively affected business expectations.

翻译:最近受大幅增加的大宗商品成本和不利的外汇影响,阿根廷比索和巴西雷亚尔对商业预期产生了负面影响。

2. Our ability to deliver new products, services and experiences that attract new, and are desired by existing, customers and to effectively compete in autonomous, ride-sharing and transportation as a service.

翻译:我们有能力提供新产品、服务和经验,吸引新的和现有客户达到他们的期望,并在自主选择、共享汽车和运输服务方面进行有效竞争。

3. Our significant business in China which subjects us to unique operational, competitive and regulatory risks.

翻译:我们在中国的重要业务,使我们有独特的运营、竞争和监管风险。

4. New barriers to entry and changes to or withdrawals from free trade agreements, changes in foreign exchange rates, economic downturnsin foreign countries, differing local product preferences and product requirements, compliance with U. S. and foreign countries' export controls and economic sanctions, differing labor laws and regulations and difficulties in obtaining financing in foreign countries.

翻译:新障碍包括自由贸易协定变更或退出、汇率变化、国外经济低迷、当地产品偏好和产品需求不同、遵守美国和其他各国的出口管制和经济制裁、不同的劳动法和法规以及在外国融资困难。

Exercises

1. Fill in the blanks with the proper form of the word given in the brackets.

1) Who _____ (finance) this organization?
2) The builders _____ (contract) for three bridges this year.
3) The painting is a _____ (represent) of a storm at sea.
4) The workers _____ (demand) for better conditions of work.
5) This train _____ (proceed) from Paris to London now.
6) Altogether, our _____ (achieve) are very great.

2. Translate the sentences into English by using the word or expression in the brackets.

1)老师病了,因为一直忙于我们的期末考试。(engage in)

2)神舟六号火箭的成功发射说明了我国航天事业取得了很大的进步。(account for)

3)因为堵车,他来完了。(attribute to)

4)莎士比亚把世界比作舞台。(compare to)

5)我们不喜欢像他这号人。(such as)

6)他是一名优秀的运动员,也是一个律师。(as well as)

3. Match the best Chinese equivalents.

A. Chinese art	B. people's activities	C. local travel
D. hot news this month	E. views on the society	F. city scene
G. the youth	H. fashion	I. music movie and book reviews
J. classified ads'	K. puzzles	L. business guidance
M. restaurant and bars	N. sports activities	O. shanghai grand stage
P. traffic		

Examples:(A)中国艺术　　　　　　　　(G)青年一代

1)(　)城市景观　　　　　　　　(　)分类广告

2)(　)市民活动　　　　　　　　(　)餐厅和酒吧

3)(　)社会观察　　　　　　　　(　)商业指南

4)(　)本月热点新闻　　　　　　(　)上海大舞台

5)(　)时尚　　　　　　　　　　(　)本地旅游

Practical Reading

2008 PRIORITIES

Continue to Execute Great Products

Our first priority for 2008 is continuing to focus on product excellence by fully leveraging our global design, engineering and power train expertise to produce vehicles for a wide variety of regions and market segments.[1] In North America, we plan to introduce several new vehicles in 2008 including the Pontiac G8 and Chevrolet Traverse to complement our successful 2007 introductions of the GMC Acadia, Saturn Outlook, Buick Enclave, Cadillac CTS and the Chevrolet Malibu. In emerging markets, we plan to expand and enhance our portfolio of lower cost vehicles, with special attention to the fuel economy.[2]

Build Strong Brands and Distribution Channels

Our second priority for 2008 is building strong brands and distribution channels. We plan to integrate our product and marketing strategies and believe that if we achieve product excellence, stronger brands will result. [3] In addition, we plan to build brand equity with a special focus on key car segments. Programs in 2008 are intended to enhance the effectiveness of our marketing, particularly using digital marketing. Finally, we propose to leverage competitive advantages like the OnStar telematics systems, which is available in more than 50 GM vehicles throughout the world. [4] We also plan to accelerate our channel strategy of combining certain brands in a single dealership, which we believe will differentiate products and brands more clearly, enhance dealer profitability and provide us with greater flexibility in product portfolio and technology planning. [5]

Execute Additional Cost Reduction Initiatives

Our third priority for 2008 is addressing costs by executing additional cost reduction initiatives. As discussed below under "Key Factors Affecting Future and Current Results," we have taken action in a number of areas to reduce legacy and structural costs. In 2007, we achieved our announced target of reducing certain annual structural costs in GMNA and Corporate and Other primarily related to labor, pension and other post-retirement costs by $9 billion, on average, less than those costs in 2005. [6] We have also reduced structural costs as a percentage of global automotive revenue to below 30% for 2007 from 34% in 2005, and have announced global targets of 25% by 2010 and 23% by 2012. We also plan to reduce structural costs as a percentage of global automotive revenue by pursuing manufacturing capacity utilization of 100% or more in higher cost countries and will continue to assess what specific actions may be required based on trends in industry volumes and product mix. [7]

In October 2007, we entered into a new collective bargaining agreement with the International Union, United Automobile, Aerospace and Agricultural Workers of America (UAW), including the Settlement Agreement, which we anticipate will significantly support our structural cost reduction plans when it is put into effect after January 1, 2010. [8] Additionally, we plan to execute a collective bargaining agreement with the National Automobile, Aerospace, Transportation and General Workers Union of Canada (CAW) that will support our cost reduction goals. We have announced a special attrition program available to all of our 74000 hourly workers represented by the UAW, and we expect that participating employees will begin exiting in April 2008. [9] We remain focused on repositioning our business for long-term competitiveness, including achieving a successful resolution to the issues related to the bankruptcy proceedings of Delphi, a major supplier and former subsidiary. We recognize, however, that near-term continuing weakness in the US. automotive market, and its impact on our Canadian operations that are linked to the U.S. market, will provide a significant challenge to improving earnings and cash flow, and could constrain our ability to achieve future revenue goals. [10]

Grow Aggressively in Emerging Markets

Our fourth 2008 priority is to focus on emerging markets and capitalize on the growth in areas such as China, India and the ASEAN region, as well as Russia, Brazil, the Middle East and the Andean region. [11] Vehicle sales and revenues continue to grow globally, with the strongest growth in these emerging markets. In 2007, 38% of all vehicle sales took place in emerging markets; we project that in 2012, 45% of vehicles will be sold in emerging markets. In response, we are planning to expand capacity in these emerging markets, and to pursue additional growth opportunities through our relationships with Shanghai GM, GM Daewoo and other potential strategic partners, such as recently announced joint ventures in Malaysia and Uzbekistan. During 2007, key metrics such as net margin, operating income and market share showed continued growth across key emerging markets. [12] In addition to the product and brand strategies discussed above, we plan to expand our manufacturing capacity in emerging markets in a cost effective way and to pursue new market opportunities. We believe that growth in these emerging markets will help to offset challenging near-term market conditions in mature markets, such as the U.S. and Germany. [13]

Continue to Develop and Implement our Advanced Propulsion Strategy

Our fifth priority for 2008 is to continue to develop and advance our alternative propulsion strategy, focused on fuel and other technologies, making energy diversity and environmental leadership a critical element of our ongoing strategy. [14] In addition to continuing to improve the efficiency of our internal combustion engines, we are focused on the introduction of propulsion technologies which utilize alternative fuels and have intensified our efforts to displace traditional petroleum-based fuels. [15] For example, we have entered into arrangements with battery and biofuel companies to support the development of commercially viable applications of these technologies. In September 2007, we launched Project Driveway, making more than 100 Chevrolet Equinox fuel cell electric vehicles available for driving by the public in the vicinity of Los Angeles, New York City and Washington, D.C. During the fourth quarter of 2007, we introduced new hybrid models of the Chevrolet Tahoe and the GMC Yukon. We anticipate that this strategy will require a major commitment to technical and financial resources. Like others in the automotive industry, we recognize that the key challenge to our advanced propulsion strategy will be our ability to price our products to cover cost increases driven by new technology.

Drive the Benefits of Managing the Business Globally

Our final priority for 2008 is to continue to integrate our operations around the world to manage our business on a global basis. We have been focusing on restructuring our operations and have already taken a number of steps to globalize our principal business functions such as product development, manufacturing, power train and purchasing to improve our performance in an increasingly competitive environment. [16] As we build functional and technical excellence, we plan to leverage our products, power trains, supplier base and technical expertise globally so that we can flow our existing resources to support opportunities for highest returns at the lowest cost.

Basis of Presentation

This Management's Discussion and Analysis of Financial Condition and Results of Operations (MD&A) should be read in conjunction with the accompanying consolidated financial statements.

We operate in two businesses, consisting of Automotive (GM Automotive or GMA) and Financing and Insurance Operations (FIO).

Our Auto business consists of our four regional segments: GMNA, GME, GMLAAM, and GMAP, which collectively constitute GMA. Our FIO business consists of the operating results of GMAC for 2005 and the eleven months ended November 30, 2006, on a consolidated basis and includes our 49% share of GMAC's operating results for the month of December 2006 and the full year of 2007 on an equity method basis. FIO also includes Other Financing, which includes financing entities that are not consolidated by GMAC and two special purpose entities holding automotive leases previously owned by GMAC and its affiliates that we retained having a net book value of $3.3 billion, as well as the elimination of inter-company transactions with GM Automotive and Corporate and Other.

In 2007, we changed our measure of segment operating performance from segment net income to segment pre-tax income plus equity income, net of tax and minority interest, net of tax. All prior periods have been adjusted to reflect this change. Income taxes are now evaluated on a consolidated basis only. The results of operations and cash flows of Allison have been reported as discontinued operations for all periods presented. Historically, Allison was included in GMNA. [17] Consistent with industry practice, our market share information includes estimates of industry sales in certain countries where public reporting is not legally required or otherwise available on a consistent basis.

Word List

1. execute [ˈeksɪkjuːt]　　　　　　　　　vt. 执行，实现；使生效
2. priority [praɪˈɔːrɪtɪ]　　　　　　　　n. 优先权，重点
3. expertise [ˌekspəːˈtɪːz]　　　　　　　n. 专门知识或技能
4. portfolio [pɔːtˈfəuljəu]　　　　　　　n. 公事包，文件夹；投资组合
5. priority [praɪɔːrɪtɪ]　　　　　　　　n. 优先权，重点
6. strategy [ˈstrætɪdʒɪ]　　　　　　　　n. 战略，策略
7. segment [ˈsegmənt]　　　　　　　　n. 部分，片段
8. opportunity [ˌɔpəˈtjuːnɪtɪ]　　　　　n. 机会，时机
9. initiative [ɪˈnɪʃɪətɪv]　　　　　　　　adj. 起始的；初步的；自发的
10. assess [əˈses]　　　　　　　　　　vt. 估价，估计

11. anticipate ［ænˈtɪsɪpeɪt］　　　　　vt. 先于…行动；预感，期望
12. announce ［əˈnauns］　　　　　　vt./vi. 宣布，宣告，发表
13. employee ［emplɔɪˈiː］　　　　　n. 雇工，雇员
14. challenge ［ˈtʃæləndʒ］　　　　　vt. 挑战
15. accompany ［əˈkʌmpəni］　　　　vt. 陪伴，陪同
16. collective ［kəˈlektɪv］　　　　　adj. 集合的；聚合性的
17. lease ［liːs］　　　　　　　　　vt. 租，租借
18. consistent ［kənˈsɪstənt］　　　　adj. 一贯的，始终如一的

Notes on the reading

1. Our first priority for 2008 is continuing to focus on product excellence by fully leveraging our global design, engineering and power train expertise to produce vehicles for a wide variety of regions and market segments.

翻译：2008年，我们首先任务是通过全面推动整体设计、制造工艺和动力传动技术水平，来提高产品卓越性能，为更广泛的地区和市场的需求提供汽车产品。

2. In emerging markets, we plan to expand and enhance our portfolio of lower cost vehicles, with special attention to fuel economy.

翻译：我们计划在新兴市场扩展和加强低成本汽车的投资，以引起社会对燃油经济性的关注。

3. Our second priority for 2008 is building strong brands and distribution channels. We plan to integrate our product and marketing strategies and believe that if we achieve product excellence, stronger brands will result.

翻译：2008年，我们第二发展重点是建立强势品牌和分销渠道。我们计划把产品和市场策略有机结合起来，相信如果我们能生产出优秀产品就能建立更强大的品牌。

4. Programs in 2008 are intended to enhance the effectiveness of our marketing, particularly using digital marketing. Finally, we propose to leverage competitive advantages like the OnStar telematics systems, which is available in more than 50 GM vehicles throughout the world.

翻译：最后，我们提议去推进像the OnStar telematics系统一样的竞争优势，全球超过50种通用车辆都是可用的。

5. We also plan to accelerate our channel strategy of combining certain brands in a single dealership, which we believe will differentiate products and brands more clearly, enhance dealer profitability and provide us with greater flexibility in product portfolio and technology planning.

翻译：我们计划在单一的经销商中加快我们的渠道整合战略，相信这样可以更清晰地区分出不同品牌的市场，增加经销商的利润。同时对不同产品的投资和计划的编制提供更大的灵活性。

6. In 2007, we achieved our announced target of reducing certain annual structural costs in

GMNA and Corporate and Other primarily related to labor, pension and other post-retirement costs by $9 billion, on average, less than those costs in 2005.

翻译:2007年,我们实现降低北美通用汽车公司结构成本的目标,养老金和其他退休后成本降低90亿美元,低于2005年的成本。

7. We also plan to reduce structural costs as a percentage of global automotive revenue by pursuing manufacturing capacity utilization of 100% or more in higher cost countries, and will continue to assess what specific actions may be required based on trends in industry volumes and product mix.

翻译:我们还计划在成本更高的国家,通过全部或更有效的生产力来降低结构成本在汽车收入中所占的比率。我们也会以制造厂各种产品的产量趋势来估定所需要的方案。

8. In October 2007, we entered into a new collective bargaining agreement with the International Union, United Automobile, Aerospace and Agricultural Workers of America (UAW), including the Settlement Agreement, which we anticipate will significantly support our structural cost reduction plans when it is put into effect after January 1, 2010.

翻译:2007年10月,我们与(美国)联合汽车工会制订了包括结算协议在内的集体交易协议,我们希望在2010年1月协议生效后对我们的结构成本缩减计划有重要的支持作用。

9. We have announced a special attrition program available to all of our 74000 hourly workers represented by the UAW, and we expect that participating employees will begin exiting in April 2008.

翻译:我们已经宣布了一个针对UAW代表的全体74000个临时工人的特别且可行的削减计划,预计被选的工人在2008年4月开始离开。

10. We recognize, however, that near-term continuing weakness in the U.S. automotive market, and its impact on our Canadian operations that are linked to the U.S. market, will provide a significant challenge to improving earnings and cash flow, and could constrain our ability to achieve future revenue goals.

翻译:然而,我们认识到了在美国汽车市场短期持续的弱势,也会对与美国市场相对接的加拿大汽车制造厂产生影响。这对我们增加收入、现金流通以及对未来收入目标的把握能力提出了重大挑战。

11. Our fourth 2008 priority is to focus on emerging markets and capitalize on the growth in areas such as China, India and the ASEAN region, as well as Russia, Brazil, the Middle East, and the Andean region.

翻译:2008年,我们的第四个发展重点是对新兴市场的关注,并增长在中国、印度、东盟地区、俄罗斯、巴西、中东和安第斯地区等新兴市场的投资。

12. During 2007, key metrics such as net margin, operating income and market share showed continued growth across key emerging markets.

翻译:2007年,关键指标如净利润率、营业收入和市场份额表明新兴市场的持续增长。

13. We believe that growth in these emerging markets will help to offset challenging near-term market conditions in mature markets, such as the U.S. and Germany.

翻译：我们相信在这些新兴市场的增长有助于弥补对如德、美这些成熟市场的短期市场弱势的挑战。

14. Our fifth priority for 2008 is to continue to develop and advance our alternative propulsion strategy, focused on fuel and other technologies, making energy diversity and environmental leadership a critical element of our ongoing strategy.

翻译：2008 年，我们的第五个发展重点是继续研发和优化我们的推进策略，重点关注燃料和其他技术，使能量多元化和以环境为主导的现行策略成为关键要素。

15. In addition to continuing to improve the efficiency of our internal combustion engines, we are focused on the introduction of propulsion technologies which utilize alternative fuels and have intensified our efforts to displace traditional petroleum-based fuels.

翻译：另外，为了继续提高内燃机的效率，我们致力于引进利用替代燃料的推进技术，并加大取代传统石油燃料的力度。

16. We have been focusing on restructuring our operations and have already taken a number of steps to globalize our principal business functions such as product development, manufacturing, power train and purchasing to improve our performance in an increasingly competitive environment.

翻译：我们一直专注于重组业务，并已采取一系列措施使主要业务功能全球化，例如产品开发、制造、动力传动系统和采购，以在竞争日益激烈的环境中提高我们的业绩。

17. The results of operations and cash flows of Allison have been reported as discontinued operations for all periods presented. Historically, Allison was included in GMNA.

翻译：对于现有周期，其 Allison 的运营成效和现金流转都预示着停产。实质上，北美通用汽车公司包括 Allison。

学习资源：
相关链接及网址
1. http://media.gm.com/cn/gm/zh/index.html；
2. http://www.21manager.com/index.html；
3. http://www.cnscdc.com。

推荐书目：
1. 李蓉. 汽车市场调查与预测[M]. 2 版. 北京：化学工业出版社，2015.
2. 冯利英. 市场调查——理论、分析方法与实践案例[M]. 北京：经济管理出版社，2017.
3. 李刚. 汽车及配件营销[M]. 2 版. 北京：北京理工大学出版社，2010.
4. 庄贵军. 市场调查与预测[M]. 2 版. 北京：北京大学出版社，2014.
5. 于明进. 汽车服务工程专业英语[M]. 2 版. 北京：人民交通出版社股份有限公司，2017.

任务十 进出口交易的一般流程

1. 掌握进出口交易的一般流程等方面相关的专业术语、词汇。
2. 能阅读进出口交易中的单据——进口许可证、信用证、提单并掌握其填写规则。
3. 能阅读简单的进出口交易的英文资料。

通过完成该任务,掌握进出口交易的操作流程并熟悉各类表格内容。

本学习任务沿着以下脉络进行学习:

通读全文 → 学习单词和语法 → 完成课后练习 → 分组讨论 → 课后阅读练习

Task 10　General Procedures of Export and Import Transaction

Imports and exports are the most important international activities for most nations in the world. Each country needs to import the articles and commodities it does not produce itself, while in order to pay for them, it has to earn foreign exchanges. [1] It does this by exporting its own manufactured articles and surplus raw materials. Thus the import and export trades are two sides of the same coin, and both can have beneficial effects on the home market. Imports create competition for home-produced goods; exporting gives a manufacturer a larger market for his products, so helping to reduce the unit cost. Both of them have the effect to keep prices down in the home and international markets.

But there may be factors that compel governments to place restrictions on the trades with foreign countries. [2] Imports may be controlled or subjected to a custom duty to protect some home industries, or because the available foreign exchange had to be channeled into purchasing more essential goods. Exports may be restricted, too, to conserve a particular raw material required by a developing home industry.

These factors mean that importing and exporting are subject to a lot of formalities, such as customs entry and exchange control approval, which are not applicable to the home retail and wholesale trades. [3] They also mean that the procedure of foreign trades is much more complicated than that of domestic trades, and it involves specialized knowledge and highly trained personnel.

This unit presents a general picture and a brief introduction to import and export trades for the purpose of clarifying their complicated procedures.

An import or export business is so complicated that it may take quite a long time to conclude a transaction. It has to go through various and complicated procedures. The whole process of the transaction generally undergoes four stages: preparation of import or export, business negotiation, implementing the contract, and settlement of disputes, if any. Each stage covers some specific steps. Following diagram illustrates the general procedures of export and import transaction.

General procedures of the export transaction

1. Preparation for Exporting

The most difficult part of exporting or importing is taking the first step. Any exporter who wants to sell his products in a foreign country or countries must first conduct a lot of market research. Market research is a process of conducting research into a specific market for a particular product. Export market research, in particular, is a study of a given market abroad to determine the needs of that market and the methods by which the products can be supplied. The exporter needs to know which foreign companies are likely to use his products or might be interested in marketing and distributing the products in their country. [4] He must think whether there is a potential for making a profit. He must examine the market structures and general economic conditions in those places (Fig. 10-1). If the economy is in a recession, the demand for all products is usually decreased. So the products of exporters might not sell well at such times. Market research mainly covers:

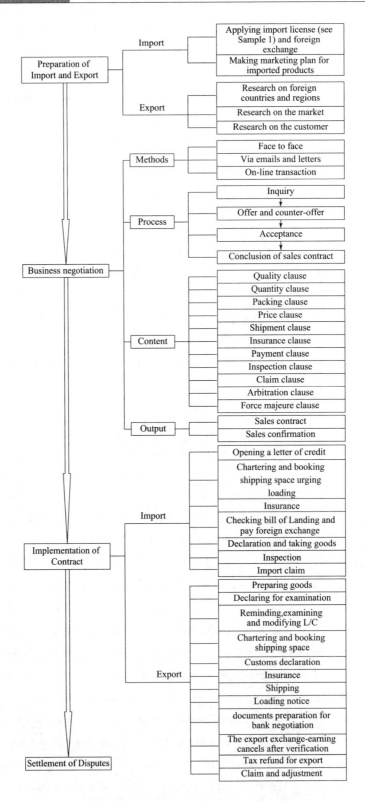

Fig. 10-1　Flow Chart of Export and Import Transaction

1) Research on the countries or regions

Countries or regions with different political and economic systems hold a quite different attitude toward foreign trade business. The exporter should investigate their political, financial and economic conditions; their policies, laws, and regulations governing foreign trade, foreign exchange control; Customs tariffs and commercial practices; their foreign trade situation (the structure, quantity, volume of exporting and importing commodities, trading partners and trade restrictions, etc.).

2) Research on the market

A research should also be conducted about the production, consumption, price and its trend, the major importing or exporting countries of a particular commodity in order to fix the right price of exporting commodities and properly handle other business terms.

3) Research on the customer

In international trade, credit information is of greater importance than in home trade.[5] The exporter should know what kind of reputation the buyer or importer has, the approximate size of his business, how he pays his accounts and information about his trade activities. Obviously, customers with a sound reputation and good financial standing will facilitate the export trade. The exporter can obtain this information from various sources such as references given by the buyer, his bank, various trade associations and enquiry agencies. In this way, the potential customers can be identified.

In addition to conducting market research to collect information or data from external sources, the exporter can also take the initiative in marketing and promoting his products in the overseas market. The frequently adopted strategies are sales literature, the point of sale advertising, packaging, sponsorship, showrooms, trade fair and exhibition, publicity, public relations, etc.

2. Business Negotiation

If a foreign company is interested in buying the exporter's products, negotiation should be organized. Business negotiation plays a very important role in the conclusion and implementation of a sale contract. It has a great bearing on the economic interest of the parties concerned.

No matter what way the negotiations are held, in general, they consist of the following links: enquiry, offer, counter-offer, acceptance and conclusion of the sales contract. Among which offer and acceptance are two indispensable links for reaching an agreement and concluding a contract.[6]

1) Enquiry

An enquiry requests for business information, such as price lists, catalogue, samples, and details about the goods or trade terms. It can be made by either the importer or the exporter. On receiving the enquiry, it is a regular practice that the exporter should reply to it without delay.

2) Offer and counter-offer

An offer is a proposal made by sellers to buyers in order to enter into a contract. In other words, it refers to trading terms put forward by offerers to offerees, on which the offerers are willing to conclude business with the offerers. There are two kinds of offers; one is the firm offer, the other, non-firm offer. A reply to an offer which purports to be an acceptance but contains additions, limitations or other modifications is a rejection of the offer and constitutes a counter offer.

3) Acceptance

Acceptance is a statement made by the offerees indicating unconditional assent to an offer. A contract is concluded once the offer is accepted.

4) Conclusion of sales contract

As soon as an offer is accepted, a written sales contract or sales confirmation is usually required to be signed between the buyer and the seller to confirm the sale and stipulate their rights and obligations respectively. A sales contract or sales confirmation contains some general terms and conditions as well as the specific terms that vary with the commodity. But such terms as the names of seller and buyer, the description of the goods, quality and specification, quantity, packing, unit price, amount, payment, date of delivery, shipping, insurance, inspection, claim and arbitration are indispensable. The sales contract or sales confirmation is normally made out in two originals, one for the buyers and the other for his seller.

3. Implementation of Contract

Under CIF contract with terms of payment by L/C (see sample 2), the implementation of export contract usually goes through the steps of goods preparation, inspection application, reminding of L/C, examination and modification of L/C, chartering and booking space shipping, shipment, insurance, documents preparation for bank negotiation and the settlement of claims, etc.[7]

1) Preparing goods for shipment

After a contract is made, it is the main task for the exporter to prepare the goods for shipment and check them against the terms stipulated in the contract. The quality, specification, quantity, marking and the packing should be in line with the contract or the L/C, the date for the preparation should agree with the shipping schedule.

2) Inspection application

If required by the stipulations of the states or contract, the exporter should obtain a certificate of inspection from the institutions concerned where the goods are inspected. Usually, the commodity will be released only after the issuance of the inspection certificate by the inspection organization.

3) Reminding, examining and modifying L/C

In international trade, a banker's letter of credit is commonly used for the payment of purchase price.[8] In the course of the performance of contract, one of the necessary steps for the seller is to urge the buyer to establish L/C. According to the contract, the buyer should establish the L/C on time, but sometimes he may delay for various reasons. For the safe collection of payment, the seller has to urge the buyer to expedite the opening of L/C. Upon receipt of a letter of credit, the seller must examine it very carefully to make sure that all terms and conditions are stipulated in accordance with the contract. If any discrepancies exist, the seller should contact the buyer immediately for necessary amendments so as to guarantee the smooth execution of the contract.

4) Chartering and booking shipping space

After receiving the relevant L/C, the exporter should contact the ship's agents or the shipping company for the chartering and the booking of shipping space and prepare for the shipment in accordance with the importer's shipping instruction. Chartering is required for goods of large quantity which needs full shipload; and for goods in small quantities, space booking would be enough.

5) Customs formalities

Before the goods are loaded, certain procedures in customs formalities have to be completed. As required, completed forms giving particulars of the goods exported together with the copy of the contract of sale, invoice, packing list, weight memo, commodity inspection certificate and other relevant documents, have to be lodged with the Customs. After the goods are on board, the shipping company or the ship's agent will issue a bill of lading (see Sample 3), which is a receipt evidencing the loading of the goods on board the ship.

6) Insurance

The export trade is subject to any risk. For example, ships may sink or consignments may be damaged in transit, exchange rates may alter, buyers default or government suddenly impose an embargo, etc. It is customary to ensure goods sold for export against the perils of the journey. The cover paid for will vary according to the type of goods and the circumstances. If the exporter has bought insurance for the goods, he will be reimbursed for the losses.

7) Documents preparation for bank negotiation

After the shipment, all kinds of documents required by the L/C shall be prepared by the exporter and the importer and presented, within the validity of the L/C to the bank for negotiation. As to the shipping documents, they include a commercial invoice, bill of lading, insurance policy, packing list, weight memo, certificate of inspection, and, in some cases, consular invoice, certificate origin, etc. Documents should be correct, complete, concise and clean. Only after the documents are checked to be fully in conformity with the L/C, the opening bank makes the payment. Payment shall be disregarded by the bank for any discrepancies in the documents.

4. Settlement of Disputes

Sometimes complaints or claim inevitably arise in spite of the careful performance of a contract by the exporter and importer. They are likely to be caused by various reasons such as more or less quantity delivered, wrong goods delivered, poor packing, inferior quality, a discrepancy between the samples and the goods which actually arrived, delay in shipment, etc. In accordance with specific conditions, complaints and claims may be made to the exporter, importer, insurance company or shipping company. Once disputes arise, it is advised that arbitration is better than litigation, and conciliation is better than arbitration.

General procedures of the import transaction

So far we have studied the general procedures of the export transaction and dealt with different stages and steps, from the point of view of the exporter. Having been familiar with the process of the export business, we find it much easier to understand how an importer handles his import business. After all, the export and import trades are two sides of the same coin. When handling an import trade, the trade conditions and terms you are striving for are sometimes just the opposite to those you do in an export trade. The terms of delivery remain the same meaning regardless of whether you work as an importer or an exporter. A bill of lading is a bill of lading no matter who uses it for some practical purposes. The knowledge, we have acquired from the previous sections is also applicable to import procedures. With the fundamental knowledge of export procedures' we can grasp the essential points of import procedures easily and manage import trade well and smoothly.

The General procedures of import transaction can be summarized as follows:

(1) To conduct the market investigation.

(2) To formulate import plan for a certain commodity.

(3) To send inquiries to the prospective sellers overseas.

(4) To compare and analyze the offers or quotations received.

(5) To make counter-offers and decide on which offer is most beneficial.

(6) To sign a purchase contract.

(7) To apply to a bank for opening a letter of credit.

(8) To book shipping space or charter a carrying vessel for taking over the cargoes if the contract is in terms of FOB.

(9) To effect insurance with the insurance company upon receipt of shipping advice.

(10) To apply for inspection if necessary.

(11) To attend to customs formalities to clear the goods through the Customs.

(12) To entrust forwarding agents with all the transport arrangements from the port to the end user's warehouse.

(13) To settle disputes (in any).

Words List

1. transaction [træn'zækʃ(ə)n]　　　　　n. 买卖,贸易,交易
2. negotiation [nɪgəʊʃɪ'eɪʃ(ə)n]　　　　n. 协商,谈判,洽谈
3. contract ['kɔntrækt]　　　　　　　　n. 合同,契约
4. dispute ['dɪspjuːt]　　　　　　　　　v. 争论,辩论,争吵
5. exporter [ɪk'spɔː(r)tə(r)]　　　　　　n. 输出者,出口商
6. recession [rɪ'seʃ(ə)n]　　　　　　　n. 衰退,经济衰退,暴跌(物价),不景气
7. commodity [kə'mɔdətɪ]　　　　　　n. 商品,货物,有用物品,日用品
8. reference ['ref(ə)rəns]　　　　　　　n. 证明人
9. conclude [kən'kluːd]　　　　　　　v. 签订
10. sponsorship ['spɔnsə(r)ʃɪp]　　　　n. 赞助者的地位、任务等
11. showroom ['ʃəʊruːm]　　　　　　　n. 展出室
12. publicity [pʌb'lɪsətɪ]　　　　　　　n. 公共宣传
13. offer ['ɔfə(r)]　　　　　　　　　　　v. 发盘
14. acceptance [ək'septəns]　　　　　　n. 接受
15. offerer ['ɔfərə]　　　　　　　　　　n. 发价人,发盘人
16. offeree ['ɔfər'iː]　　　　　　　　　n. 被报价人,被发盘人,受盘人
17. stipulate ['stɪpjuleɪt]　　　　　　　v. 规定,保证
18. obligation ['ɔblɪ'geɪʃ(ə)n]　　　　　n. 义务;职责;责任
19. claim [kleɪm]　　　　　　　　　　n. 索赔
20. arbitration ['ɑː(r)bɪ'treɪʃ(ə)n]　　　n. 仲裁
21. charter ['tʃɑː(r)tə(r)]　　　　　　　n. 租(船、车等)
22. booking ['bukɪŋ]　　　　　　　　　n. 登记,预约
23. packing ['pækɪŋ]　　　　　　　　　n. 包装
24. certificate [sə(r)'tɪfɪkət]　　　　　　n. 证明书,证明,证书,执照,证券
25. issuance ['ɪʃjuəns]　　　　　　　　n. 发给,发放
26. amendment [ə'men(d)mənt]　　　　n. 修改,修正
27. guarantee ['gærən'tiː]　　　　　　　n. 保证,保证书,担保,抵押品
28. shipload ['ʃɪpləʊd]　　　　　　　　n. 船舶运载量
29. consignment [kən'saɪnmənt]　　　n. (寄售)货物
30. default [dɪ'fɔːlt]　　　　　　　　　v. 违约
31. embargo [ɪm'bɑː(r)gəʊ]　　　　　v. 禁止;限制
32. peril ['perəl]　　　　　　　　　　　n. 危险

33. reimburse ['rɪːɪm'bə:(r)s]　　　　v. 偿还,偿付
34. validity [və'lɪdətɪ]　　　　　　n. 有效性,合法性,正确性
35. discrepancy [dɪs'krepənsɪ]　　 n. 差异性,不一致,差异,瑕疵(票据)
36. litigation [,lɪtɪ'geɪʃ(ə)n]　　　n. 诉讼,起诉
37. delivery [dɪ'lɪv(ə)rɪ]　　　　　n. 交货
38. applicable [ə'plɪkəb(ə)l]　　　adj. 可适用的,可应用的
39. entrust [ɪn'trʌst]　　　　　　v. 委托
40. warehouse ['weə(r)haus]　　　n. 仓库

Useful Expressions

1. in the courts of	在……期间
2. keep in mind	牢记
3. market structure	市场结构
4. foreign exchange	国外汇兑,国际汇兑,外汇
5. customs stuff	关税率;海关(关税),税则
6. financial standing	财务状况
7. trade association	行业公会
8. enquiry agency	咨询机构
9. take the initiative	采取主动
10. public relation	公共关系
11. counter offer	还盘
12. firm offer	实盘
13. non-firm offer	虚盘
14. unconditional assent	无条件同意
15. CIF (abbr. Cost Insurance and Freight)	到岸价格
16. L/C	信用证
17. shipping schedule	船期
18. inspection application	报检
19. ship's agent	轮船代理人
20. customs formality	报关手续
21. exchange rate	汇率,兑换率
22. commercial invoice	商业发票
23. bill of landing	提单
24. consular invoice	领事发票,领事签证,发票,领事签证货单

25. forwarding agent　　　　　　　　承运人

26. end-user　　　　　　　　　　　　最终用户

Key vocabulary

1. contract

n. 契约；合同

I was then under contract to a bus company. 那时候我按合同为一家公共汽车公司工作。

vt.

1）缔结；订（约）[（+with）]

The two businesses contracted a merger. 两家商行签约合并了。

2）得（病）；沾染（习惯）；负（债）

I contracted a cold. 我得了感冒。

vi. 缩小；收缩

Metals contract in cold weather. 金属在寒冷的天气里收缩。

2. dispute

vi. 争论；争执[（+about/on/over/with/against）]

The two countries disputed for years over a small strip of land on their border. 这两个国家为了边界上一块土地已经争执多年。

vt.

1）争论；争执[+wh-]

The couple disputed where to spend the holiday. 夫妻俩为上哪儿度假而发生争论。

2）争夺（土地，胜利等）

The two teams were disputing the cup. 两队正在争夺奖杯。

n. 争论；争执；争端[C][U][（+about/over/with）]

The dispute was settled last week. 争端在上周解决了。

3. conclude

v.

1）结束[（+by/with）]

We concluded our meeting at 9 o'clock. 我们九点钟结束了会议。

2）推断出，断定[W][Y][+that]

What can you conclude from these observations? 你从这些观察中能得出什么结论？

3）缔结（条约）[（+with）]

4)(最后)决定(为)[+to-v][+that]

He concluded that he would wait a little longer. 他决定再等一会儿。

4. stipulate

v. 规定;约定[+(that)]

He stipulated payment in advance. 他规定要预先付款。

> stipulation

n. 契约

5. amendment

n.

1)改正,修正;改善[U][C]

Your plan needs some amendment. 你的计划需要作些修正。

2)(议案等的)修正案[C][(+to)]

An amendment to the United States Constitution limits the President to two full terms in office. 一项美国宪法修正案规定总统不能超过两届任期。

> amend

vt.

1)修订,修改;订正

The constitution was amended in 1920 to give women the right to vote. 美国宪法于1920年修订,赋予妇女投票权。

2)改进,改善

vi.

1)改进,改善

2)改过自新

He was determined to amend. 他决心改过自新。

6. default

n.[U]

1)不履行,违约,拖欠

be in default on a loan 拖欠借款

2)不参加(比赛);(中途)弃权

The other team didn't arrive, so our team won by default. 由于对方球队未到,我队以其弃权而获胜。

3)【律】缺席

A default judgment was issued against the defendant. 被告受到了缺席审判。

4)【电脑】隐含值,系统默认值

vi.

1)不履行,拖欠[(+on/in)]

Let's both try not to default on our commitments. 让我们双方一起努力,不违反自己的承诺。

2)不出场;不参加;不到案;弃权

The player defaulted in the tournament because of her injury. 在这次循环赛中,这位运动员由于受伤而弃权。

vt.

1)不履行,拖欠

Foreign debts defaulted. 外债没有如期偿还。

2)对……处以缺席裁判

3)不参加(比赛)

7. validity

n.

1)正当;正确;确实

We should question the validity of those figures. 我们应当查询那些数字的正确性。

2)【律】有效性;效力;合法性

＞valid

adj.

1)有根据的;确凿的;令人信服的

Her argument is valid. 她的论点是站得住脚的。

2)合法的;有效的;经正当手续的

a valid contract 具有法律效力的合同

＞validate

v.

1)使有效;使生效

2)承认……为正当;确认;证实

8. applicable

adj.

1)可应用的,合用的;可实施的

The new law is applicable from next Monday. 新法令下个星期一开始实施。

2)适当的,合适的[(+to)]

This rule is not applicable to foreigners. 这项规定不适用于外国人。

＞apply

v.

1)涂,敷;将……铺在表面[(+to)]

The nurse applied the ointment to the wound. 护士把药膏敷到伤口上。

2)应用;实施[(+to)]

We should apply both theories in the language classroom. 我们应把两种理论都运用到语言教室中去。

3) 使起作用；使适用 [W] [(+to)]

This rule can not be applied to every case. 这条规则并不是在每种情况下都能适用的。

4) (后常接 oneself) 使致力(于)，使专心从事 [(+to)]

He applied himself to learning French. 他致力于学习法语。

➢applicably

adv. 可适用地

➢applicability

n.

(可)应用性，适用性 [U]

9. take the initiative

采取主动

Mr. Henry took the initiative in closing the park to cars. 亨利先生倡议不让汽车在公园里通行。

Notes on the Text

1. Each country needs to import the articles and commodities it does not produce itself, while in order to pay for them, it has to earn foreign exchanges.

翻译：各国都需要进口不能自产的物资和商品，而为了支付它们，它必须赚取外汇。

重点：本句在定语从句 it does not produce itself 前面省略了关系代词 that，用以指代 articles and commodities，在从句中作为 produce 的宾语。"While"是复句之间的连词，表示对比，如例句：Some people love cats, while others hate them.

2. But there may be factors that compel governments to place restrictions on the trades with foreign countries.

翻译：但是有些因素会迫使政府对国际贸易采取限制措施。

重点：that 在其后的定语从句中作主语，指代 factors。整句作为复句形式较难翻译，可以按照汉语习惯作为简单句来翻译。

3. These factors mean that importing and exporting are subject to a lot of formalities, such as customs entry and exchange control approval, which are not applicable for the home retail and wholesale trades.

翻译：这些因素意味着进口和出口会受制于很多手续，例如海关通关和外汇管制许可。

这在国内的零售和批发贸易中是不适用的。

重点:本句是比较复杂的复句结构。从属连词 that 引导名词性从句 importing and exporting are subject to a lot of formalities,作为 mean 的宾语。定语从句 which are not applicable for the home retail and wholesale trades 修饰名词 formalities。整句很难用一个中文句子表达,因此可以拆分成两句来进行翻译。

4. The exporter needs to know which foreign companies are likely to use his products or might be interested in marketing and distributing the products in their country.

翻译:出口商需要了解哪些外国公司有可能使用他的产品,或是有意在他们的国家对其产品进行营销和推介。

重点:本句中有两个表示可能性的表达方式,be likely to 和 might be。Marketing 译为营销,是动词的分词形式。

5. In international trade, credit information is of greater importance than in home trade.

翻译:在国际贸易中,资信情况比在国内贸易中更为重要。

重点:介词 of 在这里表特征,意谓"(具有)……的"。如例句:The work I'm doing is not of very much value. 我正在做的工作没什么太大的价值。

6. Among which offer and acceptance are two indispensable links for reaching an agreement and concluding a contract.

翻译:其中发盘和接受在达成协议和签订合同中是必不可少的两个环节。

重点:which 指代了前文提到的商务洽谈的四个环节 enquiry, offer, counter-offer, acceptance and conclusion of sales contract。

Indispensable:

(1)必不可少的,必需的。可后接介词 to 或 for,比如:A library is indispensable to a college. 大学里图书馆是必不可少的。

(2)责无旁贷的。Taking care of my parents is my indispensable duty. 照顾父母,我责无旁贷。

7. Under CIF contract with terms of payment by L/C (see sample 2), the implementation of export contract usually goes through the steps of goods preparation, inspection application, reminding of L/C, examination and modification of L/C, chartering and booking space shipping, shipment, insurance, documents preparation for bank negotiation and the settlement of claims, etc.

翻译:当出口合同为 CIF 合同,付款方式采用信用证时,出口合同的履行通常包括备货、报检、催证、审证和改证、租船和订舱、装运、保险、制单结汇和理赔等。

重点:本句中出现了许多进出口贸易中常用的专业术语。Tab. 10-1 给出了更为详尽的专业术语列表:

进出口贸易常用术语表　　　　　　　　　　　Tab. 10-1

国际贸易	
出口信贷 export credit	贸易顺差 favorable balance of trade
出口津贴 export subsidy	贸易逆差 unfavorable balance of trade
商品倾销 dumping	进口配额制 import quotas
外汇倾销 exchange dumping	自由贸易区 free trade zone
优惠关税 special preferences	对外贸易值 value of foreign trade
保税仓库 bonded warehouse	国际贸易值 value of international trade
普遍优惠制 generalized system of preferences-GSP	
最惠国待遇 most-favored-nation treatment-MFNT	
价格条件	
运费 freight	折扣 discount, allowance
单价 price	批发价 wholesale price
码头费 wharfage	装运港 port of shipment
总值 total value	目的港 port of destination
卸货费 landing charges	卸货港 port of discharge
金额 amount	零售价 retail price
关税 customs duty	现货价格 spot price
净价 net price	进口许可证 import licence
印花税 stamp duty	出口许可证 export licence
含佣价 price including commission	期货价格 forward price
港口税 port dues	现行价格（时价）current price prevailing price
回佣 return commission	离岸价（船上交货价）FOB-free on board
国际市场价格 world（International）Market price	
成本加运费价（离岸加运费价）C&F-cost and freight	
到岸价（成本加运费、保险费价）CIF-cost, insurance and freight	
交货条件	
交货 delivery	驳船 lighter
轮船 steamship（缩写 S.S）	舱位 shipping space
装运、装船 shipment	油轮 tanker
租船 charter（the chartered ship）	报关 clearance of goods
交货时间 time of delivery	陆运收据 cargo receipt
定程租船 voyage charter	提货 to take delivery of goods
定期租船 time charter	空运提单 airway bill
装运期限 time of shipment	正本提单 original B\\L
托运人（一般指出口商）shipper, consignor	选择港（任意港）optional port
收货人 consignee	选港费 optional charges

Continue

交货条件	
班轮 regular shipping liner	
选港费由买方负担 optional charges to be borne by the Buyers 或 optional charges for Buyers account	
一月份装船 shipment during January 或 January shipment	
一月底装船 shipment not later than Jan. 31st. 或 shipment on or before Jan. 31st.	
一/二月份装船 shipment during Jan./Feb. 或 Jan./Feb. shipment	
在……(时间)分两批装船 shipment during…in two lots	
在……(时间)平均分两批装船 shipment during…in two equal lots	
分三个月装运 in three monthly shipments	
分三个月,每月平均装运 in three equal monthly shipments	
立即装运 immediate shipments	即期装运 prompt shipments
收到信用证后30天内装运 shipments within 30 days after receipt of L/C	
不允许分批装船 partial shipment not allowed / permitted	
交易磋商、合同签订	
订单 indent	交易磋商 business negotiation
订货 booking	不受约束 without engagement
电复 cable reply	业务洽谈 business discussion
实盘 firm offer	限＊＊复 subject to reply ＊＊
递盘 bid	限＊＊复到 subject to reply reaching here ＊＊
递实盘 bid firm	有效期限 time of validity
还盘 counter offer	有效至＊＊: valid till ＊＊
发盘(发价) offer	购货合同 purchase contract
发实盘 offer firm	销售合同 sales contract
询盘(询价) inquiry;enquiry	购货确认书 purchase confirmation
交易磋商、合同签订	销售确认书 sales confirmation
指示性价格 price indication	一般交易条件 general terms and conditions
速复 reply immediately	以未售出为准 subject to prior sale
参考价 reference price	需经卖方确认 subject to sellers confirmation
习惯做法 usual practice	
需经我方最后确认 subject to our final confirmation	
贸易方式	
INT(拍卖 auction)	累计佣金 accumulative commission
寄售 consignment	补偿贸易 compensation trade
招标 invitation of tender	来料加工 processing on giving materials
投标 submission of tender	来料装配 assembling on provided parts
一般代理人 agent	独家经营/专营权 exclusive right
总代理人 general agent	独家经营/代理协议 exclusivity agreement
代理协议 agency agreement	独家代理 sole agency;exclusive agency;

Continue

品质条件	
品质 quality	参考样品 reference sample
规格 specifications	封样 sealed sample
说明 description	公差 tolerance
标准 standard type	货号 article No.
商品目录 catalogue	花色(搭配) assortment
宣传小册 pamphlet	样品 sample
原样 original sample	5%增减 5% plus or minus
复样 duplicate sample	代表性样品 representative sample
对等样品 counter sample	大路货(良好平均品质) fair average quality
商检仲裁	
索赔 claim	罚金条款 penalty
争议 disputes	不可抗力 force Majeure
仲裁 arbitration	产地证明书 certificate of origin
仲裁庭 arbitral tribunal	品质、重量检验证书 inspection certificate
品质检验证书 inspection certificate of quanlity	
重量检验证书 inspection certificate of weight(quantity)	
＊．商品检验局 ＊．commodity inspection bureau(＊.C.I.B)	
数量条件	
个数 number	毛作净 gross for net
容积 capacity	皮重 tare
体积 volume	毛重 gross weight
净重 net weight	溢短装条款 more or less clause
外汇	
外汇 foreign exchange	间接标价 indirect quotation
外币 foreign currency	买入汇率 buying rate
汇率 rate of exchange	卖出汇率 selling rate
法定贬值 devaluation	固定汇率 fixed rate
法定升值 revaluation	通货膨胀 inflation
浮动汇率 floating rate	金本位制度 gold standard
硬通货 hard currency	纸币制度 paper money system
软通货 soft currency	黄金输送点 gold points
金平价 gold standard	铸币平价 mint par
国际收支 balance of payments	国际货币基金 international monetary fund
直接标价 direct quotation	
黄金外汇储备 gold and foreign exchange reserve	
汇率波动的官定上下限 official upper and lower limits of fluctuation	

8. In international trade, a banker's letter of credit is commonly used for the payment of purchase price.

翻译:在国际贸易中,银行信用证被广泛用于支付货款。

重点:letter of credit,信用证,可简写为 L/C。信用证是一种由银行依照客户的要求和指示开立的有条件的承诺付款的书面文件,是国际结算的一种主要的结算方式。因其为银行风险而非商业风险,较为安全可靠,故广泛被采用为交易方法。

Exercises

1. Choose the best answer according to the passage.

1) Which of the following is NOT the factors that compel governments to place restrictions on the trades with foreign countries:
   A. Channeling foreign exchange for essential goods
   B. Conserving raw materials required by home industry
   C. Promoting tourist economy
   D. Protecting home industries

2) In the whole process of the export or import transaction, which of the following is the first stage:
   A. implementing the contract   B. preparation of import or export
   C. business negotiation   D. settlement of disputes

3) Which of the following is NOT cover by the market research:
   A. Research on the countries or regions   B. Research on the market
   C. Research on the customer   D. Preparing goods for shipment

4) A conclusion of a contract is indicated by:
   A. Acceptance   B. counter-offer
   C. Offer   D. Enquiry

5) In the settlement of disputes, which is the best way to take:
   A. arbitration   B. litigation
   C. conciliation   D. Defamation

2. Answer the following questions according to the passage.

1) Which stages are included in an export or import transaction?
2) What kinds of steps are included in the implementation of export contract?
3) What are the procedures in Customs formalities?

3. Translate following sentences into Chinese

1) Please make sure that details of the goods, prices, and terms as mentioned in the Documentary Credit are included in the invoice and any other information supplied in the invoice is con-

sistent with that of the other documents.

2) The currency of the invoice should be the same as that of the Documentary Credit, and the value of the invoice should correspond with that of the draft and should not exceed the available balance of the Documentary Credit.

3) Please take care that the Weight List or Certificate should be a unique document and not combined with any other documents and the date on it should accord with that of other documents.

4) The insurance covers the merchandise from the designated port of embarkation or point of taking in charge to port of discharge or point of delivery.

5) The name of the consignee in a transport document should be as required in the Documentary Credit. If the transport document requires endorsement, then it should be appropriately endorsed.

Practical Reading

Customs Further Standardise Import-Export Declaration Procedures

Chinese Customs authorities have recently strengthened the administrative procedures for import-export declaration[1]. A major emphasis is the use of dutiable price as the basis for declaration. Before, some import-export enterprises, including Hong Kong-invested ones, failed to comply with the necessary requirements and as a result their goods were detained pending investigation and delay in customs clearance in turn caused delay in production[2].

In view of this, Customs authorities reiterated the proper declaration procedures for import-export goods in accordance with the relevant regulations[3]:

(1) Consignors and consignees of import-export goods should declare the actual transaction price and submit documents such as invoices, contracts, packing lists as well as other supporting written and electronic information to Customs. If considered necessary, Customs may request the consignor and consignee to provide further evidence to substantiate their buyer-seller relationship, the transaction process and price[4].

(2) If the declared transaction price is found to be lower than current prices in the international market, the consignor and consignee must provide sufficient proof that the declared price is true and correct by submitting contracts, invoices, books, foreign exchange settlement receipts, bills, business correspondences and other papers pertaining to the transaction, as well as other written or electronic data to substantiate the buyer-seller relationship and the transaction[5]. Besides, they have to provide detailed explanation for the price discrepancy. If no information is furnished to justify the price difference, Customs will make their own valuation in accordance with

the relevant regulations.

(3) Import goods declared as second-class, left over or substandard items should be backed by proofs provided by the manufacturer and information regarding the definition of a regular item of their kind. If this condition is not met, Customs will levy the same tariff as that on regular items.

(4) Import goods not accompanied by certificate of origin or other proofs of origin will be taxed at the applicable general tariff rate[6]. Customs will not process the declaration if information on the brand, description, specifications, model, technical data and year of production is withheld or removed deliberately.

(5) Import-export declarations failing to satisfy Customs authorities in terms of product classification, price assessment and other requirements as stipulated in the "Manual for Filling in Customs Import-export Declaration Forms" will be rejected. In cases where the information submitted to Customs is suspected to be inaccurate or false, investigation will be carried out and the matter will be handled in accordance with law[7].

Word List

1. standardise ['stændədaɪz]   vt. 使合乎规格；使标准化
2. dutiable ['djuːtjəbl]   adj. 应纳关税的
3. enterprise ['entəpraɪz]   n. 企[事]业单位，公司
4. detain [dɪ'teɪn]   vt. 留住，耽搁
5. reiterate [riːˈɪtəreɪt]   vt. 反复地说，重申
6. consignor [kən'saɪnə(r)]   n. 发货人，寄件人
7. consignee [kɒnsaɪ'niː]   n. 受托者，收件人，代销人
8. substantiate [səb'stænʃɪeɪt]   vt. 用事实支持(某主张、说法等)；证明，证实
9. pertain [pə'teɪn]   vi. 关于，有关
10. discrepancy [dɪs'krepənsɪ]   n. 差异，不符合(之处)；不一致(之处)
11. furnish ['fɜːnɪʃ]   vt. 提供；陈设，布置
12. justify ['dʒʌstɪfaɪ]   vt. 证明……有理；为……辩护
13. substandard [səb'stændəd]   adj. 标准以下的，不合规格的
14. levy ['levɪ]   vt. 征收；征税
15. tariff ['tærɪf]   n. 关税
16. withhold ['wɪðhəʊd]   vt. 扣留，保留；拒绝给予
17. deliberately [dɪ'lɪbərətlɪ]   adv. 故意地；慎重地
18. stipulate ['stɪpjuleɪt]   vt. (尤指在协议或建议中)规定，约定，讲明(条件等)

Proper Names

1. Customs authorities   海关当局
2. administrative procedures   行政程序
3. customs clearance   清关,海关放行
4. foreign exchange settlement receipts   外汇结算凭证

Notes on the reading

1. Chinese Customs authorities have recently strengthened the administrative procedures for import-export declaration.

翻译:最近,中国海关当局强化了进出口申报单的行政程序。

2. Before, some import-export enterprises, including Hong Kong-invested ones, failed to comply with the necessary requirements and as a result their goods were detained pending investigation and delay in customs clearance in turn caused delay in production.

翻译:之前,包括香港投资的一些进出口公司,由于没有提供必要的资料,导致它们的货物结关时间推迟,进而引起产品的生产延迟。

3. In view of this, Customs authorities reiterated the proper declaration procedures for import-export goods in accordance with the relevant regulations.

翻译:鉴于此,海关当局重申与相关规则一致的、正确的进出口货物办事程序。

4. If considered necessary, Customs may request the consignor and consignee to provide further evidence to substantiate their buyer-seller relationship, the transaction process and price.

翻译:若有必要的话,海关将要求发货人及收件人提供更有说服力的证据材料以证实买卖双方之间的关系、交易过程及价格。

5. If the declared transaction price is found to be lower than current prices in the international market, the consignor and consignee must provide sufficient proof that the declared price is true and correct by submitting contracts, invoices, books, foreign exchange settlement receipts, bills, business correspondences and other papers pertaining to the transaction, as well as other written or electronic data to substantiate the buyer-seller relationship and the transaction.

翻译:一旦发现交易价格低于当前国际价格,发货人及收件人必须提供充足的证据材料以表明价格是合理的,这些材料包括:买卖合同、发票、台账、银行结汇票据、账单、商业信函及其他与本交易相关的文件材料,能证明买卖双方及交易的其他书面材料或电子数据同样有效。

6. Import goods not accompanied by certificate of origin or other proofs of origin will be taxed at the applicable general tariff rate.

翻译:没有提供货物原产地证明材料或者来源证明的进口商品,应按照一般税率征税。

7. In cases where the information submitted to Customs is suspected to be inaccurate or false, investigation will be carried out and the matter will be handled in accordance with law.

翻译:一旦海关认为递交的相关信息存在可疑或是错误的,海关将根据相关法律进行处理。

学习资料:
相关链接及网址
1. http://www.unzco.com/basicguide/index.html
2. http://en.wikipedia.org/wiki/Bill_of_lading
3. http://www.trust-trade.com.cn
4. http://www.en8848.com.cn/yingyu/43/n-92443.html
5. http://www.jingpinke.com

推荐书目
1. 诸葛霖,杨伶俐. 对外贸易实务英语读本[M]. 3版. 北京:对外经贸大学出版社,2014.
2. 王增澄. 新编实用英语语法详解[M]. 上海:东华大学出版社,2009.
3. 边浩毅. 现代汽车营销技巧[M]. 北京:劳动与社会保障出版社,2004.
4. 王蕾. 汽车商务英语[M]. 北京:中国劳动社会保障出版社,2015.
5. 缪东玲. 国际贸易单证实务与实验[M]. 2版. 北京:电子工业出版社,2015.
6. 宫焕久. 汽车商品国际贸易[M]. 北京:机械工业出版社,2011.

任务十一

来人来电购车接待

1. 掌握现场沟通及电话沟通的常见表达相关的专业术语、词汇。
2. 能叙述不同对话状态下的客户沟通技巧。
3. 能阅读推销过程中的不同英文表达习惯等的相关资料。

以一个销售员向顾客推销福特车为例,通过完成该任务,能够熟练用英语进行汽车产品简单介绍和推销,该任务是在模拟实际场景进行的。

本学习任务沿着以下脉络进行学习:

现场表达 → 单词学习 → 相关语法 → 完成课后练习 → 英语写作 → 相关阅读

Task 11 Reception for Guest & Telephone Purchasing

Pre-reading

(1) Do you want to be an auto-seller after graduation? Give your reasons.

(2) In your opinion, what kinds of quality an auto-seller should have?

(In a 4s Shop, George, a salesman, is walking towards a customer.)

George: Nice to meet you. What can I help you, sir?

Albert: I'd like to buy a new car. Can you introduce some information about your cars?

George: Of course, offering excellent products and services is our work. [1] Can we talk about the details in the customer reception room? This way, please.

(George and Albert go into the reception room. It is a customer-friendly lounge: Hot and cold drinks will be offered to customers. Magazines, newspapers, and other reading materials will be available. The A/V system will be kept on at all times to encourage customers to stay. [2])

George: Please look through these car-pictures first. By the way, tea or coffee?

Albert: A cup of black coffee, thank you. [3]

George: What do you think of the pictures? Are you satisfied with some?

Albert: I like this one, the Focus wagon 2.3L automatic transmission.

George: Right choice, it has a good market this year. What do you expect from this product?

Albert: Well, I'm a new driver and what is especially important for me is its safety and driving quality.

George: Ford products are engineered to flatter the novice and reward the expert driver, providing an enjoyable driving experience. [4] About the Focus, the first-class technology of its safety belts, airbag, door protection, and battery reduce the risk of accidents and injuries. For its driving quality, using our understanding of the market to anticipate customer needs, Focus is set for max. ride comfort in our country. [5] Relative to competitors, it is nimble, secure, controllable, comfortable and easy to drive.

Albert: What about the environment protection of your cars?

George: We respect the natural environment and help preserve it for future generation. The Focus wagon 2.3L automatic transmission was listed as a 'greener choice' by the American Council for an Energy-Efficient Economy. Some kinds of our new products can run on both gasoline and solar energy.

Albert: It sounds impressive.

George: Besides, the Focus has some other advantages: its features are up-to-date; its price is reasonable; and we offer prompt and reliable after-sale service.

Albert: I have read your price list. Can you give me a discount?

George: I'm sorry that discount is unacceptable. The price is attractive and that is one important reason why it is very popular among private car drivers. [6]

Albert: Thank you for your information. I think I should discuss it with my family numbers later.

George: Ok, I'm looking forward to your good news. [7] Thank you for your visiting. Please don't hesitate to contact us if there is any question about our products. This is a little token for you. See you next time.

Albert: Thank you. See you.

Word List

1. offer ['ɒf(r)]   vt./vi. 提出,提供;报价;呈现
2. excellent ['eksələnt]   adj. 优秀的;极好的;卓越的;杰出的
3. reception [ri'sepʃən]   n. 接受;接待;接纳;接收
4. lounge [laundʒ]   n. 等候室;(俱乐部等的)休息室;v. 懒洋洋地坐或立
5. transmission [trænz'mɪʃn]   n. (机动车的)传动装置,变速器;传送;传播;传递
6. product [ˌprɒdʌkt]   n. 产品;产物(自然的或人工的);制品
7. engineer [ˌendʒɪ'nɪr]   n. 工程师;建筑师
8. flatter ['flætə]   v. 恭维,讨好(某人);使(某人)感到高兴或荣幸
9. novice ['nɒvɪs]   n. 新手;生手;初学者
10. reward [rɪ'wɔːd]   n. 报答;报偿;酬金
11. expert ['ekspɜːt]   n. 专家,能手;adj. 熟练的;需有专门知识或技术的
12. safety ['seɪftɪ]   n. 安全;平安
13. protect [prə'tekt]   v. 保护、保卫某人/某事物
14. anticipate [æn'tɪsɪpeɪt]   v. 期望,预料(某事物);预见到
15. battery ['bætərɪ]   n. 电池;电池组;电瓶
16. relative ['relətɪv]   adj. 与某事物有关的,相对的,成比例的;n. 亲戚,亲属
17. competitor [kəm'petɪt(v)]   n. 竞争者;比赛者;对手
18. nimble ['nɪmbəl]   adj. 迅速的;敏捷的;灵敏的;(指头脑)聪敏的
19. secure [sɪ'kjuə]   adj. 安全的;牢固的;有把握的;无疑虑的
20. controllable [kən'trəuəbl]   adj. 可控制的,能操纵的,可管理的
21. preserve [prɪ'zɜːv]   v. 保护,维护;保持
22. gasoline ['gæsəliːn]   n. 汽油
23. solar ['səul(r)]   adj. 太阳的;与太阳相关的;利用太阳能的
24. advantage [əd'vɑːntɪdʒ]   n. 益处;利益;优势

25. discount ['dɪskaunt]   n. 减价;折扣
26. attractive [ə'træktɪv]   adj. 有吸引力的;诱人的;引起兴趣的
27. private ['praɪvɪt]   adj. 私人的;私有的;私用的;不公开的
28. hesitate ['hezɪteɪt]   v. 犹豫;踌躇;迟疑
29. token ['təukən]   n. 表征;标志;证据;赠券;礼券

Proper Names

1. 4s Shop 4S 店是一种以"四位一体"为核心的汽车特许经营模式,包括整车销售(Sale)、零配件(Sparepart)、售后服务(Service)、信息反馈(Survey)等。
2. American Council for an Energy-Efficient Economy   美国能源效益经济委员会
3. A/V system   音频/视频系统

Useful Expressions

1. look through   浏览,快速阅读;快速检查某事物
2. by the way   顺便说,顺便问一下
3. black coffee   不加糖的咖啡
4. Focus   福克斯
5. look forward to   期待某事物
6. up-to-date   现代的,现代化的

Key vocabulary

1. offer

v.

1) offer sth (to sb)(for sth)(向某人)提出某事物

The company has offered a high salary. 公司已提出高薪相聘。

She offered a reward for the return of her lost bracelet. 她为寻回遗失的手镯提出以酬金答谢。

We offered him the house for £35000. 这所房子我们向他索价35000英镑。

2) 为(某事物)提供机会;给予

We offered him a lift, but he didn't accept. 我们建议他搭我们的车,但他没有接受。

The trees offered welcome shade from the sun. 这些树凉儿十分宜人。

3)发生；出现；呈现

Take the first opportunity that offers, if that there is. 有机会切勿放过。

n.

1)[C] offer (to sb/to do sth)(为某人做某事物或给某人某事物的)提议,建议

an offer of help from the community 社区提出的帮助建议

2)[C] offer (for sth)提供考虑的数量；出价：

I've had an offer of £1200 for the car. 有人向我出价1200英镑买这辆汽车。

> offering

提供；提供之物；奉献物

the offering of bribes 行贿

a church offering 给教堂的捐献

2. excellent

adj.

1)very good; of very high quality 优秀的；极好的；卓越的；杰出的

an excellent meal 精美的一餐

She speaks excellent French. 她的法语说得非常漂亮。

2)used to indicate approval or pleasure 用以表示赞同或愉快

They won't be coming then? Excellent! 那么他们就不来了？太好了！

3. available

adj

1)(of things)that can be used or obtained (指物)可用的或可得到的

You will be informed when the book becomes available. 这本书有货时就通知你。

This was the only available room. 只剩下那个房间可用了。

2)(of people)free to be seen, talked to, etc. (指人)可会见的,可与之交谈的等。

I'm available in the afternoon. 我下午有空。

The Prime Minister was not available for comment. 首相无暇作出评论。

4. expect

vt.

1)expect sth. (from sb/sth)预料,预计,期待,盼望

You can't expect to learn a foreign language in a week. 不要指望一个星期就能学会一门外语。

I was expecting a present from her, so I was disappointed I didn't receive one.

我原来一直盼望着能收到她送的礼物,所以因得不到而失望。

2)要求(某人)某事物(尤指有权或有责任要求者)

The sergeant expects obedience from his men/that his men will obey him/his men to obey him.

中士要士兵服从他的命令。

You will be expected to work on Saturdays. 你们星期六要上班。

3）to be expected 可能发生；相当正常

A little tiredness after taking these drugs is to be expected. 服下这些药后会有些疲倦。

It is only to be expected your son will leave home eventually.

儿子总归要离开家的，这种事很难免。

　＞expectancy 预料；预计；期待；盼望；指望

a look/feeling of expectancy 期望的神色［心情］

She went to meet him with an air of expectancy. 她去见他时带着有所期待的神情。

　＞expectant 期待的；期望的；怀有希望的

children with expectant faces waiting for the pantomime to start

眼巴巴地等候童话剧开演的儿童们。

　＞expected adj. 预料的；预期的；期望的

expected objections to the plan 预料到的对该计划的反对意见

5. product

n. 产品，产物（自然的或人工的）；制品

gross national product 国民生产总值

product development 产品开发

They are the products of post-war affluence. 他们是战后富裕生活的产物。

　＞produce

v. 制造、生产、出产或创造某事物

America produced more cars this year than last year. 美国今年生产的汽车比去年多。

She has produced very little（work）recently. 她近来作品很少。

The soil produces good crops. 这种土壤能长出好庄稼来。

n. 产品；（尤指）农产品

fresh produce 新鲜的农产品

　＞producer

n. 制造者；产地

The firm is Britain's main producer of electronic equipment.

该公司为英国主要的电子设备制造厂家。

The producers of the radios could not find a market for them.

这些收音机制造厂产品打不开销路。

　＞production

1）制造，生产（尤指大批量）

oil production 采油

Production of the new aircraft will start next year. 明年开始制造新型的飞机。

2)[U] quantity produced 产量

increase production by using more efficient methods 采用更有效的方法提高产量

a fall/increase in production 产量的减少[增加]

3)(习语)go ,into/ ,out of production 投产[停产]

6. flatter

vt. 恭维,奉承,讨好(某人),使(某人)感到高兴或荣幸

If you flatter your mother a bit she might invite us all to dinner.

你要是奉承你母亲几句,说不定她会把我们全请去吃饭。

I was very flattered by your invitation to talk at the conference.

承蒙你邀我在会上讲话,深感荣幸。

▷ flatterer 谄媚者;奉承者

Don't believe him, he's a real flatterer. 别相信他,他纯粹是奉承。

▷ flattering 使一个人美过其实的

That's a very flattering dress Ann's wearing. 安穿着那条连衣裙显得更漂亮了。

▷ flattery 奉承;恭维话

With a little flattery, I might persuade him to do the job.

我说几句好听的,也许能说服他去做这工作。

(saying 谚) Flattery will get you nowhere. 你恭维奉承也无济于事。

7. reward

n. 报偿;报酬;奖赏

He received a medal in reward for his bravery. 他因表现勇敢而获得了一枚奖章。

A 1000 reward has been offered for the return of the stolen painting.

悬赏 1000 英镑寻找失窃的画。

v. 给某人报酬;奖赏某人

She rewarded him with a smile. 她向他报之以一笑。

His persistence was rewarded when the car finally started.

他那些力气没有白费,汽车终于起动了。

▷ rewarding *adj.* (指活动等)值得做的,令人满意的

Gardening is a very rewarding pastime. 园艺劳动是非常有益的消遣。

8. protect

v. protect sb/sth (against/from sth)保护、保卫某人[某事物]

You need warm clothes to protect you against the cold. 你需要穿暖些以免着凉。

The country's car industry is so strongly protected that foreign cars are rarely seen there.

该国对汽车工业严加保护,外国汽车甚为罕见。

▷ protective

保护的；防护的；意在保护或防护的

a protective layer of varnish 一层保护清漆

A mother naturally feels protective towards her children. 母亲对自己的孩子自然会悉心保护。

9. anticipate

v. 期望，预料（某事物）

We anticipate that demand is likely to increase. 我们预料需求可能增加。

She anticipates all her mother's needs. 她预见到母亲的一切需要而事先做好安排。

> anticipatory *adj.* 预先的

anticipatory precautions 预先的防范

10. relative

adj.

1）（与他人［他事物］）相对的，成比例的，比较的

Supply is relative to demand. 供应要与需求保持一定比例。

They are living in relative comfort. 他们现在生活比较舒适（与他人或与过去相比而言）。

2）与某事物有关的；关于或涉及某事物的

the facts relative to the problem 与这问题有关的事实

the papers relative to the case 关于此案的文件

n. 亲戚；亲属

a close/near/distant relative of hers 她的近亲［较近的亲戚/远亲］

> relatively

adv. 相对地，比较地；适度地

Considering the smallness of the car, it is relatively roomy inside. 别看这辆汽车小，里面还比较宽敞。

In spite of her illness, she is relatively cheerful. 她尽管有病，但仍很快乐。

Relatively speaking, this matter is unimportant. 相对来说，这事并不重要。

11. competitor

n. 竞争者；比赛者；对手；敌手

The firm has better products than its competitors. 这公司的产品比其对手的好。

> competition

n.

1）比赛；竞赛

boxing, chess, beauty competitions 拳击、棋类、选美竞赛

2）［U］ competition (between/with sb) (for sth) 竞争；角逐

We're in competition with several other companies for the contract.

我们与另外几家公司角逐争取这项合同。

3）the competition 竞争者；对手

She had a chance to see the competition before the interview. 她在面试之前有机会见到了对手。

➢ compete

v.

compete (against/with sb)(in sth)(for sth) 竞争；对抗；比赛

Several companies are competing (against/with each other) for the contract/to gain the contract.

几家公司正为争取一项合同而互相竞争。

a horse that has competed in the Grand National four times 参加过四次"英国大赛马"的马

➢ competitive

adj.

1）比赛的；竞争的

competitive examinations for government posts 公职遴选考试

competitive sports 竞技性体育运动

2）~ (with sb/sth) 不逊于、不亚于、胜过或超过他人的

Our firm is no longer competitive in world markets. 我们公司在世界市场上已不占优势。

a shop offering competitive prices 在价格上有竞争力的商店

3）（指人）求胜心切的，急于取胜的

You have to be highly competitive to do well in sport nowadays.

如今必须有高度的竞争意识才能在体育运动中取胜。

12. secure

v.

1）将（某物）固定住；缚住；系住

Secure all the doors and windows before leaving. 要把所有门窗关好再出门。

2）使某事物安全；保护

secure a building (from collapse) 将建筑物加固（以免倒塌）

Can the town be secured against attack? 能保护这个市镇不受攻击吗？

adj. 无忧虑的；稳固的；可靠的；有把握的

feel secure about one's future 对自己的前途无忧无虑

a secure investment 无风险的投资

have a secure job in the Civil Service 在政府部门有一份稳定的工作

When you're insured, you're secure against loss. 只要买了保险就不会遭受损失。

13. preserve

v.

1) 保护,维护

Wax polish preserves wood and leather. 上光蜡可以保护木料和皮革。

The calm courage of the pilot preserved the lives of the passengers.

飞行员临危不惧的勇气保住了乘客们的生命。

2) 保存,保留

Few of the early manuscripts have been preserved. 早期的手稿保存下来的不多。

Salt and spices help to preserve meat. 盐和调味品有助于保藏肉类。

14. impressive

adj. having a strong effect on sb, esp through size, grandeur, or importance

给人以深刻印象的(尤指因巨大、壮观或重要)

an impressive ceremony, building, speech, performance

令人难忘的仪式、建筑、讲话、演出

His collection of paintings is most impressive. 他的绘画收藏令人叹为观止。

15. advantage

n.

1) ~ (over sb) 比……有优势

gain an advantage over an opponent 获得超越对手的优势

He has the advantage of a steady job. 他有工作稳定的有利条件。

2) 益处;利益

There is little advantage in buying a dictionary if you can't read.

如果不识字,买字典就没有什么用了。

3) (idom 习语) have the advantage of sb 比某人强,占上风(尤指知其所不知)

take advantage of sth/sb

She took advantage of my generosity. 她利用了我的慷慨(取得比我想给的多)。

to advantage 用某种方法使优点突出

The picture may be seen to (its best) advantage against a plain wall.

这幅画衬在素墙上就更加(格外)好看了。

advantageous *adj.* ~ (to sb) 有利的;有益的

16. discount

n.

1) 从某物的价格中扣去的数目;折扣

We give (a)10% discount for cash. 现金付款,我们予以九折优待。

discount shop /discount store/discount warehouse 廉价商店

2)(idm 习语)at a discount 打折扣;减价.不受重视的;不时兴的

Concern for others seems to be at (something of) a discount today. 如今好像不兴关心别人了。

v.

1)不重视,不相信,不理会(某人/某事物)

You can discount what Jack said：he's a dreadful liar. 杰克说的话你不必当真,他可是个说谎大王。

2)(commerce 商)将(票据)贴现

17. attractive

adj. 有吸引力的;诱人的;使人愉快的;引起兴趣的

I don't find him at all attractive. 我觉得他一点儿也不讨人喜欢。

Your proposal sounds very attractive. 你的建议很动听。

goods for sale at attractive prices 价钱低廉诱人的货物

18. private

adj.

1)私人的;私有的;私用的;秘密的

a private letter 私人信件

private property 私有财产

That's my private opinion. 这是我私下持有的见解。

2)(指场所)清静的,不受侵扰的

Let's find some private spot where we can discuss the matter. 咱们找个清静的地方谈谈这个问题吧。

3)个体(经营)的;私营的;民办的

private industry 私营企业

private education, medicine, medical treatment, etc. 民办教育、私人行医、民间疗法

n.(idioms 习语)无他人在场;私下地

She asked to see him in private. 她请求单独与他见面。

19. hesitate

1)[I, Ipr] ~ (at/about/over sth)犹豫;踌躇;迟疑;(因有疑虑而)停顿

Don't hesitate to tell us if you have a problem. 你有问题就直截了当地告诉我们。

I'd hesitate before accepting such an offer. 我得先斟酌一下,才能决定是否接受这样的提议。

2)[It] be reluctant 不情愿

I hesitate to spend so much money on clothes. 我舍不得把这么多钱花在穿衣服上。

➢ hesitation 犹豫;踌躇;迟疑;不情愿

His frequent hesitations annoyed the audience. 他三番五次欲言又止，听众已感到厌烦。

Notes on the Text

1. Of course, offering excellent products and services is our work.

翻译：当然了，我们的工作就是为您提供优质的产品和服务。

重点：在此句中，动名词短语 offering excellent products and services 作主语，谓语动词用单数。

当动名词短语、不定式短语或者一个句子作主语时，句子的谓语动词用单数。

2. The A/V system will be kept on at all times to encourage customers to stay.

翻译：影视设备也将被一直开着，用以吸引顾客留在这里。

重点：…will be kept…被动语态的将来式。be done（被动语态）的时态变化在助动词 be 上表现：一般现在时态，am/is/are + done；一般过去时态，was/were + done；一般将来时态，will be + done；现在完成时态，have/has been + done；过去完成时态，had been + done；将来完成时态，will have been + done；现在进行时态，am/is/are being + done；过去进行时态，was/were being + done；将来进行时态 will be being + done。

3. A cup of black coffee, thank you.

翻译：要一杯不加糖的咖啡，谢谢。

重点：black coffee 不加糖/牛奶的咖啡；coffee with some sugar 加糖的咖啡；coffee with some milk 加牛奶的咖啡；black tea 意思为"红茶"。

4. Ford products are engineered to flatter the novice and reward the expert driver, providing an enjoyable driving experience.

翻译：福特产品让新手自信，让有经验的驾驶人满足，让驾驶变得令人愉悦。

重点：该句的翻译成中文时最好意译，原英文句子利用 to + 不定式表达目的，译成中文时用排比句"让……让……让……"，意思表达全面，读起来朗朗上口，很适合产品推销或者广告语。

5. For its driving quality, using our understanding of the market to anticipate customer needs, Focus is set for max. ride comfort in our country.

翻译：对于福克斯的驾驶质量，我们凭借对市场和顾客需求的了解和预测，按照中国地区最大的行驶舒适度设计。

重点：非谓语动词 doing 表示主动、进行，时间上为现在；done 表示被动、完成，时间上为过去；to do 表示目的，时间上为将来。注意该句中非谓语动词的运用，动词 use 和主语 Focus 之间时主动关系，因此是 using 而不是 used 或者 to use。

6. The price is attractive and that is one reason why it is very popular among private

car drivers.

翻译:这个价格非常有吸引力,这也是这款车在私家车购车者中很畅销的一个原因。

重点:当先行词为 reason 时,关系代词选择 that 还是 why 要看 reason 在其后的句子中充当什么成分,此处 reason(the price is attractive)作后面句子的原因状语,因此关系代词用 why。

7. Ok, I'm looking forward to your good news.

翻译:好的,期待你的好消息。

重点:look forward to + doing / something 常用于谈生意的结束语和书信结尾。

Exercises

1. Choose the best answer according to the passage.

1) By saying "Focus is set for max. ride comfort in our country", George implies _____.

 A. Focus is the max. auto in our country.

 B. Focus is better than any other band of scars.

 C. Focus is the right choice for Albert.

 D. Focus is set after market studying.

2) Which of the following description about Albert is not true?

 A. Albert is a new driver.

 B. Albert pays attention to environment protection in daily life.

 C. Albert wants the safety and driving quality of his new car good.

 D. Albert is a challenging buyer.

3) According to George, what is one important reason why Focus wagon 2.3L automatic transmission is very popular among private car drivers?

 A. The price is attractive.

 B. It is very beautiful.

 C. It was listed as a "greener choice" by the American Council for an Energy-Efficient Economy.

 D. The first-class technology of its safety belts, airbag, door protection and battery.

4) Which of the following description about George is not true?

 A. George is a skilled salesman.

 B. George is not familiar with the band Focus.

 C. George is very familiar with the band Focus.

D. George is patient.

5) What may a reader infer from the passage?

　　A. In the 4S shop, Focus wagon 2.3L is the most expensive car.

　　B. In the 4S shop, all the autos are Focus.

　　C. Albert wanted to buy Focus wagon 2.3L.

　　D. Albert didn't like Focus wagon 2.3L.

2. Fill in the blanks with the proper form of the word given in the brackets.

1) America _____ (product) more cars this year than last year.

2) His frequent _____ (hesitate) annoyed the audience.

3) The beautiful clothes are so _____ (attract) to young ladies.

4) Have you got any _____ (relate) or friends abroad?

5) Although he was faced with a fierce _____ (compete), he was very calm.

6) One of the _____ (advantage) of being a nurse is working irregular hours.

3. Translate the sentences into English by using the word or expression in the brackets.

1) 明年开始制造新型的汽车。(production)

2) 帮人修车是他的兼职工作。

3) 这款车很漂亮,这是很多年轻人买它的关键原因。

4) 我期待着尽快收到您的回信。(look forward to)

4. Communicative practice

Work with your partner for the following situation:

Topic 1: communicate with a customer on the telephone

Topic 2: communication between a challenging customer and a skilled seller

Practical Reading

How to Handle with Challenging Customers

　　Good salespeople demonstrate the following forms of behavior when handing with a challenging situation or challenging customers[1].

　　(1) View grievances and challenging people as a normal part of work, as an opportunity for dispelling customer dissatisfaction[2].

　　(2) Maintain confidence in the product, react with calm and composure.

　　(3) Keep in mind that the customer doesn't mean me personally - I represent the dealership and the brand here. Try to solve problems rather than justify or defend myself[3].

　　(4) Put myself in the customer's shoes. Don't question their subjective impression. Don't

contradict them[4].

(5) Listen actively in order to identify parts of the conversation which can result in a solution to the conflict. Even when something inapplicable or inappropriate is said, don't interrupt[5].

(6) If demands can not be met, say "no" calmly and objectively. Explain the reasons. Express regret that no other decision is possible. Customers have the right to make high demands, and salespeople have the right to reject them[6].

(7) Explain your own situation. Ask for, but do not expect their understanding.

(8) Make concession which cost little but are of high value to the customer.

(9) Keep friendly and close difficult conversations with a positive formulation.

(10) The following mistakes must be avoided:

①Inciting rash accusations.

②Assessing the customer's behavior incorrectly.

③Speak badly of colleagues, employees, firms or products you present.

Word List

1. demonstrate ['demənstreɪt]　　　　　v. 证明,表明
2. challenging ['tʃælɪndʒɪŋ]　　　　　adj. 提出难题的,激励的,挑战的
3. grievance ['griːvns]　　　　　n. 委屈,苦衷,牢骚,不满,怨恨
4. normal ['nɔːml]　　　　　adj. 正常的,正规的;n. 常态,标准
5. composure [kəm'pəʊzə(r)]　　　　　n. 镇静,沉着
6. personally ['pɜːsənlɪ]　　　　　adv. 亲自,就个人而论
7. represent ['reprɪ'zent]　　　　　v. 歪曲地描述
8. justify ['dʒʌstɪfaɪ]　　　　　v. 表明有理的或公正的,调整
9. defend [dɪ'fend]　　　　　v. 保护, 保卫
10. contradict ['kɔntrə'dɪkt]　　　　　v. 反驳,与事实相矛盾
11. identify [aɪ'dentɪfaɪ]　　　　　v. 确认, 证明, 鉴别
12. conflict ['kɔnflɪkt]　　　　　n./v. 冲突, 战斗, 争论
13. concession [kən'seʃ(ə)n]　　　　　n. 承认,妥协,让步;减价
14. formulation ['fɔːmjʊ'leɪʃən]　　　　　n. 格式化,公式化;确切的表达
15. incite [ɪn'saɪt]　　　　　v. 煽动,鼓动
16. accusation [ækjuː'zeɪʃən]　　　　　n. 指责;谴责;控告;
17. assess [ə'ses]　　　　　v. 确定,评定;评估
18. colleague ['kɔliːg]　　　　　n. 同事;同僚

Notes on the Reading

1. Good salespeople demonstrate the following forms of behavior when handing with challenging situation or challenging customers.

翻译:优秀的销售人员在应对困难处境和挑战性客户时会表现出如下行为。

2. View grievances and challenging people as a normal part of work, as an opportunity for dispelling customer dissatisfaction.

翻译:把牢骚和难缠的人看作是日常工作的一部分,看作是消除客户不满的机会。

3. Keep in mind that the customer doesn't mean me personally-I represent the dealership and the brand here. Try to solve problems rather than justify or defend myself.

翻译:始终记着客户并不是针对我个人,我在此代表经销商和该品牌。努力去解决问题而不是为自己辩护和辩解。

4. Put myself in the customer's shoes. Don't question their subjective impression. Don't contradict them.

翻译:站在客户的立场,不质疑他们的主观印象,不与客户发生冲突。

5. Listen actively in order to identify parts of the conversation which can result in a solution to the conflict. Even when something inapplicable or inappropriate is said, don't interrupt.

翻译:积极倾听,以确定有哪些谈话内容可以解决矛盾。不打断客户讲话,即使他们讲了不合适或者不适宜的内容。

6. If demands can not be met, say "no" calmly and objectively. Explain the reasons. Express regret that no other decision is possible. Customers have the right to make high demands, and salespeople have the right to reject them.

翻译:如果客户需要无法满足,镇静和客观地说"不"。解释原因,对不可能做出其他决定表示遗憾。客户有权提出高要求,销售人员也有权拒绝客户的要求。

学习资源:
相关链接及网址
1. http://www.ford.com.cn
2. http://auto.sohu.com
3. http://www.autopx.cc
4. http://jpkc.zjbti.net.cn/scyxx/kwyxsj.htm
5. http://xxx.fjcpc.edu.cn/cource2008/qcscyx

推荐书目
1. 教育部高等教育司.高等学校英语应用能力考试国家级试题库(高职高专用)[M].北京:高等教育出版社 2000.

2. 杨铭涂.百行各业英语视窗[M].北京:外语教学与研究出版社,2001.

3. 陈友新.汽车营销艺术通论[M].北京:北京理工大学出版社,2003.

4. 边浩毅.现代汽车营销技巧[M].北京:劳动与社会保障出版社,2004.

5. 刑怡.高职高专英语词汇[M].上海:学林出版社,2004.

6. 张国方.汽车销售与服务[M].北京:人民交通出版社,2006.

7. 李江天,宋晓冰.汽车销售实务(汽车服务工程专业用)[M].北京:人民交通出版社,2008.

任务十二
汽车产品配置介绍

1. 掌握汽车产品配置相关的专业术语、词汇。
2. 辨识不同汽车产品之间的相关性能评价指标。
3. 能读懂厂家之间的往来书信及产品说明书。

以别克(BUICK)汽车为例,阅读外国汽车公司产品的配置说明,并给顾客做介绍。

本学习任务沿着以下脉络进行学习:

通读全文 → 学习单词和语法 → 用英语叙述课文 → 完成课后练习 → 分组讨论 → 课后阅读

Task 12　Introduction to Automobile Product

Overview

From its clean exterior lines to its beautifully appointed interior, the 2017 Regal performs with style, whether you're cruising a scenic beach highway or out on the town (Fig. 12-1)[1].

Fig. 12-1　2017 Regal

The standard six-way power driver seat and available premium sound system help to make travel special. So do the standard cruise control and 3.8 Liter V6.[2] Your wants and needs are both fulfilled with Buick 2017 Regal.[3]

> **相关链接**：别克(BUICK)品牌始于 1900 年。在美国密歇根州底特律市,苏格兰人 David Dunbar Buick 和他的总工程师 Walter L. Marr 离开了他们朝夕相处的船机及农机修理行,开始着手制造第一辆试验汽车(当时马车是主要的交通工具)。1903 年,他们成立了 BUICK 汽车公司。一年后,汽车生产正式宣告开始,首批 37 辆汽车上市销售。

Special Package

The taupe instrument panel, two-tone steering wheel, shift handle and boot, 16" aluminum wheels with highlighted wheel caps; Signature accents on front head restraints, carpet savers, door cladding and tail lamp. Available with solid taupe or two-tone taupe/chestnut leather-appointed interior (requires power passenger seat on GS).

Optional Equipment

(1) Luxury Package includes illuminated vanity mirrors, rear assist grips, steering wheel-mounted radio controls, front and rear carpeted floor mats, 16-inch aluminum wheels and P225/60R-16 Touring tires (available on LS, standard on GS).

(2) Six-way power passenger seat (available on LS and GS).

(3) Heated driver and front-passenger seat cushions (available on LS and GS; requires four-wheel antilock disc brakes).

(4) Monsoon high performance, 220 watts, eight-speaker sound system (available on LS and GS).

(5) AM/FM stereo with cassette/CD players, Radio Data System (RDS), seek-and-scan, digital clock, auto tone control, speed-compensated volume and theft lock.[4]

Equipments (Tab. 12-1)

Some Different Equipment on 2017 Regal Product Tab. 12-1

Equipments	LS	GS
3800 V6 engine with 200 horsepower	◆	
supercharged 3800 V6 engine with 240 horsepower		◆
four-speed automatic transmission with overdrive	◆	◆
four-wheel disc antilock brakes		◆
four-wheel independent touring suspension		◆
full-range traction control		◆
dual stainless-steel exhaust outlets	◆	
dual chrome-plated stainless-steel exhaust outlets		◆
driver and front-passenger airbags	◆	◆
16-inch aluminum wheels		◆
power remote body-color inside rearview mirrors	◆	◆
power remote body-color outside rearview mirrors	◆	◆
remote Keyless Entry	◆	◆
theft-deterrent system	◆	◆
AM/FM stereo with CD player and Radio Data System (RDS)	◆	◆
one-year On Star Safe & Sound Plan		◆
six-way power driver seat	◆	◆
leather seating surfaces		◆
dual-zone climate control with Air Filtration System	◆	
automatic dual-zone climate control with Air Filtration System		◆
power windows with driver's express-down feature and passenger lockout	◆	◆

(1) Power, tilt-sliding sunroof (includes inside rearview electro-chronic mirror and outside rearview blue-tint mirror; available on LS with Leather/Luxury Package and GS models).[5]

(2) Four-wheel antilock brake system (includes enhanced Traction Control and Tire Inflation Monitor; available on LS).

(3) Driver seat-mounted side-impact airbag (optional on LS and requires Leather/Luxury Package; optional on GS).

Word List

1. information [ˌɪnfə(r)'meɪʃn]   n. 知识,通告之事
2. overview ['əʊvəvjuː]   n. 概述,概观
3. exterior [ɪk'stɪrɪə(r)]   adj. 外部的,外面的
4. line [laɪn]   n. 线条,曲线,轮廓线

5. appointed [ə'pɔɪntɪd]　　　　　　　　adj. 设施良好的
6. interior [ɪn'tɪərɪə(r)]　　　　　　　adj. 内部的,内在的
7. perform [pə'fɔːm]　　　　　　　　　v. 实施,做
8. style [staɪl]　　　　　　　　　　　n. 样式,种类,类型
9. cruise [kruːz]　　　　　　　　　　v. 中速行驶
10. scenic ['siːnɪk]　　　　　　　　　adj. 如画的,风景优美的
11. beach [biːtʃ]　　　　　　　　　　n. 海滩,沙滩
12. standard ['stændəd]　　　　　　　adj. 标准的,用作标准的
13. available [ə'veɪləbl]　　　　　　adj. 现成的,可用的,可获得的
14. premium ['priːmɪəm]　　　　　　　adj. 奇缺的,十分需要的
15. fulfill [ful'fɪl]　　　　　　　　v. 满足(条件、愿望、祈求等)
16. taupe [təup]　　　　　　　　　　adj. (尤指灰中带褐色)褐灰色(的)
17. instrument ['ɪnstrumənt]　　　　 n. 工具,器具
18. shift [ʃɪft]　　　　　　　　　　n. 换挡操纵杆
19. aluminum [ə'luːmɪnəm]　　　　　 n. 铝
20. highlight ['haɪlaɪt]　　　　　　adj. 精彩的
21. accent [æk'sent]　　　　　　　　n. 特点,强调
22. tail [teɪl]　　　　　　　　　　 n. 尾部
23. chestnut ['tʃesnʌt]　　　　　　 n. 栗色,红棕色
24. leather ['leðə(r)]　　　　　　　n. 皮革
25. supercharged ['suːpətʃɑːdʒd]　　adj. 过度的
26. overdrive ['əuvə(r)draɪv]　　　 n. 超速挡
27. antilock ['æntɪlɔk]　　　　　　adj. (制动系统)防抱死的
28. dual ['djuːəl]　　　　　　　　 n. 两体的,双重的
29. chrome [krəum]　　　　　　　　　n. 铬
30. deterrent [di'terənt]　　　　　adj. 威慑的,遏制的,制止的
31. stereo ['sterɪəu]　　　　　　　n. 立体声唱机(录放机等)
32. climate ['klaɪmɪt]　　　　　　 n. 气候,风气
33. filtrate ['fɪltreɪt]　　　　　　v. 过滤
34. optional ['ɔpʃnl]　　　　　　　adj. 可选择的
35. luxury ['lʌkʃəri]　　　　　　　adj. 舒适而昂贵的
36. illuminate [ɪ'ljuːmɪneɪt]　　　v. 照明,照亮
37. grip [grɪp]　　　　　　　　　　n. 夹,钳
38. cushion ['kuʃən]　　　　　　　　n. 垫子,坐垫,背垫
39. monsoon [mɔn'suːn]　　　　　　　n. 季风
40. digital ['dɪdʒɪtl]　　　　　　　adj. 数字的,数码的

41. sunroof ['sʌnruːf] 　　　　　　　　　n. 遮阳篷顶
42. chronic ['krɒnɪk] 　　　　　　　　　adj. 慢性的，延续很长的
43. tint [tɪnt] 　　　　　　　　　　　　n. 浅色，淡色
44. enhance [ɪn'hɑːns] 　　　　　　　　v. 增强，加强，进一步改进
45. inflate [ɪn'fleɪt] 　　　　　　　　　v. 使充气

Proper Names

1. automatic transmission　　　　　　自动变速器
2. independent touring suspension　　非独立式悬架
3. full-range traction control　　　　全范围牵引力控制
4. dual stainless-steel exhaust outlets　双不锈钢排气管
5. 16-inch aluminum wheels　　　　　16英寸铝制车轮
6. rearview mirrors　　　　　　　　　后视镜
7. AM/FM stereo with CD player　　　带CD的立体声AM/FM调频
8. six-way power driver seat　　　　　6路动力驾驶座
9. leather seating surfaces　　　　　　真皮座椅
10. dual-zone climate control　　　　　双路空气调节
11. air filtration system　　　　　　　空气过滤系统
12. power windows　　　　　　　　　电动窗
13. radio data system　　　　　　　　收音机数据系统
14. Antilock Brake System　　　　　　防抱死制动系统
15. air bag　　　　　　　　　　　　　气囊

Useful Expressions

1. from…to…　　　　　　　　　　　从……到……
2. whether…or…　　　　　　　　　不论……或……
3. help to…　　　　　　　　　　　　有助于……

Key Vocabulary

1. introduction

n. 介绍；引进；绪论，导言

introduction to a book 书的绪论，导论

introduction to economics 经济学导论(入门)

get an introduction to 被引见给……

give sb. an introduction to 把……介绍给

letter of introduction 介绍信

make an introduction 做介绍

serve as an introduction 作为引言

We don't need an introduction to each other, do you? 你们不必相互介绍了,对吗?

In the introduction there is a brief account of the event. 这本书的引言中简要地讲到了这件事。

vi. introduce 介绍;引进

adj. introductory 引导的;介绍的

introduce new ideas into education 给教育进入新概念

introduce new products to public 向公众介绍新产品

introduce sb. to 把某人介绍给……

2. information

n. 信息,数据;资料;消息

information bureau 情报局

information science 信息学

ask for information about 打听……消息

classified information 保密情报

collect a piece of information 收集一条情报

feed information into a computer 给计算机输入信息

give information to 向……提供信息

suppress information 隐藏信息

information 除了作"起诉"解以外,前面不可加 a,也没有复数形式;"for your information"是公文和商业信件里常用语。

vt. inform 通知,告诉;*vi.* 检举,告发

n. informant 提供消息的人

adj. informative 提供消息的,增进知识的

inform against 告发……

inform sb. of 告知某人……

keep sb. informed 随时告知……情况

rightly informed 得到正确信息的

well informed about 消息灵通

adj. informal 非正式的,口语的,通俗的

n. informality 非正式(行为)

adv. informally 非正式地

an informal visit 非正式访问

an informal gathering 不拘礼节的集合

3. appoint

vt. 任命，委派

appoint 指某人选派另一人去完成某一特定的任务。这种选择指在正式场合中，如办公室或政府中，而且产生不是由选举产生的。

We must appoint a new teacher soon. 我们必须尽快委任一位新老师。

n. appointee 被任命的人

adj. appointive 委任的

n. appointer 指定人

n. appointment 约会；任命

appointment 通常指与人谈生意或与医生等事先约定的见面。

keep sb. by appointment 经约定而会见某人

keep one's appointment 守约

make an appointment with sb. 与某人约会

The appointment of a chief Justice of the Supreme Court is an important decision. 任命最高法院的首席法官是一项重大的决定。

4. perform

v. 履行，完成；演出，表演

n. performance 实行；完成

n. performer 执行者，表演者

perform one's duty 履行职责

perform a task 执行任务

perform an operation on a patient 给病人施行手术

5. available

adj. 可利用的；可得到的；有效的

adv. availably 可用地；通用地；有效地

某些以-able 或-ile 结尾的形容词用作定语，与 every、the only 或形容词最高级连用来修饰一个名词时，通常放在所修饰的名词的后面。

He is too busy to be available for the interview. 他忙得连接见的时间都没有。

n. availability 有效性，可用性

v. avail 有利于，有助于

avail sb. nothing 对……不起作用；毫无帮助

avail oneself of 利用

of no avail 完全无用的

to no avail 完全无用地

without avail 无益地,徒劳地

He tried but to no avail. 他努力过,但不起作用。

6. shift

v. 变换,转换;变速,调挡

n. 转变,更换;轮班,换班

shift for oneself 自谋出路

make shift 尽力设法应付

shift the blame onto 把罪责推倒……身上

on the night shift 上夜班

He always tries to shift the blame to someone else. 他总是设法把罪责推给别人。

7. convenience

adj. 普通的,常见的;习惯的,常规的

at one's convenience 顺便;方便时

at your earliest convenience 尽早……

for the convenience of 为……的方便起见

make a convenience of 利用

adj. convenient 方便的

adv. conveniently 方便地,合适地

be convenient to sb. 对某人来说,十分方便

问某人是否觉得方便时,介词用 to:Is it convenient to you? 这对你方便吗?

也用 for sb. to do sth. 的结构:Will it be convenient for you to start work tomorrow? 明天就开始工作,你觉得方便吗?

convenient 也常用于 it 作形式主语的句型中:It is not convenient for me to pay just now. 现在就付款我有所不便。

8. enhance

vt. 提高,增强

n. enhancement 增强,提高

enhance one's consciousness 提高觉悟

enhance the beauty of 使……更美

The class enhances my English level. 上课使我英语水平提高了。

Notes on the Text

1. From its clean exterior lines to its beautifully appointed interior, the 2017 Regal performs with style, whether you're cruising a scenic beach highway or out on the town.

翻译:2017款君威拥有清洁的外观线条,美观的内饰,不论你是在风景秀丽的海边高速公路还是在郊外,开着它都非常合适。

重点:exterior *n.* 外部,外形,表面;*adj.* 外部的,表面的,外在的

interior *n.* 内部,内政;*adj.* 内部的,内陆的,内心的

whether *conj.* 是否,无论,不管

We are often asked whether consumer Web sites should be optimized for beginners or intermediates. 我们常常被问到这样的问题:消费类网站究竟应该为新手而优化,还是应该为中间用户而优化?

whether…or… 是……还是……或者……或者……不是……就是……不管……还是……

whether or no(not)无论是不是;无论如何;不管怎样;总之;必定

2. The standard six-way power driver seat and available premium sound system help to make travel special. So do the standard cruise control and 3.8 Liter V6.

翻译:它拥有标准全方位动力驾驶座椅、高级音响系统、标准的导航控制系统和3.8LV6发动机,这一切都会给你的旅行带来全新的感受。

重点:standard *n.* 标准,平,规范,规格,度量衡标准;*adj.* 标准的,合规格的,本位的

help to do 对做……有用;help out 帮助……解决困难;帮忙完成

So do the standard cruise control and 3.8 Liter V6. 此句是一个倒装句,so放句首,句子用半倒装。另外,句首是否定和半否定词时,句子也用半倒装。所谓半倒装,即句子的谓语动词放在主语之前。

3. Your wants and needs are both fulfilled with Buick 2017 Regal.

翻译:2017款别克君威将满足你所有的需求。

重点:wants and needs 需求,此处两个近义词并列,不需要都翻译。meet one's needs 满足某人的需求。fulfill *vt.* 履行,实现,完成(计划等),满足;fulfill one's promises 履行承诺。

例如:He had started for the continent of Europe, intending to fulfill his education. 他已经动身到欧洲大陆去,准备完成他的学业。

4. AM/FM stereo with cassette/CD players, Radio Data System(RDS), seek-and-scan, digital clock, auto tone control, speed-compensated volume and theft lock.

翻译:调幅/调频立体声,磁带/CD播放机,广播数据系统(RDS),自动扫描系统,电子时钟,自动音调控制,速度补偿数量和防盗锁。

重点:AM(Amplitude Modulation)调幅,调谐

FM(Frequency Modulation)调频,频率调制

CD(Compact Disc)激光唱片;用激光读取的光盘

5. Power, tilt-sliding sunroof(includes inside rearview electro-chronic mirror and outside rearview blue-tint mirror; available on LS with Leather/Luxury Package and GS models).

翻译:动力系统,倾斜滑动天窗(包括内部后视镜,外后视蓝色彩镜;LS和GS车型还配

有真皮、豪华配件等)。

重点:sunroof *n.*(汽车顶上可开启的)天窗,凉栅;Electric sunroof in glass version 防紫外线电动玻璃天窗;例如:We bought a car with such accessories as air conditioning, stereo, and a sunroof. 我们购买了一辆带有空调、立体音响和天窗的汽车。GS 标志是德国劳工部授权 TUV、VDE 等机构颁发的安全认证标志;GS 标志是被欧洲广大顾客接受的安全标志;通常 GS 认证产品销售单价更高而且更加畅销。

Exercises

1. Choose the best answer according to the passage.

1) Why do so many history books say that the automobile was invented by either Gottlieb Daimler or Karl Benz?

    A. Because the automobiles they invented were highly successful and practical.

    B. Because the two companies are the most famous automobile-manufacturing companies in the world.

    C. Because they invented the automobile powered by steam.

    D. Because Gottlieb Daimler cooperated with Karl Benz company.

2) When was first automobile invented and by what means was it powered?

    A. 1680, an internal combustion engine

    B. 1769, steam engines

    C. 1863, an improved engine

    D. 1885, with a vertical cylinder

3) Which of the following statements is not true?

    A. 1824, English engineer, Samuel Brown adopted a more efficient gas engine to burn gas, and he used it to power a vehicle up Shooter's Hill in London.

    B. 1866, German engineers, Eugen Langen, and Nikolaus August Otto improved an old type of steam engine on Lenoir's designs and invented.

    C. 1876, The first successful three-stroke engine was invented by Sir Dougald Clerk.

    D. 1886, On January 29, Karl Benz received the first patent (DRP No. 37435) for a gas-fueled car.

4) Who built a two-wheeled vehicle according to the passage?

    A. Gottlieb Daimler   B. Eugen Langen

    C. Daimler   D. Nikolaus August Otto

5) What may a reader infer from the passage?

    A. There are many famous car manufacturers in history.

    B. China has become ar automobile-making power country.

C. All the automobile majors should be interested in the history of the automobile.

D. Automobile history has been lasting a long period, and every designer and maker has been doing hard work.

2. Fill in the blanks with the proper form of the word given in the brackets.

1) This little book is a very good _____ (introduce) to geometry.

2) The FBI wans warned about the spy ring by a confident _____ (inform).

3) I have an _____ (appoint) at 10:30 with the doctor.

4) The audience booked some of the _____ (performance).

5) I _____ (available) myself of this opportunity to improve my English.

6) I'm afraid this isn't a very _____ (convenience) moment to see you.

3. Translate the sentences into English by using the word or expression in the brackets.

1) 我们从早到晚一直在工作。(from…to)

2) 问题是:是去还是留。(whether…or)

3) 石油价格下跌有助于我国的经济发展。(help to)

4) 这些信函应该为我们提供所需要的全部信息。(provide with)

5) 我们去巴黎时,把我妹妹也一起带去了。(along with)

Practical Reading

Other optional equipment of Buick 2017 Regal

safety

Driver and right front passenger airbags

Airbags help protect the driver and right front seat passenger in certain collisions by supplementing the protection provided by safety belts. Never secure an infant in a rear-facing restraint in the front seat of any vehicle with an active air bag. [1]

Always use safety belts and proper child restraints, even with air bags. Children are safer when properly secured in a rear seat. See the Owner's Manual for more safety information. [2]

Driver seat-mounted side-impact air bag (optional on LS and requires Leather/Luxury Package; optional on GS)

A side-impact airbags for the driver helps reduce the risk of injury in certain side impacts.

Always use safety belts and proper child restraints, even with air bags. Children are safer when properly secured in a rear seat. See the Owner's Manual for more safety information.

Child safety seat Lower Anchors and Top tethers for Children (LATCH system)

This system offers an attachment for a child safety seat that's independent of the vehicle's safety belts. A compatible child safety seat can be installed in any two rear seating positions. If your child safety seat does not have compatible attachment points, you should use the vehicle's safety belt system to install it. [3]

Call 1-888-4ONSTAR(1-888-466-7827) or visit www.onstar.com for system limitations and details. [4]

Owner benefits
Corrosion Protection

GM vehicles are designed and built to resist corrosion. All body sheet-metal components are warranted against rust-through corrosion for up to six years or 100000 miles. Application of additional rust-inhibiting materials is not required and none is recommended. Ask your dealer for full terms of this limited warranty. [5]

New Vehicle Limited Warranty

This warranty is for GM vehicles registered in the USA. See your Buick dealer for terms and conditions. Covered for 3 years/36000 miles: The complete vehicle including tires; towing to your nearest Buick dealership; cosmetic corrosion defects and repairs made to correct any vehicle defect. There is no charge for most warranty repairs. Rust-through corrosion is covered for 6 years/100000 miles. [6]

Word List

1. collision [kə'lɪʒən]	n. 碰撞,冲突,抵触
2. supplement ['sʌplɪment]	n. 增补
3. infant ['ɪnfənt]	n. 婴儿,幼儿
4. optional ['ɔpʃənl]	adj. 可选择的,非强制的
5. risk [rɪsk]	n. 危险(性),风险
6. tether ['teðə]	n. 系绳;系链
7. attachment [ə'tætʃmənt]	n. 附着,附属
8. compatible [kəm'pætəbl]	adj. 可以并存的,相容的,协调的
9. corrosion [kə'rəuʒən]	n. 腐蚀;受腐蚀的部位
10. warranty ['wɔrəntɪ]	n. 保证书,保单
11. cosmetic [kɔz'metɪk]	adj. 化妆用的;美容的

Notes on the Reading

1. Air bags help protect the driver and right front seat passenger in certain collisions by sup-

plementing the protection provided by safety belts. Never secure an infant in a rear-facing restraint in the front seat of any vehicle with an active air bag.

翻译:安全气囊有助于保护驾驶员及前座乘客在由安全带的辅助保护下免受特殊碰撞。但是,千万不要指望让一个婴儿在前座安全气囊作用时,在面朝后状态下受保护。

2. Always use safety belts and proper child restraints, even with air bags. Children are safer when properly secured in a rear seat. See the Owner's Manual for more safety information.

翻译:经常使用安全带及合适的限制小孩活动的措施,包括安全气囊。若采用合适的安全措施,孩子在后座会更安全。请查阅用户手册了解更多关于安全方面的信息。

3. This system offers an attachment for a child safety seat that's independent of the vehicle's safety belts. A compatible child safety seat can be installed in any two rear seating positions. If your child's safety seat does not have compatible attachment points, you should use the vehicle's safety belt system to install it.

翻译:这个系统作为小孩安全座椅的附件,独立于车辆的安全带而存在。一个兼容的安全座椅可以安装在后部座椅位置处。若小孩的安全带与提供的附件不兼容,就应该利用车辆安全带系统安装它。

4. Call 1-888-4ONSTAR (1-888-466-7827) or visit www. onstar. com for system limitations and details.

翻译:拨打电话1-888-4,ONSTAR公司电话1-888-466-7827,或者登录www. onstar. com网站获得系统要求及详细信息。

5. GM vehicles are designed and built to resist corrosion. All body sheet-metal components are warranted against rust-through corrosion for up to six years or 100000 miles, whichever comes first. Application of additional rust-inhibiting materials is not required and none is recommended. Ask your dealer for full terms of this limited warranty.

翻译:通用汽车设计成可以防止碰撞的。所有的车身由薄金属组件组成,可以防止碰撞后生锈,担保最长年限可以达到6年或10万英里行驶里程。你可以向当地经销商了解这项限制性保证条款的全部内容。

6. This warranty is for GM vehicles registered in the USA. See your Buick dealer for terms and conditions. Covered for 3 years/36000 miles:The complete vehicle including tires; towing to your nearest Buick dealership; cosmetic corrosion defects and repairs made to correct any vehicle defect. There is no charge for most warranty repairs. Rust- through corrosion is covered for 6 years/100000 miles.

翻译:这项保证在美国注册,适用于通用汽车。向你的经销商索取相关条款内容。全车(包括轮胎)提供3年或3.6万英里的保证,将车子开到最近的别克经销店,像修补碰撞痕迹、修复车辆小故障等所有这些都是免费进行的。碰撞后的防锈担保时间是6年或行驶里程为10万英里。

学习资源：

相关链接及网址：

1. http://www.buick.com.cn；

2. http://221.123.68.107/kcwz/index2.asp；

3. http://jpkc.szpt.edu.cn/2007/swyy。

推荐书目：

1. 田战省.最好看的汽车百科[M].西安:陕西科学技术出版社,2005.

2. 梁开荣.汽车精益集成产品开发[M].北京:机械工业出版社,2014.

3. 吴文琳.汽车驾驶从入门到精通全程图解[M].北京:电子工业出版社,2016.

任务十三

汽车保险办理

1. 掌握与汽车保险相关的专业术语、词汇。
2. 掌握汽车保险相关单据的填写及注意事项。
3. 能根据不同客户需要设计不同的汽车保险险种。

以一个保险销售员向一位刚买了二手车的顾客推销车险为例,通过完成该任务,能够用简单的英语进行车险推销,能够掌握车险相关的专业词语,完成该任务是通过模拟电话推销进行的。

本学习任务沿着以下脉络进行学习:

现场表达 → 单词学习 → 相关语法 → 完成课后练习 → 英语写作 → 相关阅读

Task 13 Handle with Automobile Insurance

Pre-reading

1. In our country, many people hesitate to talk with an insurance salesman, analyze the reasons.

2. If you get a used car, what kind of insurance policy will you buy?

David: Excuse me. Is Mr. Wang speaking?

Mr. Wang: Yes, I am. What's that?

David: This is David, from Shanghai Orient Insurance Agency Co., Ltd. [1] Is it convenient for you to answer a call now?

Mr. Wang: Yes, go on.

David: I heard you bought a car yesterday. Maybe we can talk about car insurance?

Mr. Wang: Do you insure old cars? In fact, I bought a used car and I don't want to spend a lot on car insurance.

David: We insure all kinds of vehicles. Losses from property damage, medical and legal costs, and lost income add up to billions of dollars annually for automobile mishaps. Automobile insurance plays an important role in protecting consumers from serious financial losses that can result from such accidents. [2]

Mr. Wang: I am a new driver and what kind of insurance should I get?

David: Generally, new drivers suffer from more dangerous problems than skilled ones, so nearly every kind is useful to lower loss. In our country, Motor Vehicle Accident Liability Compulsory Insurance is a must for drivers. Vehicle Damage Insurance and Third Party Liability Insurance are basic insurance. Others are additional insurance, such as Drivers Liability, Passengers Liability, automobile fire insurance, automobile theft insurance and so on. And you must buy basic insurance before getting some additional insurance.

Mr. Wang: Once an accident happens, what should we do to claim the compensation of insurance premium?

David: Call your insurance agent as soon as possible and ask your agent or company representative how to proceed and what forms or documents are needed to support your claim. [3] Then supply the information your insurer requests. It is your responsibility to notify and explain the accidents. In our reputation, we will handle claims in a speedy and efficient manner.

Mr. Wang: How about your insurance rate and any discount?

David: Our rate is fair and it is generally adopted by all the large underwriters here. It is pity that the discount is just for the drivers who have no accidents in three years, who are over 50 years of age or who have more than one car insured with our company.

Mr. Wang: You are a good insurance salesman. I've learned a lot from you today but I can't make a decision now. Will you please send me your catalogue for my reference?[4]

David: Sure thing. Call me whenever you have any request for insurance, OK? Thank you.[5]

Mr. Wang: You are welcome. Bye.

David: Bye.

Word List

1. orient [ˈɔːrɪənt]　　　　　　　　　n. 东部,黎明;adj. 东方的,珍贵的
2. agency [ˈeɪdʒ(ə)nsɪ]　　　　　　　n. 经销;代办;代理;经销处;代理处
3. convenient [kənˈviːnɪənt]　　　　　adj. 适合需要的;方便的;合适的
4. insurance [ɪnˈʃʊərəns]　　　　　　n. 保险;保险业;保险费
5. vehicle [ˈvɪːɪk(ə)l]　　　　　　　　n. 陆上交通工具;车
6. property [ˈprɔpə(r)tɪ]　　　　　　　n. 所有物;财产;资产
7. billion [ˈbɪljən]　　　　　　　　　n. 十亿
8. annually [ˈænjuəlɪ]　　　　　　　adv. 每年
9. mishap [ˈmɪshæp]　　　　　　　　n. 不幸事故;坏运气;不幸
10. financial [faɪˈnænʃ(ə)l]　　　　　adj. 财务的;金融的;财政的
11. suffer [ˈsʌfə(r)]　　　　　　　　　v. 经历或遭受(不愉快之事);受苦
12. injury [ˈɪndʒərɪ]　　　　　　　　n. 伤害,损害
13. liability [ˌlaɪəˈbɪlətɪ]　　　　　　　n. 责任,义务;妨碍;不利
14. additional [əˈdɪʃ(ə)nəl]　　　　　adj. 附加的;另外的;外加的
15. claim [kleɪm]　　　　　　　　　v. 索赔;要求或索要
16. compensation [ˌkɔmpənˈseɪʃ(ə)n]　n. 补偿;赔偿;报偿;报酬
17. premium [ˈpriːmɪəm]　　　　　　n. 保险费;额外费用;津贴;奖金;花红
18. agent [ˈeɪdʒ(ə)nt]　　　　　　　　n. (商业、政治等方面的)代理人,经纪人
19. representative [ˌreprɪˈzentətɪv]　　adj. 有代表性的;典型的
20. proceed [prəˈsiːd]　　　　　　　v. 继续前进;继续进行;继续下去;前进;行进
21. responsibility [rɪˌspɔnsəˈbɪlɪtɪ]　　n. 责任;负责;义务
22. notify [ˈnəʊtɪfaɪ]　　　　　　　　v. 通知;报告
23. reputation [ˌrepjuˈteɪʃ(ə)n]　　　　n. 名声;名誉;名气
24. efficient [ɪˈfɪʃ(ə)nt]　　　　　　　adj. 能胜任的;有能力的;有效力的

25. rate [reit]   n. 比率；率；价值、费用或价格的量度
26. fair [feə(r)]   adj. 公正的；应得的；合理的
27. adopt [əˈdɔpt]   v. 采纳；采用；收养；过继
28. underwriter [ˈʌndəˌraɪtə(r)]   n. 险业者，保险公司
29. catalogue [ˈkætəlɔg]   n. 目录；目录册
30. reference [ˈref(ə)rəns]   n. 提到；说到；涉及；附注，旁注；资料

Proper Names

1. Motor Vehicle Accident Liability Compulsory Insurance   交强险（机动车交通事故责任强制保险）
2. Third Party Liability Insurance   第三责任险
3. Vehicle Damage Insurance   车辆损失险
4. automobile fire insurance   汽车火灾保险
5. automobile theft insurance   汽车盗窃保险

Useful Expressions

1. used car   二手车
2. add up to   总计共达
3. play a role   起……作用
4. result from   （因而）发生，产生
5. relate to   与……有关，涉及

Key vocabulary

1. convenient

adj. 适合需要的；方便的；省心的；省事的；合适的

Will it be convenient for you to start work tomorrow? 你明天开始工作方便吗？

We must arrange a convenient time and place for the meeting.

我们必须安排一个合适的时间和地点开会。

> conveniently

adv. 方便地

My house is conveniently near a bus stop. 我家离公共汽车站不远，非常方便。

2. insurance

n.

1）[U] 保险（契约）

People without insurance had to pay for their own repairs. 未投保者需自付修理费。

an insurance against theft, fire, etc 盗窃保险、火险

insurance broker 保险经纪人

insurance policy 保险单

insurance premium（定期交付的）保险费

2）[U] 保险业

Her husband works in insurance. 她丈夫在保险业工作。

3）[U] 保险费

When her husband died, she received 50000 in insurance.

她丈夫去世后，她得到 50000 英镑的保险金。

4）[C, U] 保险措施；（预防损失、失败等的）安全保障

He's applying for two other jobs as an insurance against not passing the interview for this one. 他还申请了另外两份工作，以防这份工作面试不合格。

3. property

n.

1）[U] 所有物；财产；资产

Don't touch those tools they are not your property. 不要动那些工具——那不是你的东西。

The jewels were her personal property. 这些首饰是她的私人财产。

2）[U] 房地产；不动产

She invested her money in property. 她进行房地产投资。

He has a property in the West Country. 他在英格兰西南部有一处房地产。

＞ propertied 有产的；（尤指）有地产的

The tax will affect only the propertied classes. 该税项仅影响有房地产的阶层。

4. financial

adj. 财务的；金融的；财政的

in financial difficulties 处于财务困难之中

Tokyo and New York are major financial centres. 东京和纽约是主要的金融中心。

＞ finance *n.*

1）财务的管理；（尤指）财政

an expert in finance 财务专家　the Minister of Finance 财政部长

2）资金；（个人、公司或国家）可动用的钱，财源，财力

Finance for the National Health Service comes from taxpayers.

国家卫生局的资金来自纳税人的税款。

Are the firm's finances sound? 这家公司的财务状况可靠吗？

5. suffer

v.

1）经历或遭受（不愉快之事）；受苦；吃苦头

He made a rash decision now he's suffering for it. 他做决定太仓促，现在可吃到苦头了。

We suffered huge losses in the financial crisis. 我们在金融危机中损失惨重。

2）变坏；变差；变糟

Your studies will suffer if you play too much football. 你要是总踢足球，功课就变糟了。

Her business suffered（eg made less profit）when she was ill. 她患病时，生意受到了影响。

➢ sufferer *n.* 受苦者；受难者；受害者；患病者 arthritis sufferers 关节炎患者

➢ suffering *n.*（肉体或内心的）痛苦；折磨

There is so much suffering in this world. 这个世界上多灾多难.

the sufferings of the starving refugees 饥饿中的难民所受的折磨.

6. liability

n.

1）[U]（对某事物）有责任或义务

liability for military service 服兵役的义务

Don't admit liability for the accident. 不要承认对事故有责任。

2）liabilities [pl] 债；债务.

➢ liable

adj.

1）~（for sth）负法律责任

Be careful if you have an accident I'll be liable. 小心！你要是出事故，我要负责的。

2）~ to sth 可能遭到某事

a road liable to subsidence 可能塌陷的公路

Offenders are liable to fines of up to 100. 触犯者可处罚款达 100 英镑。

3）~ to do sth likely to do sth 有做某事物倾向

We're all liable to make mistakes when we're tired. 人若疲劳谁都可能出差错。

7. claim

v.

1）要求或索要应得的权利或财物；凭保险单要求赔偿（款项）；索赔

You can claim your money back if the goods are damaged. 货物有损坏，可以要求退钱。

You can always claim on the insurance. 反正出了事可按保险索赔。

claim for damages 要求损害赔偿金。

2）声称；宣称；断言

After the battle both sides claimed victory. 战斗结束后，双方均宣称获胜。

3）（指事物）需要，值得

important matters claiming one's attention 值得注意的重要事情

4）（指灾难、事故等）使（某人）失踪或死亡

The earthquake claimed thousands of lives/victims. 地震夺去数以千计的［人］罹难者的生命。

n.

①［C］索款（作为保险金、赔偿、增薪等）

put in/make a claim for damages, a pay rise, etc 提出损害赔偿、增薪等要求

That's a very large claim! 索要的是一大笔钱！

②［C，U］对某事物的权利

His claim to ownership is invalid. 他的所有权是无效的。

a claim to the throne 对获得王位的权利

③［C］称某事为事实的陈述；声称；断言

Nobody believed his claim that he was innocent/to be innocent. 他说他清白，谁也不相信。

8. premium

n.

1）保险费

Your first premium is now due. 你的第一期保险费现已到期。

2）额外费用；津贴；奖金；花红

A premium of 2 percent is paid on long-term investments.

对投资期限较长者可获百分之二的奖励。

You have to pay a premium for express delivery. 你得支付特快投递的补加费用。

3）（idm 习语）

at a premium （指公债和股票）超过正常或市面价值；因稀少或难得而较之一般昂贵或宝贵

Shares are selling at a premium. 股票溢价出售。

Space is at a premium in this building. 在这个建筑物里场地面积十分昂贵。

put a premium on sb/sth 使某人（某事物）受到重视；高度评价

The examiners put a premium on rational argument.

评委们对以理服人的论据给以高度评价。

9. representative

adj. 有代表性的；典型的

Is a questionnaire answered by 500 people truly representative of national opinion?
一份调查问卷有 500 人作答,是否能真正代表全国人民的意见?

a representative sample, selection, survey, etc 有多种类型的样品、锦集、调查等

n.

1) 典型;有代表性的人或事物

Many representatives of the older generation were there. 老一辈的各类人都在那里。

2)(公司的)代理者;(尤指)派出的推销员

act as sole representatives of XYZ Oil 充当 XYZ 石油公司的总代理

3) 代表他人的人;代表

send a representative to the negotiations 派代表参加谈判

our representative in the House of Commons 我们在下议院的代表

10. reputation

n[U,C]名声;名誉;名气

a school with an excellent, enviable, fine, etc reputation 享有盛誉的学校

establish, build up, make a reputation (for oneself)(为自己)树立声誉,博得名声

live up to one's reputation 不负盛名(行为、表现等与声誉相符)

11. efficient

adj.

1)(指人)能胜任的;有能力的

an efficient secretary, teacher, administrator, etc. 能干的秘书、教师、行政人员等

He's efficient at his job. 他胜任工作。

2)(尤指工具,机器,系统等)有效力的

an efficient new filing system 有效的新归档系统

▷ efficiency n [U] 能力;效力;效能

▷ efficiently adv. 有效力的

get industry running more efficiently 使工业经营管理效率更高

12. fair

adj.

1) 合理的;公正的

She deserves a fair trial. 她应该得到公正的审判。

a fair share, wage, price 应得的一份、合理的工资、公道的价钱

2) average; moderately good 中等的;相当大的;不错的

His knowledge of French is fair, but ought to be better. 他法语还不错,但应该再好些。

A fair number of people came along. 来了不少人。

3)(指天气)好的;晴朗的;顺风的

hoping for fair weather 希望有好天气

They set sail with the first fair wind. 他们一有顺风就扬帆起航。

4）（指皮肤或毛发）白皙的，浅色的

a fair complexion 白皙的肤色

fair hair 浅色的毛发

n.

a world fair 世界博览会

a trade fair 交易会

13. adopt

v.

1）收养某人（尤指作为儿女或继承人）；过继

Having no children of their own they decided to adopt an orphan.

他们因没有亲生儿女，所以决定领养一个孤儿。

He is their adopted son. 他是他们的养子。

2）采纳；采取；采用

adopt a name, a custom, an idea 取名、随俗、采纳意见

adopt a hard line towards terrorists 对恐怖分子采取强硬态度

Congress has adopted the new measures. 国会通过了新的议案。

＞ adoption *n.*［C，U］收养；过继；挑选；采纳；采取；采用；接受

offer a child for adoption 将孩子送给他人收养

her adoption as Labor candidate for York 她作为约克郡工党候选人的提名

＞adoptive *adj.* 有收养关系的；过继的；采纳的；接受的

his adoptive parents 他的养父养母

14. reference

n.

1）［U］提到；说到；涉及

Avoid (making) any reference to his illness. 千万别提起他的病。

The original text is here for ease of reference. 谨附原文以便查考。

2）［C］（向读者指示参考书、文章等的）附注，资料；（做此种用途的）书，章节

check your references 要核对引证的资料

cite Green 1986 as a reference 引用 1986 年格林的论述作参考资料

3）证明文书，介绍信；证明人

quote sb/sb's name as a reference 提出某人（某人的名字）做可咨询的证明人

provide a reference for sb 为某人出具证明

a banker's reference 银行证明（证明某人财务状况良好）

Notes on the Text

1. This is David, from Shanghai Orient Insurance Agency Co. , Ltd.

翻译:我是上海东方保险有限公司的员工,大卫。

重点:Co. , Ltd. 是 Corporation Limited 的缩写,就是有限公司。

2. Automobile insurance plays an important role in protecting consumers from serious financial losses that can result from such accidents.

翻译:汽车保险在保护消费者由于交通事故导致的严重经济损失方面起着重要作用。

重点:play an important role 相当于 play an important part,起重要作用,扮演重要角色。

protect sb. /sth. from/against…保护……以免……

that can result from such accidents 是一个定语从句,修饰前面的 losses。

3. …ask your agent or company representative how to proceed and what forms or documents are needed to support your claim.

翻译:询问你的保险代理人该怎样做,以及索赔需要哪些资料和表格。

重点:how to proceed 作 ask 的宾语。疑问代词 + to do 相当于疑问句,常做句子的宾语。what to do 做什么,how to do 怎样做,when to do 何时做,why to do 为何做。

4. Will you please send me your catalogue for my reference?

翻译:把你们相关的宣传资料寄给我,我作为参考,可以吗?

重点:Will you please…口语中用于客气地请求,意为:请你……好吗? 如:Will you please explain this to me? 请你把这个给我解释一下好吗?

Will you please…语序可以调整,有三种表达方式,例如:请把那本书给我好吗?

Will you please give me that book? Will you give me that book, please? Please will you give me that book?

5. Call me whenever you have any request for insurance, OK?

翻译:你有任何关于保险方面的问题,随时给我打电话。

重点:whenever 在任何时候;无论何时,相当于 at any time, regardless of when,引导状语从句。I'll discuss it with you whenever you like. 你愿意什么时候我就什么时候和你商量这件事。

Exercises

1. Choose the best answer according to the passage.

1) By saying "new drivers suffer from more dangerous problems than skilled ones", David implies ____.

A. Nearly every kind of insurance is useful to lower loss for new drivers.

B. Mr. Wang should buy more kinds of car insurance than skilled drivers.

C. Mr. Wang must buy all kinds of car insurance.

D. A skilled driver need not buy car insurance.

2) Which of the following is basic insurance?

A. automobile fire insurance   B. Vehicle Damage Insurance

C. automobile theft insurance   D. all of the above

3) According to David, once an accident happens, what is the first step we should do to claim the compensation of insurance premium?

A. Call your insurance agent and ask for handling claims as soon as possible.

B. Supply the information your insurer requests.

C. Send the injured person to the hospital.

D. Call your insurance agent and ask what forms or documents are needed.

4) What kind of person can't get a discount from Shanghai Orient Insurance Agency Co.?

A. The person whose car is not a new one.

B. The person who have no accidents in three years.

C. The person who is over 50 years of age.

D. The person who have more than one car insured with the company.

5) According to the passage, we can know that ____.

A. Mr. Wang is not satisfied with David's service.

B. Mr. Wang will buy car insurance from Shanghai Orient Insurance Agency Co..

C. David is a skilled worker.

D. Shanghai Orient Insurance Agency Co. just offer service for the used car.

2. Fill in the blanks with the proper form of the word given in the brackets.

1) Congress has _____ (adopt) the new measures.

2) He is the _____ (represent) sent by Ford company to the negotiations

3) Be careful if you have an accident I'll be _____ (liability).

4) Please come to visit me whenever it is to your _____ (convenient).

5) Our company has _____ (agent) all over the world.

6) You need a very _____ (efficient) production manager.

3. Translate the sentences into English by using the word or expression in the brackets.

1) 汽车在运输系统中起着关键作用。(play a role)

2) 财富鲜与幸福相关。(relate to)

3) 他身上的伤是昨天的车祸导致的。(result from)

4) 这些车辆的数目合起来为1100辆。(add up to)

5) 你常常头痛吗?(suffer from)

4. Communicative Practice.

Work with your partner for the following situation:

Topic 1: Introduce some knowledge about insurance to a potential customer
Topic 2: Establish business links with a stranger

Practical Reading

A Policy of Insurance Car from Australia

Premium Estimate

Third Party Property Damage, Fire and Theft Car Insurance

Issue Date	29/12/2017
Estimate Reference	C000106422
Source Reference	MV071129842764
Brand Number	4804

CommInsure is pleased to provide you with this Premium Estimate. It is valid on the day of issue only. If you would like to proceed with this application please contract your local CBA brand or call CommInsure on 8am to 8pm Sydney time (AEST) 7days a week and a representative will be pleased to assist you. [1]

Your Vehicle: You have told us the following information about your vehicle

2015	FORD	TELSTAR
TX5	AT	
5D HATCHBACK		3 SP AUTOMATIC
CARB	2015CC	4

Vehicle Use: You have told us that your vehicle is primarily used for the following purpose: Private Use. [2]

Sum Insured: Market Value up to a maximum of $8000

Vehicle Garaging You have told us that your vehicle is normally parked at the following location

Location:　　　overnight:
　　　　　　　　EARLVILLE　　QLD4870

Excesses: The following excesses apply to this Premium Estimate

Basic Excess	$400.00
Age Excess-driver under 25 years old	$250.00 in addition to any Basic Excess
Undeclared diver excess-driver under 25 years old not declared on your policy	$750.00 in addition to the Age Excess

Inexperienced Driver-drivers years old and over, who have held an Australia driver's license for less than 2 years

$250.00 in addition to any Basic Excess

All relevant discounts available to you at this time have been incorporated into the Premium Estimate Calculation. [3]

Premium Estimate for the above coverage (inc. all Statutory charges)

Annual Premium   Monthly Premium
$268.89 $22.40

Important Information

This estimate must not be taken as confirmation and is in force if the cover has been affected. [4] This estimate is current on the day of issue only, and may be subject to change without notice. [5] Insurance will not be in force until satisfactory completion of the additional information we require has been undertaken, and the risk proposed for insurance has been accepted by us. [6] We reserve the right to decline to accept any application for insurance. [7]

Word List

1. premium ['priːmɪəm] n. 加付款,赠品;adj. 高级的,售价高的
2. estimate ['estɪmeɪt] n. 估计,估量,评价,看法;vt. 估计,估量
3. brand [brænd] n. 商标,品牌;vt. 打烙印于,加污名于
4. valid ['vælɪd] adj. 有根据的,有效的,具有法律效力的
5. application [ˌæplɪ'keɪʃ(ə)n] n. 申请(表,书);应用;敷用
6. contract ['kɔntrækt] n. 合同;vi. 缩小,订合同;vt. 染上,订(约)
7. primarily [praɪ'merəlɪ] adv. 主要地,首先
8. private ['praɪvət] adj. 私人的,秘密的,私立(营)的;n. 士兵
9. maximum ['mæksɪməm] adj. 最高(大)的,顶点的;n. 最大(限度),顶点
10. excess [ɪk'ses] n. 过量,过度,超越;adj. 过量的,附加的
11. declare [dɪ'kleə(r)] vt. 宣布,声明,宣称,申报;vi. 表态
12. relevant ['reləv(ə)nt] adj. 有关的,切题的
13. incorporate [ɪn'kɔː(r)pəreɪt] vt. 包含,加上,吸收;把……合并,使并入
14. statutory ['stætʃut(ə)rɪ] adj. 法定的,法规的,依照法令的
15. annual ['ænjuəl] adj. 年度的;n. 年鉴,年报;一年生植物
16. current ['kʌrənt] adj. 当前的,流行的;n. 流,电流,趋势
17. undertaken [ˌʌndə(r)'teɪk] vt. 承担,着手做;同意,答应,保证
18. decline [dɪ'klaɪn] n. 下降;vi. 下降,衰退,谢绝;vt. 谢绝

Notes on the Reading

1. If you would like to proceed with this application please contact your local CBA brand or call CommInsure on 8am to 8pm Sydney time (AEST) 7days a week and a representative will be pleased to assist you.

翻译：如果您想继续这份申请，请在7天内联系您当地的CBA和CommInsure公司，相关的代理人员会热诚为您服务，联系时间为悉尼时间早上8点到晚上8点。

2. You have told us that your vehicle is primarily used for the following purpose: Private Use.

翻译：我们从您那里得到的信息是，您的车辆主要是用于以下目的：私人使用

3. All relevant discounts available to you at this time have been incorporated into the Premium Estimate Calculation.

翻译：此次提供给您的所有相关折扣优惠都已经被纳入保费估算之中。

4. This estimate must not be taken as confirmation and is in force if the cover has been affected.

翻译：如果这份估算书的表面有涂改或者受损严重，那么它将不得作为确认并生效。

5. This estimate is current on the day of issue only, and may be subject to change without notice.

翻译：这份估算只是签发当天价格的计算值，以后如果有所变动，恕不另行通知。

6. Insurance will not be in force until satisfactory completion of the additional information we require has been undertaken, and the risk proposed for insurance has been accepted by us.

翻译：只有当我们要求的附加资料全部准备妥当并且拟议的风险保险已被我们接受时，保险才会生效。

7. We reserve the right to decline to accept any application for insurance.

翻译：我们有权拒绝接受任何保险申请。

学习资源：
相关链接及网址
1. http://www.libertymutual.com
2. http://www.libertymutual.com.cn/kf/kf_4.html
3. http://www.qiche.com.cn
4. http://auto.sina.com.cn/z/baoxian
5. http://jingpin.gdmec.cn/solver/classView.do
6. http://www.sdjtu.edu.cn/jpkc/bxylp/qcgz02.htm

推荐书目
1. 孙颢. 保险推销员必备全书[M]. 北京：中国时代经济出版社，2011.

2. 薄冰.薄冰实用英语语法详解[M].山西:山西教育出版社,2012.
3. 李景芝,赵长利.汽车保险与理赔实务(汽车类专业)[M].北京:高等教育出版社,2017.
4. 徐红光.汽车服务人员百问百答系列书汽车保险与理赔百问百答[M].北京:中国电力出版社,2007.
5. 赵颖悟.汽车保险与理赔[M].2版.北京:电子工业出版社,2017.

任务十四
汽车销售礼仪

1. 了解销售礼仪的重要性。
2. 了解汽车销售礼仪的简要信息。
3. 了解最受欢迎的汽车品牌。
4. 学习著名的汽车标志。

学习汽车商务礼仪的准则,通过完成该任务,能知道世界最大汽车集团和各大汽车公司标志。

本学习任务沿着以下脉络进行学习:

通读全文 → 学习单词和语法 → 用英语叙述课文 → 完成课后练习 → 分组讨论 → 课后阅读

Task 14　The Car Sales Etiquette

Lead In

Sales Etiquette is of great importance in the process of auto sales, both the dealers and the buyer, therefore, have to get a better understand of the rules of etiquette, and spare no effort to follow them. Besides, the brands and logos of a certain product are common knowledge that should be acquired.

People who sell cars are constantly in the public eye and should therefore always practice proper etiquette and display good manners to satisfy guests. In addition to high customer interaction, a person who sells cars spends more time at his or her job than at home. Because of this, there is also etiquette to follow with co-workers, management and other departments of the dealership.

Addressing the Public

When you greet a customer, you should take note of how she titles herself. If your customer gives you the last name, you should refer to that person as Mr., Mrs. or Ms. This is common with older folks, many of whom prefer to be on a first-name basis with only friends. The customer views his or her visit to your dealership as a professional transaction. Someone who introduces herself as "Dr." should be shown respect for her degree and profession. Do not use the term "guys," as in "you guys," as some people are offended by this. Folks, gentlemen or "ladies" are respectable ways of addressing several people at once.

Acknowledgement

During down times at the dealership, you may spend days without speaking to a customer. Because you spend so much time with co-workers, you most likely have established good friendships and have found things to do to pass the time. But do not forget why you come to work every day. Never ignore a customer. If you see a customer come on the lot, help him. Do not continue to play around with your co-workers, as your possible customer will take note of this. [1] Be careful in the showroom not to have personal conversations in front of guests and keep your socializing with co-workers away from customers' view and hearing.

Emotions

All salespeople feel stressed at some time or another. Do not convey your attitude and emotions to guests or the people with whom you work. Customers come to your business to spend money and should be treated kindly. If you are unable to separate your emotions from your job responsibility, let someone else help the customer.

The Service Department

The sales and service departments have a hard time seeing each others' points of view. Salespeople often feel that service wouldn't exist without car sales, whereas service workers feel that salespeople think that all scheduled work should be halted until delivery, or final sale in where the customer picks up their car. Always schedule your customers for service by transferring their requests to the service department rather than telling your customer to come in whenever he'd like. When you have your automobile inspected or washed or need a problem addressed, ask for help. Do not demand it. Bring any problems to your manager. Try to respect the service department—everyone in it has a job to do.

Management

Do your paperwork and don't take shortcuts; it only makes the manager's job more difficult. Fill out all required information on buyer orders, credit applications, trade-in worksheets and any other necessary paperwork the dealer requires. Someone will end up having to do the work, and it is appreciated when the salesperson takes the time to do her job effectively.

Taking Customers

Be respectful of other salespeople. If you came in late, do not help the first customer of the day. If you have already helped several customers for the day, give someone else have a shot. If a customer mentions that he spoke with another sales consultant, do the right thing and turn the customer over to that person or split the deal if that person is off for the day. Treat other salespeople how you want to be treated.

Word Use and Gossip

Even though you spend a lot of time with your co-workers, they are not your family and do not have to forgive your words as if they were. [2] Do not use racial, sexist or derogatory terms. Even if an issue hasn't been brought to your attention, you may have offended someone. Be respectful of everyone's background and situation. Do not spread gossip or rumors to disrupt the dealership for whom you work.

GM—One of the World's Four Largest Automobile Groups

on September 16, 1902, William Durant established the GM early. After William Dutlan's repeated efforts, it had a joint work or was merged with Buick, Katie Lake, Chevrolet, Oldsmobile, Pontiac, Oakland, Hughes and EDS computer companies, and then established the huge General Motors Corporation, making each car become the company's division, and thus set up more than 30 subordinate branches of the company. GM's brands, presumably the majority of fans and friends is no stranger. Buick series was the earliest one of GM to enter the Chinese and domestic models, and it still maintains share high in the market; Cadillac was the preferred model for Chinese to chase luxury and gain honorable experience, especially extended edition Cady, which became the people's beauty. Hummer, as a symbol of America car or even Americans, overbearing cannot describe its huge body. Of course, the general family never lacks "international friends", Japan Fuji, Daewoo, Opel of Germany and Sweden's Saab has made great contributions to the brand.

Volkswagen

Volkswagen is the most familiar family of this introduction, and the German translation of company is Volkswagen, which can be translated as the car applied by the public. The graphics trademarks are designed with the two letters V and W from the word "Volkswagen" and is embedded in a large circle to make the shape of the three "V". Volkswagen is Germany's youngest and also the largest automobile manufacturer, whose famous product is "the Beatles" series.

FIAT

In 1899, Agnelli founded the Fiat Cor. in Italy's northwestern city of Turin and the shield trademark. In 1906, the company began to use the first capital letters of four words "F. I. A. T" as a trademark. "FIAT" in English means "law" and "license". In the minds of customers, therefore, the validity and reliability of the Fiat is of high trust by the family users.[3] The Fiat family dominated more than 90% annual outputs of Italy automobile, which is quite rare in the world automobile industry. Therefore, Fiat is known as the Italy automobile industry "barometer".

Ford

All folks ford must not feel strange about family members, and friends with little knowledge can also see a collection of ford group in the past two years in the domestic automobile show. In 1903, Henry Ford created the Ford automobile company. It is said that Rumors Ford was very fond of the animal, and he often found time to visit animal experts. In 1911, trademark designers, in order to meet Henry Ford hobby, designed English "Ford" as a running white image to get into good graces of him.

BMW

BMW, short for the Bavarian Machinery Factory Co Ltd (BayerischeMotorenWerke in German), is a world-famous automobile and motorcycle manufacturer in Germany, with its headquartered in Munich.[4]

Daimler Chrysler—Benz

Mercedes Benz[5], a German automobile brand, is considered one of the world's most successful luxury car brands with its perfect technology, quality standard, innovation ability to bring forth the new through the old, as well as a series of classic coupe style which is commendable. The trigeminal star of Mercedes Benz has become one of the world's most famous brand logo. Since December 22, 1900, when Daimler Engine Factory (Daimler-Motoren-Gesellschaft, DMG) provided the world's first car with Mercedes (Mercedes) to its customers, Mercedes Benz has become a model for the automobile industry. Over the past 100 years, the Mercedes Benz brand has been a pioneer in automobile technology innovation.

Renault, Nissan, and Peugeot-CITROEN

Renault, (Renault S. A.) is a French car maker, whose products are small cars, mid-sized car, SUV, large car (including trucks, engineering automobiles, and bus) etc.. Between 1950 and

1960, Renault first entered the American market, and the brand's pronunciation is "Ren-ALT", which is the most widely accepted nowadays. However, the correct pronunciation of Renault is "Rhen-oh" (as the most common pronunciation in Britain).

In 1914, YudaKenjiro created the "Fast Forwarding Agency", which was changed into the Nissan Motor Company in 1934. Products in Nissan vary a lot, including President, childe, laurel, horizon, Silvia, Antelope, Prince, Southerly, Violets and Small sun etc.

Peugeot motor company is one of the ten companies of the world automobile, and the largest automobile company in France. Founded in 1890, the founder is Armand Peugeot. In 1976 the Peugeot Co annexed Citroen with a long history in France to become the world's first transnational industrial group who was mainly engaged in car production, concurrently running machinery processing, transportation, and financial services. Headquarter of Peugeot company is in Paris of France, with its most car factories in Fernand Hugh Di Province and the total number of employees of about ll million as well as an annual output of 2200000.

Toyota, Honda

Toyota Automobile Body Co (Toyota Motor Corporation) is an automobile manufacturing company whose headquartered was set up in Tokyo, Aichi, and Bunkyo, Tokyo, belonging to the Mitsui Zaibatsu. Toyota Automobile Co gradually has replaced GM as the world's first ranking car manufacturers since the beginning of 2008. Its brands include Lexus, Toyota series high school low-end models etc..

Honda Corporation is the world's largest motorcycle manufacturer, whose automobile production also ranks the world's ten major automobile manufacturers list. Founded in 1948, with its founder of legend Soichiro Honda, the company's headquartered is in Tokyo with a total of 180000 employees around. Now, the Honda Corporation is a transnational automobile and motorcycle production and sales group. In addition to car and motorcycle, its products also include generator, agricultural machinery, and power machinery products.

Hyundai

In 1967, Mr. Zheng Zhouyong, the most legendary business tycoon in the history of South Korea founded the Hyundai automobile. Compared with the rest of the world's leading automobile companies, although the history of Hyundai automobile is short, it concentrated the development history of the automobile industry. It only takes 18 years from the establishment of the factory to develop models on its own (1967-1985), and becomes South Korea's largest automobile group, ranking top 20 in Global Motor Co.

Word List

1. constantly   ['kɔnstəntlɪ]   *adv.* 不断地, 时常地; 时刻; 常来; 历来

2. professional [prəˈfeʃənl]　　　　　　　　*adj.* 专业(性)的；职业的
3. convey [kənˈveɪ]　　　　　　　　　　　*vt.* 传达；运送
4. scheduled [ˈʃedjuːld]　　　　　　　　　*adj.* 预定的；预先安排的
5. effectively [ɪˈfektɪvlɪ]　　　　　　　　　*adv.* 有效地；实际上，事实上
6. derogatory [dɪˈrɒgətɔːrɪ]　　　　　　　*adj.* 贬低的；贬义的
7. joint [dʒɔɪnt]　　　　　　　　　　　　*adj.* 共同的，联合的；共享的；两院的；连带的，共同的
8. luxury [ˈlʌkʃərɪ]　　　　　　　　　　　*n.* 奢侈，豪华；奢侈品，美食美衣；乐趣，享受
9. satisfy [ˈsætɪsfaɪ]　　　　　　　　　　*vt./vi.* 使满意，满足
10. respectable [rɪˈspektəbl]　　　　　　*adj.* 可敬的；品行端正的；可观的，相当大的；体面的
11. separate [ˈseprət]　　　　　　　　　*vt./vi.* 分开；(使)分离；区分；隔开
12. application [ˌæplɪˈkeɪʃn]　　　　　　*n.* 适用，应用，运用；申请，请求，申请表格
13. forgive [fəˈgɪv]　　　　　　　　　　　*vt./vi.* 原谅；饶恕；对不起；请原谅
14. disrupt [dɪsˈrʌpt]　　　　　　　　　　*vt.* 使混乱；使分裂；使瓦解；破坏；使中断
15. subordinate [səˈbɔːdɪnət]　　　　　　*adj.* 级别或职位较低的；下级的；次要的；附属的
16. trademark [ˈtreɪdmɑːk]　　　　　　　*n.* (注册)商标；(人的行为或衣着的)特征，标记
17. validity [vəˈlɪdətɪ]　　　　　　　　　　*n.* 有效，合法性；效力；正确；正当；正确性
18. commendable [kəˈmendəbl]　　　　*adj.* 值得表扬的，值得称赞的；很好的；可推荐的
19. transnational [ˌtrænzˈnæʃnəl]　　　　*adj.* 影响数国的；数国参与的，跨国的
20. rank [ræŋk]　　　　　　　　　　　　*n.* 阶层，等级，军衔，次序，顺序，行列；
　　　　　　　　　　　　　　　　　　　　vt./vi. 排列，使成横排；把……分类
21. barometer [bəˈrɒmɪtə(r)]　　　　　　*n.* 气压计；晴雨表；显示变化的事物
22. engage [ɪnˈgeɪdʒ]　　　　　　　　　*vt.* 从事；使从事(某种事业等)
23. legendary [ˈledʒəndrɪ]　　　　　　　*adj.* 传说的；传奇的；极其著名的

Notes

1. Do not continue to play around with your co-workers, as your possible customer will take note of this.

翻译：不要与同事过度玩乐，你的潜在客户会看到这一幕。

注意：as 引导的是原因状语从句，解释不要玩乐的原因是客户会注意到你的行为。

2. Even though you spend a lot of time with your co-workers, they are not your family and do

not have to forgive your words as if they were.

翻译:尽管你会有很多时间与同事相处,但他们并非你的家人,并不能像表面所表现的那样原谅你说错的话。

注意:even though 引导让步状语从句,表示尽管有很长的时间与同事相处。后面的 as if 表示好像,表面上好像可以不计较,其实同事并不能像家人那样可以原谅你说错的话。

3. In the minds of customers, therefore, the validity and reliability of the Fiat is of high trust by the family users.

翻译:因此在客户的心目中,菲亚特轿车具有较高的合法性与可靠性,深受家庭用户的信赖。

注意:therefore 此时做插入语,连接的是上一句中的内容,也可放到句首 therefore, in the minds of customers…

4. BMW, short for the Bavarian Machinery Factory Co Ltd (BayerischeMotorenWerke in German), is a world famous automobile mobile and motorcycle manufacturer in Germany, with its headquartered in Munich.

翻译:BMW,全称为巴伐利亚机械制造厂股份公司(德文:Bayerische Motoren Werke AG),是德国一家世界知名的高档汽车和摩托车制造商,总部位于慕尼黑。

注意:short for the Bavarian Machinery Factory Co Ltd (BayerischeMotorenWerke in German)是个长短语的插入,完整形式为 which is short for the Bavarian Machinery Factory Co Ltd (BayerischeMotorenWerke in German)。

5. Mercedes Benz

梅赛德斯—奔驰(Mercedes-Benz)是世界著名的德国汽车品牌。1886 年 1 月,卡尔·奔驰发明了世界上第一辆三轮汽车,并获得专利(专利号:DRP 37435);与此同时,奔驰的另一位创始人戈特利布·戴姆勒也发明了世界上第一辆四轮汽车。从此,世界发生了改变。1926 年 6 月,戴姆勒公司与奔驰公司合并成立了戴姆勒—奔驰汽车公司,以梅赛德斯—奔驰命名的汽车正式出现,并从此以高质量、高性能的汽车产品闻名于世。除了高档豪华轿车外,奔驰公司还是世界上最著名的大客车和重型载重汽车的生产厂家。目前,梅赛德斯—奔驰为戴姆勒集团(Daimler AG)旗下公司,与宝马,奥迪并称"三驾马车"。

Exercises

1. Fill in the blanks with the proper form of the word given in the brackets.

1) The tire has a _____ (notice) decline in performance to geometry.

2) Works were _____ (lubricate) the gears of a car.

3) I am prepared to _____ (resize) the pattern of my house at.

4) Compared to hand-count, using computer _____ (handle) data is a lot easier.

5) A 12-year-old boy was admitted to graduate a bit _____ (abnormal).

6) His performance _____ (brisk) site of the atmosphere.

2. Translate the sentences into English by using the word or expression in the brackets.

1) 竹竿和地面成直角。(be normal to)

2) 如果你工作太累的话,你可能病倒。(collapse)

3) 这个手表充分说明汤姆在说谎。(cut sb. down to size)

4) 美国就台湾问题持保留态度。(with some discount)

5) 科学家们就人类起源一事进行了详细的研究。(make an investigation on sth)

3. Fill in the blanks with the following words or phrases.

| constantly | satisfy | professional | application | effectively |
| joint | subordinate | validity | legendary | respectable |

1) He maintained a _____ demeanour throughout.

2) We must _____ adapt and innovate to ensure success in a growing market.

3) His _____ to the court for bail has been refused.

4) He does not cope very _____ with this dilemma.

5) Some people are very hard to _____ .

6) It's not _____ to be drunk on the street.

7) _____ stories are passed down from parents to children.

8) We wrote a letter in _____ names.

9) Order the _____ troops to act immediately!

10) I would question the _____ of that assumption.

4. Translate the following sentences into English.

1) 除了与客户高频度的沟通,一个卖车的人用在工作中的时间要多于待在家中的。

2) 由于你长时间与同事相处,你们之间很可能建立了良好的关系并找到了一些可以打发时间的方式。

3) 销售部门和客服部门很少能了解彼此的想法。

4) 日产公司生产的轿车品牌很多。

5. Translate the following sentences into Chinese.

1) Many of the elders prefer to be on a first-name basis with only friends.

2) Do not convey your attitude and emotions to guests or the people with whom you work.

3) Someone will end up having to do the work, and it is appreciated when the salesperson takes the time to do her job effectively.

4) Toyota Automobile Co gradually has replaced GM as the world's first ranking car manufacturers since the beginning of 2008.

5) It only takes 18 years from the establishment of the factory to develop models on its own.

Practical Reading

Cheurolet Camaro

Schafer—Bumblebee

Good looks-they run in the family

The design changes give the Camaro a more contemporary look. The front fascia has a wider lower grille and a narrower upper grille, while the functional hood event helps reduce heat and aerodynamic lift. [1] At the rear, a sculptural decklid horizontal lamps, and diffuser complete the facelift

Convertible—the sky's been waiting for you

It takes less than 20 seconds for the roof to automatically retract and stow neatly away. 20 seconds to transform the Camaro into an exhilarating sensory experience. [2]

Top up or top down, the Camaro Convertible looks beautiful in either guise. Our designers purposely developed a stow-away top to mimic the muscular shape of the standard Coupé roofline.

Camaro's handling is out of this world. The independent rear suspension and variable-ratio power steering lead to a thrilling ride.

Chevrolet MyLink Technology

Chevrolet MyLink1 technology is standard on all Camaro models. This high-tech infotainment system allows you to play multimedia files on USB, your smart-phone or through Bluetooth streaming. [3]

Chevrolet MyLink also features a standard rear-view parking camera - great for parking in a tight spot - while a voice recognition system means you can make and receive calls safely on the go.

Word List

1. contemporary [kən'temp(ə)r(ə)rɪ]　　adj. 现代的;当代的;当时的;同时代的
2. grille [grɪl]　　n. 网格;(窗,门等前面的)网格状护栏;烤架;烧烤店
3. aerodynamic [ˌeərəʊdaɪ'næmɪk]　　adj. 空气动力学的
4. sculptural ['skʌlptʃərəl]　　adj. 雕刻[塑]的
5. roof [ruːf]　　n. 屋顶;车顶;顶部;有…顶的
6. sensory ['sensərɪ]　　adj. 感觉的;感官的

7. guise [gaɪz]　　　　　　　　　　　　*n.* 伪装;姿态;外衣;名义
8. muscular ['mʌskjulə(r)]　　　　　　*adj.* 肌肉的;强壮的;肌肉发达的
9. independent [ˌɪndɪ'pendənt]　　　　*adj.* 独立的;自主的;自治的;不相干的人所做的(或提供的)
10. infotainment [ˌɪnfəʊ'teɪnmənt]　　*n.* 资讯娱乐节目
11. features ['fiːtʃə(r)]　　　　　　　*n.* 特点;特色;五官;容貌
12. recognition [ˌrekəg'nɪʃ(ə)n]　　　*n.* 识别;认识;承认;认可

Notes

1. The front fascia has a wider lower grille and a narrower upper grille, while the functional hood vent helps reduce heat and aerodynamic lift.

翻译:前饰板有一个更宽的下部格栅和一个较窄的上层格栅,而功能通风口有助于减少热量和空气动力升降。

2. It takes less than 20 seconds for the roof to automatically retract and stow neatly away. 20 seconds to transform the Camaro into an exhilarating sensory experience.

翻译:车顶需要不到20s的时间自动缩回并整齐地收起。大黄蜂将这20s转变成令人振奋的感官体验。

3. Chevrolet MyLink1 technology is standard on all Camaro models. This high-tech infotainment system allows you to play multimedia files on USB, your smart-phone or through Bluetooth streaming.

翻译:雪佛兰MyLink1技术是所有Camaro车型的标配。这种高科技信息娱乐系统允许您通过USB、智能手机或蓝牙播放多媒体文件。

学习资源:
相关链接及网址
1. http://www.zj.xinhuanet.com
2. http://auto.qianlong.com
3. http://shifan.hnjtzy.com.cn/gj/qcwf/moive/index.asp

推荐书目
1. 赵俊英. 现代英语语法[M]. 北京:商务印书馆国际有限公司,2016.
2. 傅冬勇. 汽车销售礼仪与实务[M]. 杭州:浙江工商大学出版社,2014.
3. 石虹. 汽车销售礼仪[M]. 2版. 北京:北京理工大学出版社,2013.
4. 刘军. 汽车销售与售后服务全案[M]. 北京:化学工业出版社,2016.

任务十五 汽车产品售后服务

学习目标

1. 掌握汽车售后服务相关的专业术语、词汇。
2. 掌握售后服务过程中客户抱怨及投诉的关键环节及诉求的应答重点。
3. 能读懂汽车新产品相关的售后服务说明书。

以奥迪 Audi A6LL 为例,通过完成该任务,掌握汽车产品售后服务是如何进行的,并能就各类情形进行合理处理。

本学习任务沿着以下脉络进行学习:

通读全文 → 学习单词和语法 → 完成课后练习 → 分组对话 → 课后阅读练习

Task 15　Automotive Product After-sales Service

Accepting Complaints

Manager: Hello, This is Sales Department, Audi Automobile Company.

Customer: I'm afraid I have to make a complaint with your corporation. It's a most unpleasant incident.

Manager: Oh, what is it about? I'm so sorry to hear that.

Customer: Yes, I bought an Audi A6LLL saloon car one month ago. [1] It worked excellently all the while, but I found that there must be something wrong with the engine of late because it has noise continuously. That's why I want to see the manager.

Manager: I am sure everything is all right during the production. You see I know you're our regular customer and it is the first time for me to meet with such an inconvenient thing.

Customer: I want to claim for compensation. [2]

Manager: Don't worry. If we were at fault, we should be very glad to compensate for your loss.

Manager: I'm terribly sorry about that. May I know your name and address, sir? I'll check it and send a repairman to your side at once.

Customer: This is Edward Johnson, from No. 120, Rose Avenue.

On-site Maintenance and Repair

Customer: You've finally arrived.

Repairman: What's the matter?

Customer: I think something must be wrong with the engine because it has noise continuously.

Repairman: Oh, the piston frayed excessively.

Repairman: We're so sorry to have caused you so much inconvenience and we have to replace it. Let me have a look at your warranty certificate? [3]

Customer: Here it is.

Repairman: Well, your warranty period is expired. We have to charge for the parts.

Customer: That's all right, We're dying for the normal work condition at any expense. [4]

Repairman: we carry your car through into our company now. We will inform you after the repair is accomplished.

Customer: I appreciate your coming here in time.

Repairman: If anything is wrong with your car for the future, don't hesitate to call us a moment and we're at your service.

Customer: Thank you.

Repairman: My pleasure.

User Feedback

Salesman: Hello, This is Audi Automobile Company. I'm calling to know whether everything has gone well with your car.

Customer: Thanks a lot. It works excellently after being repaired.

Salesman: I'm very happy to hear you say so and I do hope the problem didn't cause you much inconvenience.

Customer: Thank you very much for your good service. I'm sure your company will be making more money.

Salesman: It is always our policy to give reliable and satisfactory services to our clients.[5] Let's find out what you like by doing a market research and it will give us an indication. Meanwhile, we will do some adapting based on research.

Customer: I recommend interior's color should be diverse so as to match with different people's demands.[6]

Salesman: It's a good suggestion, I'll report to the manager! Thank you for your warm-hearted reply. I feel more optimistic and more confident about our relations in the future.

Customer: It's just my own opinion, I'd like you to think it over.

Salesman: We'll go into it further, and let you know what decision we reach.

Customer: I shall be glad to hear from you.

Salesman: Thank you, bye-bye!

Customer: See you later.

Word List

1. complaint [kəm'pleɪnt] n. 抱怨，诉苦；投诉，控告；疾病
2. corporation [ˌkɔːpə'reɪʃən] n. 公司
3. incident ['ɪnsɪdənt] n. 发生的事，小插曲；敌对行动，军事冲突；骚乱，事故，暴力事件
4. continuously [kən'tɪnjuəslɪ] adv. 不断地，连续地
5. inconvenient [ˌɪnkən'viːnɪənt] adj. 不方便的，打扰人的，造成麻烦的，让人不舒服的
6. compensation [ˌkɔmpen'seɪʃən] n. 补偿（赔偿）物，补偿（赔偿）金
7. terribly ['terəblɪ] adv. 可怕地，恐怖地；令人震惊地，极其令人讨厌地；剧烈地，严酷地，严重地；（非正）很糟地；极差地
8. continuous [kən'tɪnjuəs] adj. 连续的，没有中断的
9. piston ['pɪstən] n. （机）活塞
10. excess ['ekses] adj. 超重的，过量的，额外的；n. 超过，过多之量，过度，过分
11. cause [kɔːz] n. 原因，起因，缘故，理由，事业，原则，目标；vt. 成为……的原因，导致；引起，促使，使发生
12. replace [rɪ(ː)'pleɪs] vt. 取代，代替；更换，替换；把……放回原位
13. warrant ['wɔrənt] n. 授权证，许可证；

	vt. 使……显得合理,成为……的根据,保证,担保
14. certificate [sə'tɪfɪkət]	n. 证明书,执照
15. expire [ɪk'spaɪə]	vi. 期满,(期限)终止;断气,死亡
16. normal ['nɔːməl]	adj. 正常的,平常的;正规的,标准的
17. expense [ɪk'spens]	n. 消耗,花费;花费的钱,费用
18. excellent ['eksələnt]	adj. 优秀的,卓越的,杰出的
19. reliable [rɪ'laɪəbl]	adj. 可靠的,可信赖的
20. meanwhile ['miːnˈwaɪl]	adv. 同时,其间; n. 其时,其间
21. adapt [ə'dæpt]	vt./vi. (使)适应,(使)适合; vt. 改编,改写
22. recommend [ˌrekə'mend]	vt. 推荐,介绍,赞许某人(某事物);劝告,建议;(特质等)使……显得可取
23. diverse [daɪ'vɜːs]	adj. 不同的;多种多样的
24. optimistic [ˌɔptɪ'mɪstɪk]	adj. 乐观的,乐观主义的
25. confident ['kɔnfɪdənt]	adj. 确信的,肯定的;有信心的,自信的

Proper Names

1. Sales Department 销售部
2. manager 经理
3. regular customer 老客户
4. client = customer 顾客
5. repairman 维修人员
6. warranty period 保修期

Useful Expressions

1. it is the first time (for me) to… 第一次……
2. carry…though into… 把……带到……
3. so as to… 以至于……
4. meet with… 碰巧遇上

Key Vocabulary

1. Complaint
   n. 抱怨.投诉

I'm afraid I have a complaint to make. 我要投诉。

2. corporation

n. 公司

unpleasant *adj.* 不高兴的

unsatisfactory *adj.* 不满意的

inconvenient *adj.* 不方便的

3. sure

adj. 无疑的，确信的，有把握的

adv. 的确，当然确信

to be sure 诚然；固然

To be sure, he's rather young for such an important position. 诚然，他担任这样重要的职务还嫌年轻一些。

make sure ＝be convinced, feel sure 确信；有把握

I made sure you would come today. 我相信你今天一定会来的。

as sure as 如……般千真万确；万无一失

as sure as night follows day 正如白天过去后，黑夜必然来临一样

4. fault

n. 缺点，缺陷；故障；过失，过错

at fault＝wrong, mistaken 出毛病；有故障；错了

find fault 找碴儿；挑剔；故意挑毛病

He is always finding fault. 他老是挑毛病。

5. wrong

adj. 不该的；不对的

It would be wrong of them to take it. 他们如果拿了这个东西，那是不应该的。

Your answer is wrong. 你答错了。

get sth. wrong 搞错（指算错、理解错、误解等）

go wrong 走错路；走入歧途；失败

6. cause

v. 引起；促使；给……带来

cause trouble to sb. 给某人带来麻烦

n. 原因；起因

What's was the cause of it? 这件事的起因是什么？

complain without a(any) cause 无理取闹

7. appreciate

v. 感激

appreciate sb.'s doing sth 因做……而表示感激

We shall appreciate your giving this matter your serious consideration. 请你方对此事认真考虑为感。

appreciate works of art 欣赏艺术作品

We shall appreciate it if you will send us a brochure and sample book by air immediately. 如能立即航寄一份说明书和一份样本,不胜感激。

be well/highly/greatly appreciated 受到高度赞赏

8. in time

及时;迟早;总有一天

ahead of time 提前

all the time 一直;始终

at a time 每次;一次

at all times 随时;总是

at no time 从不;决不

at one time 曾经;一度

at the same time ①同时②然而;不过

at times 有时;间或

behind the times 过时的;落后的

behind time 晚点的

for the time being 眼下;暂时

from time to time 有时;不时

in no time 立即;马上

in time of 当……的时候

kill time 消磨时光

of the time 现代的;当代的

have a difficult/hard time in doing sth. 做某事有困难

have a good time 过得很好;过得很愉快

in good time 及时地;早早地

in time ①及时②迟早;总有一天

in time to come 将来;在未来

It is (high) time to do sth./that… 到了做……的时候了 (接 that 从句时,从句中谓语动词要用虚拟式,形式为动词的过去式)

keep good (bad) time (钟表等)走得准(不准)

lose no time in doing sth. 立即做某事;刻不容缓地做……

many a time 多次;时常地;屡次

nine times out of ten 十有八九;几乎总是

on time 准时

once upon a time 从前

serve one's time ①服役;②服刑

some other time 改天;改时间

time after/time and again 屡次;一再

take one's time 慢慢来;不着急;不慌忙

9. call

v. 喊;叫;打电话

What is this thing called? 这个东西叫什么?

call for 要求;需要;拿取

He will call for it later. 他以后要来取的。

call at 访问;(车/船)停靠

I shall call at his house later. 我过些时候到他家去看他。

call on 访问;拜访;呼吁

call out(for) 大声叫唤

He called out for help. 他大声呼救。

call off 取消(活动.安排等);停止做……

call up 打电话给某人;召集.动员;使回忆起

10. whether

conj. 是否(经常用 if 代替)

I don't know whether(if)it's right. 我不知道对不对。

whether or no = in either case 不管怎样;无论如何

Well,I'll come,whether or no. 好吧,不管怎样,我会来的。

11. match

n. 比赛, 竞赛;相似之物, 相配之物;婚姻;婚姻对象

vt. 使较量, 使比赛

vt. /*vi.* (使)相配;(使)相称

be a(more than a,no)match for sb 是某人的对手(比某人强或优秀,比不上某人)

find/meet one's match 棋逢对手;遇到了应付不了的难题

match sb. in 在……方面比得上某人

match sth. with 使……和……相配(相称)

match up to 符合……的期望或预想;比得上……

match(nicely/perfectly)with 与……(十分)相配;(完全)比得上……

12. report

v. 报告

report to sb. 向某人报告

It is reported that… 据报道……

make a report on 作有关……的报道或报告

report on 就……作报道

13. optimistic

adj. 乐观的;乐观主义的

pessimistic 悲观的;厌世的

14. confident

adj. 确信的,自信的

be confident of 确信;对…满怀信心

I am confident of what he has said. 我相信他所说的话。

be confident with sb. 对某人表示信任

15. think over

把……仔细考虑

think about 就……思考

think better of sb. 对某人印象好

think better of(doing)sth. 决定不做某事

think ill/badly/poorly of 对……评价不高

think of 考虑……

think out 想出……;研究出……

16. hear from

收到…来信或电话

hear about/of 听说有关……

make oneself heard 把自己的意思说清楚

Notes on the Text

1. Yes, I bought an Audi A6LL saloon car one month ago.

翻译:是啊,一个月前我买了一辆奥迪 A6L 轿车。

重点:saloon car,指较为豪华的轿车。

2. I want to claim for compensation.

翻译:我要求索赔。

重点:compensation 补偿、赔偿。claim for compensation 要求赔偿。这是消费者购买了劣质产品后要求商家赔偿的惯常说法。

3. Let me have a look at your warranty certificate?

翻译:能让我看看你的保修单吗?

重点:warranty certificate 保修单,是顾客要求生产厂商对汽车进行质量维修的凭证,通常会说明保修的期限(时间或里程)。

4. We're dying for the normal work condition at any expense.

翻译:只要能让它尽快恢复正常工作,花多少钱都行。

重点:die for,在这里是"急需,迫切想要…"的意思。

I'm really dying for a drink. 我真想喝点什么。

另外还有"为…而献身"的意思。

Christians believed that Christ died for them. 基督徒们相信基督是为他们而献身的。

5. It is always our policy to give reliable and satisfactory services to our clients.

翻译:为客户提供可靠和满意的服务是我们一贯的宗旨。

重点:注意翻译时的倒装,这样符合中文的语言习惯。

6. I recommend interior's color should be diverse so as to match with different people's demands.

翻译:我建议内饰的颜色应该多样化一些来满足人们不同的需求。

重点:interior 内饰。Tab. 15-1 列出了汽车上常用的英语名词。

汽车上常用的英语名词　　　　　　　　　　　　　　　　　Tab. 15-1

Automotive Interior(汽车内饰)	Automobile External parts(汽车外设)
back seat, rear seat 后座	front wheel 前轮
driver's seat, driving seat 驾驶席	rear wheel 后轮
passenger seat 旅客席	rear window 后风窗玻璃
steering wheel, wheel 转向盘	windscreen 风窗玻璃
horn, hooter 喇叭	windscreen wiper 刮水器
choke 熄火装置	fender, wing, mudguard 挡泥板
gear stick, gear change 变速杆	radiator grille 散热器
starter, self-starter 起动器,起动按钮	wing mirror 后视镜
brake pedal 制动踏板	bonnet 发动机罩盖
clutch pedal 离合器踏板	roof rack, luggage rack 行李架
hand brake 驻车制动器	license plate, number plate 车号牌
foot brake 行车制动器	wing 前翼子板
dashboard 仪表板	hubcap 轮毂罩
milometer 里程表	bumper 保险杠
speedometer, clock 速度表	front blinker 前信号灯
	taillight, tail lamp 尾灯
	backup light, reversing light 倒车灯
	stoplight, stop lamp 制动灯

Continue

Automotive Interior(汽车内饰)	Automobile External parts(汽车外设)
	rear blinker 转弯指示灯
	bumper 保险杠
	tailpipe 排气管
	spare wheel 备胎,备用轮胎

Exercises

1. Fill in the blanks with the right word or words.

1) This automobile detect line is still _____ the experimental stage.
   A. in　　　　　B. of　　　　　C. on　　　　　D. about

2) I want to talk _____ with you.
   A. things important　　　　　B. anything important
   C. important thing　　　　　D. something important

3) We want to _____ an order with you about the machine tools.
   A. give　　　　　B. connect　　　　　C. place　　　　　D. occupy

4) Our orders are good _____ 3 days.
   A. in　　　　　B. for　　　　　C. within　　　　　D. among

5) All the prices in the lists are subject _____ our confirmation.
   A. on　　　　　B. in　　　　　C. at　　　　　D. to

6) If we were _____ fault, we should be very glad to compensate for your loss.
   A. about　　　　　B. at　　　　　C. in　　　　　D. of

7) I'm afraid I have got a complaint _____ the quality.
   A. with　　　　　B. to　　　　　C. on　　　　　D. about

8) We're dying for the normal work condition _____ any expense.
   A. for　　　　　B. with　　　　　C. at　　　　　D. in

9) We have to charge _____ the parts because your warranty is out of date.
   A. on　　　　　B. with　　　　　C. about　　　　　D. for

10) I shall be glad to hear _____ you.
    A. of　　　　　B. from　　　　　C. about　　　　　D. to

2. Translate the following into English.

1) 很高兴见到您,您对我们的产品感兴趣吗?
2) 凡在本月底之前购买我们产品的顾客,均可享受到8折优惠。
3) 这个新产品必须轻拿轻放,以防破碎。
4) 如果责任在我方,我们当然乐意赔偿你方损失。

5）对于对您造成的损失我方深表歉意。

6）我们向您保证随时提供最佳服务。

7）请在这张表格上写上你的姓名、住址和电话号码。

8）我对我们未来的关系更加乐观和充满信心。

3. Practice

教师随意选择两位学生,用英语开展售后服务情景对话练习。

After-sale Service Warranty within and after Guarantee Period

Basic requirements of our after-sale service

（1）If any quality problems such as design, manufacture, function or procedure occur within the guarantee period, SCCW shall take full responsibility and bear all the economic losses incurred.[1]

（2）If any quality problems occur with in the guarantee period, SCCW shall provide on-site service after receiving the buyer's notice in 24 hrs.

（3）If any big quality problems occur out of the guarantee period, SCCW will send maintenance technician to provide visiting service after receive the buyer's notice in 24 hrs and charge for a favorable price.[2]

（4）SCCW will provide a lifetime favorable price to the buyer with the materials and spare parts used in system operation, equipment maintenance.[3]

The above mentioned are only basic after-sale service requirements, we will make more promises related to quality assurance and operation guarantee mechanism.

After-sale service commitment

Quality and service commitment：

1）After-sale service department

SCCW will set up an after-sale service department and spare parts center specified for Valin ArcelorMittal Automotive Steel Co., Ltd Crane in Main Factory Building of Cold Rolling Project and provide professional equipment maintenance engineers.

2）Payment of maintenance expense

All the maintenance expense within the guarantee period shall be borne by SCCW.

3）After-sale service measures within the guarantee period

The after-sale service work is an important part of our marketing and sales work. The quality of service provided will not only influence the company credit but also closely related to the safe running of the equipments. In order to maintain the good reputation of Hercules, SCCW will strictly observe relevant national regulations about Product-Quality Law and provide-high quality products with the principle of hospitable reception, enthusiastic service, quick response, and prompt resolution. We will conscientiously implement the after-sale service work in full-scale, and make the commitment to our clients as follows:

(1) Select and appoint engineering technicians and workers who are professionally competent and personally committed to undertake the after-sale service work. Meanwhile set up the service office made up of chief engineer office, project office, technical center, after-sale service department, and workshop specialists led and coordinated by me marketing and sales department.[4]

(2) During the Valin ArcelorMittal Automotive Steel Co., Ltd Crane in Main Factory Building of Cold Rolling Project on-site installation and trial, appoint specialized after-sale service personnel to work at the workplace.

Word List

1. procedure [prə'sɪːdʒə(r)]   n. 步骤;手术;(商业、法律或政治上的)程序
2. guarantee [ˌgærən'tiː]   v. 保证;保障;担保;确保
3. responsibility [rɪˌspɒnsə'bɪləti]   n. 责任;职责;负责;义务
4. technician [tek'nɪʃ(ə)n]   n. 技术员;技师;(艺术、体育等的)技巧精湛者
5. assurance [ə'ʃʊərəns]   n. 保证;担保;自信;人寿保险
6. payment ['peɪmənt]   n. 支付;付款;款项;收款
7. influence ['ɪnfluəns]   n. 影响;作用;影响力;支配力
8. reputation [ˌrepjuː'teɪʃ(ə)n]   n. 名声;名誉
9. relevant ['reləv(ə)nt]   adj. 紧密相关的;切题的;有价值的;有意义的
10. principle ['prɪnsəp(ə)l]   n. 原理;原则;工作原理;法则
11. implement ['ɪmplɪmənt]   v. 实施;执行;贯彻;使生效
12. professionally [prə'feʃ(ə)nəli]   adv. 专业地;内行地;职业地
13. meanwhile ['miːnwaɪl]   adv. 与此同时;其间;(比较两方面)对比之下
14. coordinated [kəʊ'ɔː(r)dɪnət]   v. 调整;使成同等;使成同位;使配合
15. trial ['traɪəl]   v. 试验;试用;测试(能力、质量、性能等)

Notes

1. If any quality problems such as design, manufacture, function or procedure occur within

the guarantee period, SCCW shall take full responsibility and bear all the economic losses incurred.

翻译：如果在保质期内出现设计、制造、功能或程序等质量问题，SCCW 应承担全部责任，承担一切经济损失。

2. If any big quality problems occur out of the guarantee period, SCCW will send maintenance technician to provide visiting service after receive the buyer's notice in 24 hrs and charge for a favorable price.

翻译：如果在保修期内出现重大质量问题，SCCW 在收到买方通知后将派维修技师在 24 小时内提供来访服务，并收取优惠价格。

3. SCCW will provide a lifetime favorable price to the buyer with the materials and spare parts used in system operation, equipment maintenance.

翻译：SCCW 将为买方提供终身优惠的价格，包括用于系统操作、设备维护的材料和备件。

4. Meanwhile set up the service office made up of chief engineer office, project office, technical center, after-sale service department and workshop specialists led and coordinated by the marketing and sales department.

翻译：同时由市场营销部牵头协调设立由总工程师办公室、项目办公室、技术中心、售后服务部和车间专家组成的服务办公室。

学习资源：
相关链接及网址
1. http://www.audi.cn/audi/cn/zh2.html
2. http://www.betterlifecar.com
3. http://jxs.che168.com/3078

推荐书目
1. 王杰,王文村. 汽车与配件营销[M]. 北京：人民交通出版社股份有限公司,2017.
2. 刘晗兵,陈燕. 物流服务营销[M]. 北京：清华大学出版社,2017.
3. 裴保纯,王丁. 汽车营销百事通[M] 2 版. 北京：机械工业出版社. 2015.
4. Gary Armstrong,Philip Kotler,王永贵. 市场营销学[M]. 12 版. 北京：中国人民大学出版社,2017.
5. 张国方. 汽车营销学[M]. 2 版. 北京：人民交通出版社股份有限公司,2017.

任务十六
出国手续办理

1. 掌握出国手续办理所包含的相关专业术语、词汇。
2. 叙述出国手续办理流程中所需的资料。
3. 分析手续办理过程中的注意事项及重点。
4. 根据签证的规范要求完成户口簿及相关资料的翻译。

通过完成该任务，熟悉出国手续办理的相关事宜，掌握该任务所必须翻译的相关材料。

学习引导

本学习任务沿着以下脉络进行学习：

阅读材料→掌握单词及表达→相关语法→完成作业→实际训练→相关阅读

Task 16　Service Of Procedure For Going Abroad

invitation

　　Mr. Chen Huaxin

　　Bureau of Road Transport Management

　　Zhejiang Provincial Communication Department

Marseille, 2015-10-27

　　Dear Mr. Chen Huaxin,

　　VISIT OF CHINESE DELEGATION

　　With pleasure we've heard about your 7-days-stay during November/December 2015 in France and would like to welcome you at our school to inform you about (Tab. 16-1):[1]

　　—organisation and administration

　　—duties and functions

　　—content of the curriculum

　　—presentation of our driving school car pool

Essential Information of people Going Abroad　　Tab. 16-1

No.	Name	Birthday	Position
01			
…			

　　All the costs for the travel, health insurance, stay as well as expenses which may occur due to this visit will be borne by the Chinese side.[2]

　　Best regards

　　ACOURT(人名)

　　President

　　There are some forms which are necessary for you to go abroad (sample 1 to sample 9).

Sample 1：申请出国护照签证事项表

1.申办单位：		联系人：	电话：
2.审批情况	任务审批单位、文号、日期：		
	政审审批单位、文号、日期：		
3.出国团、组名称、人数及出国事由：			
今领到_____等_____人 前往_____国出境证明。 领取人： 年　　月　　日		今领到_____等人 _____本护照。 领取人： 年　　月　　日	
4.国外邀请人详细情况（内容请填中、外文，外文用印刷体书写）： (1)姓名：_____ (2)单位：_____ (3)地址（填到门牌号码）：_____			
(4)电话和传真号码：_____			
5.出国路线、日期及交通工具（国内填启程地点，国外填入、出境和过境口岸）			
6.注意事项	(1)此表系申办护照签证的主要依据，请务必填写详细准确，字迹清晰。 (2)本次出访人员如持有效因私护照和前往国家签证，或曾申请前往国签证被拒签的情况，请如实填写在备注栏内，以避免引起拒签等不良后果。		
7.备注			

8. 护照受理情况：　　　　　　　（本页由发照机关及签证代理部门填写）

接案人：	年　月　日	发照机关公章 及审核人签署：
制照人：	年　月　日	
发照人：	年　月　日	年　月　日

办案意见：

　　发给＿＿＿＿本普通、＿＿＿＿本公务、＿＿＿＿本外交共＿＿＿＿本护照

　　　　　　＿＿＿＿国＿＿＿＿人＿＿＿＿次入境停留＿＿＿＿天、＿＿＿＿次过境签证
　　申办：　＿＿＿＿国＿＿＿＿人＿＿＿＿次入境停留＿＿＿＿天、＿＿＿＿次过境签证
　　　　　　＿＿＿＿国＿＿＿＿人＿＿＿＿次入境停留＿＿＿＿天、＿＿＿＿次过境签证

备注：

　　　　　　　　　　　　　　　　　　　　　　　经办人：　　　年　月　日

9. 签证受理情况：

　　月　日受理＿＿＿＿国＿＿＿＿人＿＿＿＿次入境停留＿＿＿＿天、＿＿＿＿次过境
　　月　日受理＿＿＿＿国＿＿＿＿人＿＿＿＿次入境停留＿＿＿＿天、＿＿＿＿次过境
　　月　日受理＿＿＿＿国＿＿＿＿人＿＿＿＿次入境停留＿＿＿＿天、＿＿＿＿次过境

备注：

签证公函 审核人：	年　月　日	经办人：

10. 名单

姓名	汉语拼音	性别	出生年月日	出生地	工作单位	职务	发照机关、 日期、有效期	护照 号码

已面见申请人	
签名	

Sample 2: 中国公民出国(境)申请审批表

以下内容由申请人填写(请用正楷字及蓝黑色或黑色墨水水笔书写):

中文姓		中文名		别名		性别	□男□女	照片
拼音姓			拼音名			婚姻状况		
居民身份证号码						民族		
户口所在地		省　　市　　(县市区)			户口所属派出所			
出生地			政治面貌			文化程度		
现住址						联系电话		
本人系:□国家机关工作人员□金融保险系统工作人员□国有企事业单位工作人员□其他									
单位全称						单位电话		
单位地址						单位邮编		
职业			职务(级别)				职称	
申请事由		□定居□探亲□访友□商务□劳务□旅游□介绍就业□个人就业□自费留学						
		□国家公派留学□单位公派留学□奔丧□其他事由(　　　　)						
前往国家/地区					□首次申请□补证□正常换发□损坏换发□过期重领			
原护照号码:			有效期至:　　年　月　日			签发机关		
是否通过邮政特快专递方式送达护照?□是□否　　选择"是"请填写以下项目:								
投寄地址						收件人		
联系电话			邮政编码			是否加急		
国内外主要家庭成员	称谓	姓名		工作单位			职务	
	父亲							
	母亲							
	配偶							

Sample 3：护照

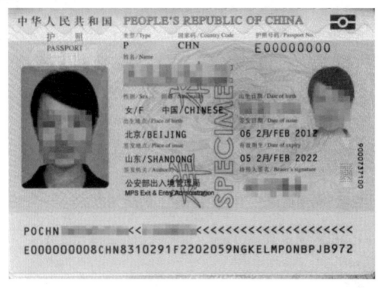

Sample 4:2015年英国签证用户口簿英文翻译

Household Register

Under Supervision of the Ministry of Public Security of P. R. C.

(1)Points for Attention:

Residence Booklet has legal effect to prove a citizen's identity status and mutual relations among family members, and is the main basis for residence registration authority to investigate and confirm his/her registered permanent residence. In so doing, the household owner or members of this household shall, of his/her own free will, show the booklet.

(2)The household owner shall well keep the booklet and is prohibited to modify, transfer or lend it. If loss arises, such shall be immediately reported to the residence registration authority.

(3)The registration right of the booklet belongs to residence registration authority, and any other organization or individual shall not make any record on it.

(4)If the members are increased or decreased, or registration items change in this household, the registration shall be declared to residence registration authority by holding the booklet.

(5) When the whole household moves out of residence jurisdictional area, the residence booklet shall be returned to residence registration authority for cancellation

Sample 5: Basic Information of Household

No. 11183996

Type of Household:	Non – agricultural family	Name of Householder:		
Household Number:		Current residential address:	No. xxx, 1 floor, Xinjiekou Avenue 34, Xicheng District	
Authorized supervisor:	Public Security Bureau of Beijing	Authorized Administrator:	Deshengmenwai Police Station	
Registrar:	Liu Xiaohua (sealed)	Date of Issue:	2013.8.9	

Register of Residence Change

New Address	Date of registration update	Registrar

Sample 6: Registration card for permanent residence（常住人口登记卡1）

NAME 姓名		RELATIONSHIP WITH HOUSEHOLDER 与户主关系		HOUSEHOLDER	
OTHER NAME 曾用名		SEX 性别		F	
PLACE OF BIRTH 出生地	Dongcheng District, Beijing	NATIONALILTY 民族		Han	
ANCESTRAL BIRTHPLACE 籍贯	Dongcheng District, Beijing	DATE OF BIRTH 出生日期			
OTHER ADDRESS WIHIN CITY 本市其他住址				RELIGION 宗教信仰	
No. OF ID CARD 身份证号		HEIGHT 身高	166	TYPE OF BLOOD 血型	O
EDUCATION 文化程度	University Degree	MARRIAGE 婚姻状况		Military Service Status	
COMPANY 服务处所	Beijing Department Store			OCCUPATION 职业	Workers
PREVIOUS ADDRESS 何时由何地迁来本址	2013.8.9　From No. x, Qianhaixi Street Xicheng District				

Updated item	Updated content	Date of Update	Registrar

Sample 7：Registration card for permanent residence（常住人口登记卡2）

NAME 姓名		RELATIONSHIP WITH HOUSEHOLDER 与户主关系	The husband	
OTHER NAME 曾用名		SEX 性别	M	
PLACE OF BIRTH 出生地	Tongxian, Beijing	NATIONALILTY 民族	Han	
ANCESTRAL BIRTHPLACE 籍贯	Tongxian, Beijing	DATE OF BIRTH 出生日期		
OTHER ADDRESS WIHIN CITY 本市其他住址		RELIGION 宗教信仰		
No. OF ID CARD 身份证号		HEIGHT 身高	175	TYPE OF BLOOD 血型	O
EDUCATION 文化程度	University Degree	MARRIAGE 婚姻状况		Military Service Status	
COMPANY 服务处所	Beijing Construction Company		OCCUPATION 职业	Cadres
PREVIOUS ADDRESS 何时由何地迁来本址	2013.8.9 From No. x, Qianhaixi Street Xicheng District			

Updated item	Updated content	Date of Update	Registrar

Sample 8：Registration card for permanent residence（常住人口登记卡 3）

NAME 姓名		RELATIONSHIP WITH HOUSEHOLDER 与户主关系		The daughter
OTHER NAME 曾用名		SEX 性别		F
PLACE OF BIRTH 出生地	Xicheng District, Beijing	NATIONALILTY 民族	Han	
ANCESTRAL BIRTHPLACE 籍贯	Tongxian, Beijing	DATE OF BIRTH 出生日期		
OTHER ADDRESS WIHIN CITY 本市其他住址		RELIGION 宗教信仰		
No. OF ID CARD 身份证号		HEIGHT 身高	TYPE OF BLOOD 血型	O
EDUCATION 文化程度	Primary School	MARRIAGE 婚姻状况	Military Service Status	
COMPANY 服务处所		OCCUPATION 职业		Student
PREVIOUS ADDRESS 何时由何地迁来本址	2013.8.9 From No. x, Qianhaixi Street Xicheng District			

Updated item	Updated content	Date of Update	Registrar

Sample 9：因公临时出国人员备案表

姓名		性别		出生年月		19XX 年 月 日	政治面貌	
工作单位及职务、是否为涉密人员及涉密等级							健康状况	健康
家庭主要成员情况	称谓	姓名		年龄	政治面貌	工作单位、职务及居住地（是否取得外国国籍、境外长期或永久居留权）		
	父亲							
	母亲							
	丈夫							
	儿子							
组团单位						在团组中拟任职务		
出访任务、所赴地区及停留时间								
出访任务审批单位								
最后一次因公赴港澳时间及任务								
人员派出单位意见	1.该人员是否存在一般不得批准出国（境）执行公务的情形之一？ ☑否　□是（具体情形：　　　　　　　　　　） 2.该人员是否存在不得批准出国（境）执行公务的情形之一？ ☑否　□是（具体情形：　　　　　　　　　　） 3.该人员配偶、子女是否已经出国（境）或与其同一时期出国（境）？ ☑否　□是（具体情况：　　　　　　　　　　） 负责人签字：　　　　　　　　　　　　　　单位盖章 　　年　月　日　　　　　　　　　　　　　年　月　日								
说明	本表一式三份。由因公临时赴港澳人员所在单位填写，按照干部管理权限，一份报送组织人事部门备案，一份抄报外事（港澳事务）审批部门，一份存所在单位。								

Word List

1. invitation [ˌɪnvɪˈteɪʃən] n. 邀请；请柬，请帖
2. bureau [ˈbjuərəu] n. 局，办事处，分社
3. management [ˈmænɪdʒmənt] n. (企业等的)管理，经营；管理人员，管理部门；资方；与人交往的技巧，手腕
4. province [ˈprɒvɪns] n. 省份，大行政区；范围，职责，领域
5. communication [kəˌmjuːnɪˈkeɪʃən] n. 交流，交际，通信；信息，消息；通信工具，交通联系
6. department [dɪˈpɑːtmənt] n. 部，部门，系
7. pleasure [ˈpleʒə] n. 愉快，快乐，满足；娱乐，消遣；愿望，意愿
8. inform [ɪnˈfɔːm] vt. 告诉，通知；vi. 检举，告密
9. organization [ˌɔːgənaɪˈzeɪʃən] n. (主英)组织，机构，团体
10. administration [ədˌmɪnɪsˈtreɪʃən] n. 实行，执行；管理，经营，支配；政府，内阁
11. curriculum [kəˈrɪkjuləm] n. 总课程
12. function [ˈfʌŋkʃən] n. 功能；作用；职责函数；与另一事物有密切关系的事物；vi. 工作，运行，起作用
13. expense [ɪkˈspens] n. 消耗，花费；花费的钱，费用
14. expiry [ɪkˈspaɪərɪ] n. 终止；满期，届期
15. issue [ˈɪʃuː; ˈɪsjuː] n. 问题，议题，争论点，发行物放出，流出；发出，发行；vt. 出版，发行，发表，发布，分配，发给；vi. 冒出，流出，传出
16. security [sɪˈkjuərɪtɪ] n. 安全；抵押品；有价证券
17. certify [ˈsɜːtɪfaɪ] vt. 证明，证实；发证书给……
18. identification [aɪˌdentɪfɪˈkeɪʃən] n. 鉴定，验明，认出；身份证明；认同
19. foundation [faunˈdeɪʃən] n. 建立，设立，创办；基础，根据；地基；基金(会)
20. investigate [ɪnˈvestɪgeɪt] vt. 调查；审查
21. voluntarily [ˈvɒləntərɪlɪ] adv. 自愿地，志愿地；义务地，无偿地
22. authorization [ˌɔːθəraɪˈzeɪʃən] n. 授权，认可
23. remove [rɪˈmuːv] vt. 移走，排除，开除；vi. 迁移；移居
24. military [ˈmɪlɪtərɪ] adj. 军事的，军用的，军人的；n. 军人，军队，武装力量

25. occupation [ˌɔkjuˈpeɪʃən]　　　　　　n. 工作；职业；消遣；占领

Proper Names

1. Passport　　　　　　　　护照
2. date of birth　　　　　　出生日期
3. Household Register　　　户口本
4. Foreign Affairs　　　　　外交部
5. householder　　　　　　户主
6. religious belief　　　　　民族信仰

Useful Expressions

1. would like to do　　　　想要……
2. due to　　　　　　　　由于；欠下债〔账〕，应给予
3. between…and…　　　　在……和……之间
4. belong to…　　　　　　属于

Key Vocabulary

1. invitation

n. 邀请；请柬，请帖

Thank you for your kind invitation. 谢谢你的盛情邀请。

The invitations are out. 请帖已发出。

2. communication

n. 交流，交际，通信；信息，消息；通信工具，交通联系

Telegraph communication was broken off. 电信中断了。

This communication is confidential. 这消息是机密的。

All communications with the north have been stopped by snowstorm. 北部的一切交通均为暴风雪所阻。

communication area 通信区

communication cable 通信电缆

communication centre 通信中心

3. inform

vt. 告诉，通知

Can you inform me when to begin our final examination? 你能告诉我们什么时候期终考试吗?

vi. 检举,告密

inform about 将……告知(某人)

inform against 告发;检举

inform of 将……告知(某人)

4. expense

n. 消耗,花费;花费的钱,费用

expense account 报销单

expense allowance 预算拨款

expense book 费用账簿

5. expiry

n. 终止;满期,届期

expiry date 有效期限;满期日;终止日期

expiry issue 迄期期次,最末供应的一期

6. issue

n. 问题,议题;争论点;发行物;放出,流出;发出,发行;〈正〉结果,结局

There was no issue at all between us. 我们之间毫无争议。

There is a new issue of Christmas stamps every year. 每年都出一套新的圣诞邮票。

I bought the book the day after its issue. 这书出版后的第一天,我就去买了它。

vt. 出版,发行;发表,发布;分配,发给

The government issues money and stamps. 政府发行货币及邮票。

We also issued agricultural loans. 我们还发放了农业贷款。

vi. 冒出,流出;传出

Strange sounds issued from the castle. 城堡传来怪异的声音。

7. certify

vt. 证明,证实;发证书给……

The bank certified my accounts. 银行核实了我的账目。

certify for 保证

Can you certify for his ability as a teacher? 你可以保证他能胜任老师的工作吗?

certify to 证明

I can certify to his good character. 我可以证明他品德好。

8. foundation

n. 建立,设立,创办;基础,基本原理,根据;地基;基金(会)

The foundation of the university took place 600 years ago. 这所大学是600年前创办的。

The foundation of democracy is the will of the people to preserve liberty. 民主的基础在于人

民维护自由的意志。

The foundations of the building settled. 这房屋的地基下陷了。

The Foundation gives money to help artists. 那家基金会捐款帮助艺术家。

foundation bed 基座,地基

foundation bolt 地脚(基础)螺栓

foundation plan 基础平面图

9. remove

vt. 移走；排除；开除

He removed the picture and put it in the drawer. 他把画取下来,放到抽屉里。

They removed him from his position. 他们撤销了他的职务。

vi. 迁移；移居

Our office has removed. 我们的机关迁移了。

remove from 从……中移开(拿走,除掉);将(某人)撤〔免〕职

He has removed from this town. 他已迁离此城。

They removed him from his position. 他们撤销了他的职务。

remove into 搬进(到)

We are going to remove into a new house. 我们将要搬到一座新房子里去。

remove to （把……）迁移到,搬到;把……调往

They have decided to remove to a warm climate. 他们已决定搬到一个气候温暖的地方居住。

Notes on the Text

1. With pleasure we've heard about your 7-day-stay during November/December 2015 in France and would like to welcome you at our school to inform you about.

翻译:听到你将于2015年11月12月期间在法国停留7天,我们很高兴。到时欢迎你来我们学校并告知如下内容。

重点:with pleasure 愉快地,高兴地;at one's pleasure 随你,听便;at pleasure 随你,听便;for pleasure 为了取乐,作为消遣;take (a)pleasure in 以…为乐;7-day-stay 停留7天,以短线连接的复合词,其中的名称不可用复数。例如:a 3-hour-meeting,三个小时的会议,a 2-month-vocation 2个月的假期;would like to 想要做 Would you like to sit down? She would like to borrow my bike. would rather (sooner)…than 宁愿,宁可……也不;would rather do sth. 倒更希望,更喜欢。

2. All the costs for the travel, health insurance, stay as well as expenses which may occur due to this visit will be borne by the Chinese side.

翻译:这次访问产生的所有费用,包括差旅费、医疗保险费用、住宿费以及可能会出现的其他费用都将由中方承担。

重点:as well as 不但……而且;和;和……一样;也。The target market for a product describes demographics as well as lifestyles and sometimes job roles. 产品的目标市场描述了人群统计和生活风格,有时也涉及职业角色。The behavior patterns you observe and communicate should describe your users' strengths as well as their weaknesses and blind spots. 观察和交流的行为模式不仅要描述用户的能力,还应当包括他们的弱点与空白。expenses which may occur 注意定语从句的用法。

Exercises

1. Fill in the blanks with the proper form of the word given in the brackets.

1) She _____ (manage) a clothes shop two years ago.

2) We shall _____ (inform) you of the date of the delegation's arrival.

3) He has a lot of _____ (administration) work to do.

4) The government is responsible for the _____ (Provincial) of education for all the children.

5) The inspiring call _____ (issue) by the President.

6) The general _____ (remove) the troop to the front.

2. Translate the sentences into English by using the word or expression in the bracket.

1) 他们想要星期天去湖边烧烤。(would like to do)

2) 由于驾驶员失误导致两名乘客死亡。(due to)

3) 汤姆在去和留之间徘徊着。(between…and…)

4) 作为一个作家,他的确属于18世纪。(belong to)

Practical Reading

Recognizing Important Facts or Details

In the previous unit, you were given practice in reading for the main idea. To understand the main idea thoroughly, however, you must recognize the important facts or details, which help develop or support it. These facts and details give you a deeper understanding of the main idea. They may prove a point, show a relationship between ideas, or serve as examples to help you understand the main idea more fully.

Here are some ways to help you recognize important facts or details:

(1) Read for the main idea. If you have identified the main idea. you can more easily recognize the important facts that Support it.

(2) Keep it in mind that not all facts or details ~/re equally important. Look only for the facts related to the main idea.

(3) To check on your understanding of the material you have read, review the facts or details which you have decided are the most important. Then consider if they support what you have identified as the main idea. If adding up the facts or details does not lead logically to the main idea, you have failed either to identify the main idea or to recognize the important supporting details.

Example:

Read the following passage carefully. The main idea of each paragraph is given below. Write two details from the paragraph that support the main idea.

INFORMATION ABOUT TAXI DRIVER'S LICENSE EXAMINATION

(1) To drive a taxi, or car for hire, the state law requires drivers to have a taxi driver's license. [1] To get this license, drivers must pass the Taxi Driver's License Examination. The attached booklet will help you prepare and study for the exam.

(2) You must file an exam application in person. Applications can be filed on Monday, Wednesday, and Friday from 9 A.M. to noon and on Tuesday and Thursday from 1 to 5 P.M. The fee is $25, payable in cash or by money order. Bring the following with you when you apply: your driver's license and birth certificate, passport, or other proof that you are legally able to work in the United States. [2]

(3) You will receive notification of the date and time of the exam in the mail. [3] To take the exam, bring the following items: your admission card, a pen, your driver's license, and proof that you are legally able to work in the United States (birth certificate, passport, or other papers).

Word List

1. attach [ə'tætʃ]   *adj.* 附上……的
2. booklet ['buklɪt]   *n.* 小册子
3. file [faɪl]   *n.* 文件,档案,锉刀; *vt.* 把……归档,锉,琢磨
4. fee [fiː]   *n.* 费(会费、学费等),酬金
5. certificate [sə'tɪfɪkɪt]   *n.* 证书,证明书; *vt.* 发给证明书,以证书形式授权给……

6. legal [ˈliːgəl]   adj. 法律的，合法的
7. admission [ədˈmɪʃən]   n. 允许进入，承认某事之陈述，供认
8. license [ˈlaɪsəns]   n. 许可（证），执照；vt. 许可，特许；v. 许可
9. notification [ˌnəutɪfɪˈkeɪʃən] n. 通知，布告，告示

Notes

1. To drive a taxi, or car for hire, the state law requires drivers to have a taxi driver's license.

翻译：要驾驶出租车或者出租用的车辆，州法律要求驾驶员应持有出租车驾驶执照。

2. Bring the following with you when you apply: your driver's license and birth certificate, passport, or other proof that you are legally able to work in the United States.

翻译：申请时需带上以下文件：驾驶执照、出生证明、护照或者其他证明你可以合法在美国工作的文件。

3. You will receive notification of the date and time of the exam in the mail.

翻译：你会收到通知考试日期和时间的邮件。

学习资源：
相关链接及网址
1. http://www.cise.ac.cn/
2. http://www.chinalabor.net/cn/index.asp
3. http://wjm.zj.gov.cn/main/index.shtml
4. http://jpkc.ynnubs.com

推荐书目
1. 中国质量认证中心. 国际市场准入与认证制度研究（中国电气及汽车产品出口指南）[M]. 北京：中国标准出版社，2006.
2. 汉迪森. 出国旅游英语900句[M]. 北京：清华大学出版社，2016.
3. 耿小辉. 365天英语口语大全：出国口语（白金版）[M]. 北京：中译出版社（原中国对外翻译出版公司），2016.
4. 俞涔，叶红玉. 进出口贸易操作实务[M]. 北京：中国人民大学出版社，2015.
5. 何其莘，杨孝明，杨孝端. 赴美实用英语手册：商务篇[M]. 北京：外语教学与研究出版社，2017.

部分练习题参考答案

一、任务一

1. 1）C   2）A   3）B
2. 1）内燃机　　　　　　2）车辆　　　　　　　3）做功行程
   4）排气门　　　　　　5）汽油　　　　　　　6）水冷式发动机
   7）飞轮　　　　　　　8）气冷式发动机　　　9）曲轴
3. 1）Four-stroke Engine　　2）intake stroke　　　3）exhaust stroke
   4）combustion chamber　　5）cylinder　　　　　6）piston
   7）air/fuel mixture　　　　8）spark plug　　　　9）connecting rod
4. 1）在内燃机里，可燃混合气被引入到封闭的汽缸内，并在汽缸里压缩和着火。
   2）四冲程发动机中的进气行程是在活塞到达上止点后开始的。
   3）当活塞到达下止点后，活塞重新向上运动，同时起动机继续以顺时针方向转动曲轴。
5.

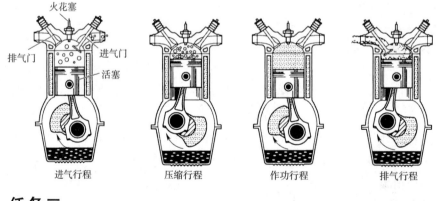

二、任务二

1. 1）B　　　　　　　　2）D　　　　　　　　3）C
   4）A　　　　　　　　5）C
2. 1）灰口铁　　　　　　2）正时齿轮　　　　　3）水泵
   4）油环　　　　　　　5）气门正时　　　　　6）曲柄
   7）平衡重　　　　　　8）扭转减振器　　　　9）风扇皮带轮

3. 1) engine block　　　　2) friction clutch assembly　　3) crankcase
   4) oil pan　　　　　　　5) piston clearance　　　　　　6) piston ring
   7) ignition distributor　 8) cam lobe　　　　　　　　　9) push rod

4. 1) 汽缸是汽缸体内部圆柱形空腔,并在活塞上下运动时起到导向作用。
   2) 还有许多零件是通过紧固件安装在汽缸体上。
   3) 无论什么原因引起的间隙过小,都将产生许多问题。

5.

三、任务三

1. 1) D　　　　　　　　　2) B　　　　　　　　　3) A
   4) B

2. 1) 电子燃油喷射　　　　2) 高压　　　　　　　　3) 空气流量计
   4) 电控单元　　　　　　5) 油箱　　　　　　　　6) 燃油经济性
   7) 压力调节器

3. 1) fuel system　　　　　2) fuel filter　　　　　　3) high-pressure pump
   4) fuel pressure sensor　5) pressure regulator　　6) injector
   7) Compression Ratio

4. 1) 燃油滤清器安装在油箱内,它是燃油泵总成的组成部分之一。
   2) 燃油轨中储存来自高压泵的燃油,高压燃油被应用于每个喷油器。
   3) 传感器信号为PCM提供一个模拟信号,当燃料轨压力发生变化时,它的电压会发生变化。

四、任务四

1. 1) B 2) C 3) C

2. 1) 冷却系统 2) 节温器 3) 散热器盖
   4) 散热器芯 5) 润滑系统 6) 曲轴箱通风
   7) 黏度指数改进剂 8) 漆膜 9) 油泥

3. 1) water pump 2) anti-freeze coolant 3) water-cooled engine
   4) lubricating system 5) lubricant 6) oxidation inhibitor
   7) engine deposit 8) oil filter 9) metal-to-metal contact

4. 1) 发动机内摩擦过大将意味着快速的损坏。
   2) 为减小锈蚀的生成,商用的防冻剂内含有防锈剂。

五、任务五

1. 1) C 2) A 3) D
   4) A

2. 1) 火花塞 2) 蓄电池 3) 分电器
   4) 电枢 5) 换向器 6) 点火系统
   7) 起动系统 8) 电刷 9) 励磁线圈

3. 1) ignition coil 2) primary winding 3) distributor cap
   4) starter solenoid 5) spark advance 6) ignition timing
   7) ignition distributor 8) starting motor 9) ignition switch

4. 1) 电容器的作用是减少断电器触点断开时的火花,进而延长触点的使用寿命。
   2) 分火头是可以旋转的导体,同时将高压电送到分电器盖内的旁电极。
   3) 电枢是起动机内部唯一的旋转件。

六、任务六

1. 1) A 2) C 3) B
   4) B 5) D

2. 1) 转向摇臂 2) 自动变速器 3) 行星齿轮系
   4) 底盘 5) 万向节 6) 转向系统
   7) 制动系统 8) 行车制动系统 9) 驻车制动系统

3. 1) power train 2) manual transmission 3) differential
   4) rear wheel drive 5) steering wheel 6) leaf spring
   7) brake shoe 8) suspension system 9) brake pedal

4. 1) 万向节用于将传动轴与变速器输出轴连接。

2) 货车转向系统有人力的,也有助力的。助力转向系统使用辅助单元,使用液压或气压装置来增加转向力。

3) 转向盘直径越大,同样转向力下产生更大的转向力矩。

5.

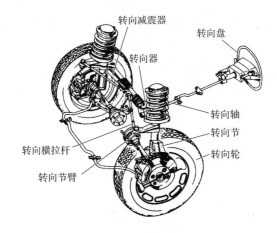

七、任务七

1. 1) B   2) D   3) A
   4) C

2. 1) 微型计算机   2) 技师   3) 车速表
   4) 主销后倾角   5) 车轮外倾角   6) 光密度计
   7) 燃油消耗   8) 泄漏检查器   9) 动力吸收单元

3. 1) diesel smoke meter   2) chassis dynamometer   3) engine test bed
   4) front wheel aligner   5) engine analyzer   6) side-slip tester
   7) fifth wheel sensor   8) single board computer   9) wheel dynamic balancer

4. 1) 这种吸收式红外分析仪可以检测汽车排气中碳氢(HC)和一氧化碳(CO)的排放量。
   2) 这种仪器用于检测汽车前轮的动力学部位。

5.

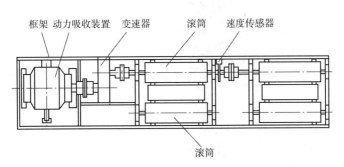

八、任务八

1. 1) 诊断法   2) 故障   3) 传感器

4)国内的   5)电压   6)点火

7)参数   8)示波器

2.1) electrical control system   2) air intake system   3) fuel system

4) Distributor ignition   5) flash memory   6) spark plug

3.1)点火、燃油喷射和电气控制系统的传感器波形,通过对传感器波形的分析,可以精确地诊断传感器故障。

2)高速五通道汽车专用示波器,具有参考波形的存储功能

4.1) China's first real-time display of real waveform automotive special oscilloscope。

2) The development of KT600's oscilloscope function has truly realized the real-time display of the secondary ignition waveform for the first time in China。

九、任务九

1.1) financed   2) have contracted   3) representative

4) demand   5) is proceeding   6) achievement

2.1) The teacher was sick, because he has been engaged in our final exams.

2) The launched of the shen zhou Ⅵ rocket accounted for great progress of China's aerospace industry.

3) He attributes his late to the traffic jam.

4) Shakespeare compares the world to a stage.

5) We dont like people such as him.

6) He is a good athlete as well as a lawyer.

3.1)(F)城市景观   (J)分类广告

2)(B)市民活动   (M)餐厅和酒吧

3)(E)社会观察   (L)商业指南

4)(D)本月热点新闻   (O)上海大舞台

5)(H)时尚   (C)本地旅游

十、任务十

1.1) C   2) B   3) D

4) A   5) C

2.1) The whole process of an export or import transaction generally covers four stages: preparation of import or export, business negotiation, implementing the contract, and settlement of disputes.

2) The implementation of the export contract includes: Preparing goods for shipment; Inspection application; Reminding, examining and modifying L/C; Chartering and booking shipping

space; Customs formalities; Insurance; Documents preparation for bank negotiation.

3) Customs formalities require completed forms giving particulars of the goods exported together with the copy of the contract of sale, invoice, packing list, weight memo, commodity inspection certificate and other relevant documents, all of which have to be submitted to the Customs.

3.答案：

1)信用证中规定的有关货物的详细情况、货物的价格和条件一定要包括在发票中,而发票中任何其他内容应和其他单证相符。

2)发票的货币种类应该与信用证中的规定相同。发票的金额应该与汇票的金额一致,并且不能超过信用证中已有的金额。

3)应该注意重量单或证书应为单独一份,不应和其他单证合并。其日期也应该和其他单证相符。

4)货物保险应该从装运港或接货点开始到目的港或交货地结束。

5)运输单证中的收货人名称应该和信用证中的有关规定相符。如果要求对运输单证背书,那么应该保证背书符合要求。

十一、任务十一

1. 1) C   2) D   3) A
   4) B   5) C

2. 1) produced   2) hesitation   3) attractive
   4) relatives   5) competition   6) disadvantages

3. 1) Next year a new style of cars will be produced.

   2) His part-time job is repairing autos for others.

   3) The features of the car are beautiful and that is the key reason why it is very popular among the young.

   4) I am looking forward to receiving your answer letter as soon as possible.

十二、任务十二

1. 1) A   2) D   3) C
   4) B   5) D

2. 1) introduction   2) information   3) appointment
   4) performance   5) avail   6) convenient

3. 1) We always work from morning to night.

   2) The question is whether to go or stay.

   3) The fall of oil price help to the development of our economy.

   4) These letters should provide with all the information we need.

5）When we went to Pairs, our sister was along with us.

十三、任务十三

1．1）B　　　　　　　　2）B　　　　　　　　3）D
　　4）A　　　　　　　　5）C
2．1）adopted　　　　　　2）representative　　　3）liable
　　4）convenience　　　　5）agencies　　　　　　6）efficient
3．1）Cars play a key role in the transportation system.
　　2）Health doesn't relate to wealth.
　　3）His injuries result from yesterday's accident.
　　4）The numbers of these vehicles add up to 1100.
　　5）Do you usually suffer from a headache

十四、任务十四

1．1）noticeable　　　　　2）lubricating　　　　　3）resize
　　4）to handle　　　　　5）abnormal　　　　　　6）was brisk
2．1）The bamboo pole is normal to the ground.
　　2）If you work too hard, you may collapse.
　　3）The watch cut Tom down to size.
　　4）In the light of Taiwan problem, the USA is still with some discount.
　　5）Scientists make an investigation in to the origin of humanity.
3．1）professional　　　　2）constantly　　　　　3）application
　　4）effectively　　　　　5）satisfy　　　　　　　6）respectable
　　7）Legendary　　　　　8）joint　　　　　　　　9）subordinate
　　10）validity
4．1）In addition to high customer interaction, a person who sells cars spends more time at his or her job than at home.
　　2）Because you spend so much time with co-workers, you most likely have established good friendships and have found things to do to pass the time.
　　3）The sales and service departments have a hard time seeing each others' points of view.
　　4）Products in Nissan vary a lot
5．1）大多数老年人只愿意让朋友称呼他们的名字。
　　2）不要将你的个人态度和情感转移到客户或你的工作伙伴身上。
　　3）一些人会在强制状况下完成工作，而当销售人员用心将工作做好时是值得赞扬的。
　　4）丰田汽车公司自2008始逐渐取代通用汽车公司而成为全世界排行第一位的汽车

生产厂商。

5）它从建立工厂到能够独立自主开发车型仅用了18年。

十五、任务十五

1. 1）C　　　　　　2）D　　　　　　3）C
   4）A　　　　　　5）D　　　　　　6）B
   7）D　　　　　　8）C　　　　　　9）B
   10）B

2. 1）I'am glad to see you, are you interested in our products?

   2）The customer buys our product prior to the end of the month can share an 80% discount.

   3）The new product must put down gently, so as not to break.

   4）If we were at fault, we should be very glad to compensate for your loss.

   5）I'm apologizing for your loss, which we bring.

   6）We promise that we will provide the best service with you at any time.

   7）Please write your name, address and phone number on the paper.

   8）I am more optimistic and confident about our future relationship.

十六、任务十六

1. 1）managed　　　　2）inform　　　　3）administrative
   4）province　　　　5）was issued　　6）removed

2. 1）They would like to barbecue on the lakeside.

   2）Two passengers died due to the driver's fault.

   3）Tom's still hesitating between leave and stay.

   4）As a writer, he really belongs to 18th century.

人民交通出版社汽车类高职教材部分书目

书　号	书　名	作　者	定价（元）	出版时间	课件
一、全国交通运输职业教育教学指导委员会规划教材　新能源汽车运用与维修专业					
978-7-114-14405-9	新能源汽车储能装置与管理系统	钱锦武	23.00	2018.02	有
978-7-114-14402-8	新能源汽车高压安全及防护	官海兵	19.00	2018.02	有
978-7-114-14499-8	新能源汽车电子电力辅助系统	李丕毅	15.00	2018.03	有
978-7-114-14490-5	新能源汽车驱动电机与控制技术	张利、缑庆伟	28.00	2018.03	有
978-7-114-14465-3	新能源汽车维护与检测诊断	夏令伟	28.00	2018.03	有
978-7-114-14442-4	纯电动汽车结构与检修	侯涛	30.00	2018.03	有
978-7-114-14487-5	混合动力汽车结构与检修	朱学军	26.00	2018.03	有
二、高职汽车检测与维修技术专业立体化教材					
978-7-114-14826-2	汽车文化	贾东明、梅丽鸽	39.00	2018.08	有
978-7-114-14744-9	汽车维修服务实务	杨朝、李洪亮	22.00	2018.07	有
978-7-114-14808-8	汽车检测技术	李军、黄志永	29.00	2018.07	有
978-7-114-14777-7	旧机动车鉴定与评估	吴丹、吴飞	33.00	2018.07	有
978-7-114-14792-0	汽车底盘故障诊断与修复	侯红宾、缑庆伟	43.00	2018.07	有
978-7-114-13154-7	汽车保险与理赔	吴冬梅	32.00	2018.05	有
978-7-114-13155-4	汽车维护技术	蔺宏良、黄晓鹏	33.00	2018.05	有
978-7-114-14731-9	汽车电气故障诊断与修复	张光磊、周羽皓	45.00	2018.07	有
978-7-114-14765-4	汽车发动机故障诊断与修复	赵宏、刘新宇	45.00	2018.07	有
三、交通运输职业教育教学指导委员会推荐教材、高等职业教育规划教材					
1. 汽车运用与维修技术专业					
978-7-114-11263-8	■汽车电工与电子基础（第三版）	任成尧	46.00	2017.06	有
978-7-114-11218-8	■汽车机械基础（第三版）	凤勇	46.00	2018.05	有
978-7-114-11495-3	汽车发动机构造与维修（第三版）	汤定国、左适够	39.00	2018.05	有
978-7-114-11245-4	■汽车底盘构造与维修（第三版）	周林福	59.00	2018.05	有
978-7-114-11422-9	■汽车电气设备构造与维修（第三版）	周建平	59.00	2018.05	有
978-7-114-11216-4	■汽车典型电控系统构造与维修（第三版）	解福泉	45.00	2016.1	有
978-7-114-11580-6	汽车运用基础（第三版）	杨宏进	28.00	2018.03	有
978-7-114-11239-3	■汽车实用英语（第二版）	马林才	38.00	2018.08	有
978-7-114-05790-3	汽车及配件营销	陈文华	33.00	2015.08	
978-7-114-05690-7	汽车车损与定损	程玉光	30.00	2013.06	
978-7-114-13916-1	汽车专业资料检索（第二版）	张琴友	32.00	2017.08	
978-7-114-11215-7	■汽车文化（第三版）	屠卫星	48.00	2016.09	有
978-7-114-11349-9	■汽车维修业务管理（第三版）	鲍贤俊	27.00	2016.12	有
978-7-114-11238-6	■汽车故障诊断技术（第三版）	崔选盟	30.00	2017.11	有
978-7-114-14078-5	汽车维修技术（第二版）	刘振楼	25.00	2017.08	有
978-7-114-14098-3	汽车检测诊断技术（第二版）	官海兵	27.00	2017.09	有
978-7-114-14077-8	汽车运行材料（第二版）	崔选盟	25.00	2017.09	有
978-7-114-05662-1	汽车检测设备与维修	杨益明	26.00	2018.05	
978-7-114-13496-8	汽车单片机及局域网技术（第二版）	方文	20.00	2018.05	
978-7-114-05655-9	汽车车身电气及附属电气设备维修	郭远辉	26.00	2013.08	
978-7-114-10520-3	汽车概论	巩航军	29.00	2016.12	有
978-7-114-10722-1	发动机原理与汽车理论（第三版）	张西振	29.00	2017.08	
978-7-114-10333-9	汽车维修企业管理（第三版）	沈树盛	36.00	2016.05	
978-7-114-13831-7	汽车空调构造与维修（第二版）	杨柳青	30.00	2017.08	
978-7-114-12421-1	汽车柴油机电控技术（第二版）	沈仲贤	26.00	2018.05	
978-7-114-11428-1	汽车使用与技术管理（第二版）	雷琼红	33.00	2016.01	
978-7-114-14091-4	汽车使用性能与检测技术（第二版）	巩航军	30.00	2017.09	
978-7-114-11729-9	汽车保险与理赔（第四版）	梁军	32.00	2018.02	有

书 号	书 名	作 者	定价（元）	出版时间	课件
978-7-114-14306-9	汽车装潢与美容技术（第二版）	全华科友	33.00	2018.05	有
2. 汽车营销与服务专业					
978-7-114-11217-1	■旧机动车鉴定与评估（第二版）	屠卫星	33.00	2018.05	有
978-7-114-14102-7	汽车保险与公估（第二版）	荆叶平	36.00	2017.09	有
978-7-114-08196-5	汽车备件管理	彭朝晖、倪红	22.00	2018.07	
978-7-114-11220-1	■汽车结构与拆装（第二版）	潘伟荣	59.00	2016.04	有
978-7-114-07952-8	汽车使用与维修	秦兴顺	40.00	2017.08	
978-7-114-08084-5	汽车维修服务	戚叔林、刘焰	23.00	2015.08	
978-7-114-11247-8	■汽车营销（第二版）	叶志斌	35.00	2018.03	有
978-7-114-11741-1	汽车使用与维护	王福忠	38.00	2018.05	有
978-7-114-14028-0	汽车保险与理赔（第二版）	陈文均、刘资媛	22.00	2017.08	有
978-7-114-14869-9	汽车维修服务接待（第2版）	王彦峰、杨柳青	28.00	2018.08	有
978-7-114-14015-0	客户沟通技巧与投诉处理（第二版）	韦峰、罗双	24.00	2017.09	有
978-7-114-13667-2	服务礼仪（第二版）	刘建伟	24.00	2017.05	有
978-7-114-14438-7	汽车电子商务（第三版）	张露	29.00	2018.02	有
978-7-114-07593-3	汽车租赁	张一兵	26.00	2016.06	
3. 汽车车身维修技术专业					
978-7-114-11377-2	■汽车材料（第二版）	周燕	40.00	2016.04	有
978-7-114-12544-7	汽车钣金工艺	郭建明	22.00	2015.11	有
978-7-114-12311-5	汽车涂装技术（第二版）	陈纪民、李扬	33.00	2016.11	有
978-7-114-09094-3	汽车车身测量与校正	郭建明、李占峰	22.00	2018.05	有
978-7-114-11595-0	汽车车身焊接技术（第二版）	李远军、李建明	28.00	2018.03	有
978-7-114-13885-0	汽车车身修复技术（第二版）	韩星、陈勇	29.00	2017.08	有
978-7-114-09603-7	汽车车身构造与修复	李远军、陈建宏	38.00	2016.12	有
978-7-114-12143-2	车身结构及附属设备（第二版）	袁杰	27.00	2017.06	有
978-7-114-13363-3	汽车涂料调色技术	王亚平	25.00	2016.11	有
4. 汽车制造与装配技术专业					
978-7-114-12154-8	汽车装配与调试技术	刘敬忠	38.00	2018.06	
978-7-114-12734-2	车身焊接技术	宋金虎	39.00	2016.03	有
978-7-114-12794-6	汽车制造工艺	马志民	28.00	2016.04	有
978-7-114-12913-1	汽车 AutoCAD	于宁、李敬辉	22.00	2016.06	有
四、新能源汽车技术专业职业教育创新规划教材					
978-7-114-13806-5	新能源汽车概论	吴晓斌、刘海峰	28.00	2018.08	有
978-7-114-13778-5	新能源汽车高压安全与防护	赵金国、李治国	30.00	2018.03	有
978-7-114-13813-3	新能源汽车动力电池与驱动电机	曾鑫、刘涛	39.00	2018.05	有
978-7-114-13822-5	新能源汽车电气技术	唐勇、王亮	35.00	2017.06	有
978-7-114-13814-0	新能源汽车维护与故障诊断	包科杰、徐利强	33.00	2018.05	有
五、职业院校潍柴博世校企合作项目教材					
978-7-114-14700-5	柴油机构造与维修	李清民、栾玉俊	39.00	2018.07	
978-7-114-14682-4	商用车底盘构造与维修	王林超、刘海峰	43.00	2018.07	
978-7-114-14709-8	商用车电气系统构造与维修	王林超、王玉刚	45.00	2018.07	
978-7-114-14852-1	柴油机电控管理系统	王文山、李秀峰	22.00	2018.08	
978-7-114-14761-6	商用车营销与服务	李景芝、王桂凤	40.00	2018.08	
六、高等职业教育汽车车身维修技术专业教材					
978-7-114-14720-3	汽车板件加工与结合工艺	王选、赵昌涛	20.00	2018.07	有
978-7-114-14711-1	轿车车身构造与维修	李金文、高窦平	21.00	2018.07	有
978-7-114-14726-5	汽车修补涂装技术	王成贵、贺利涛	22.00	2018.07	有
978-7-114-14727-2	汽车修补涂装调色与抛光技术	肖林、廖辉湘	32.00	2018.07	有

■为"十二五"职业教育国家规划教材。咨询电话：010-85285962、85285977；咨询QQ：616507284、99735898。